D1573015

THE SANDMAN.

THE SANDMAN.

KING OF DREAMS

BY ALISA KWITNEY
INTRODUCTION BY NEIL GAIMAN

CHRONICLE BOOKS
San Francisco

TO MY UNCLE PAUL, FOR BEING MY HERO WHEN I WAS LITTLE,
AND TO MY AUNT SALLY, FOR BEING PAUL'S HERO NOW.

The Sandman created by Neil Gaiman, Sam Kieth, and Mike Dringenberg.

Every effort has been made to trace the ownership or source of all illustrated material for the purpose of giving proper credit. We regret any inadvertent error concerning the attribution given to any such materials and will be pleased to make the appropriate acknowledgments in any future printings.

Library of Congress Cataloging-in-Publication Data available.

ISBN: 0-8118-3592-8

Manufactured in China.

Book design by CHARACTER, San Francisco, California.
Compositing by ultrachango.

Note on type: Giambattista Bodoni of Parma, Italy, designed and cut his typefaces at the end of the 18th century. The Bodoni types have distinctively fine hairlines that contrast sharply with bolder stems, and serifs are often unbracketed. Bodoni is recognized by its high contrast between thick and thin strokes, pure vertical stress, and hairline serifs. This particular version of Bodoni was first created by Morris Fuller Benton for American Type Founders between 1908 and 1915.

Distributed in Canada by Raincoast Books
9050 Shaughnessy Street
Vancouver, British Columbia V6P 6E5

10 9 8 7 6 5 4 3 2 1

Chronicle Books LLC
85 Second Street
San Francisco, California 94105

www.chroniclebooks.com
www.vertigocomics.com

TABLE OF CONTENTS.

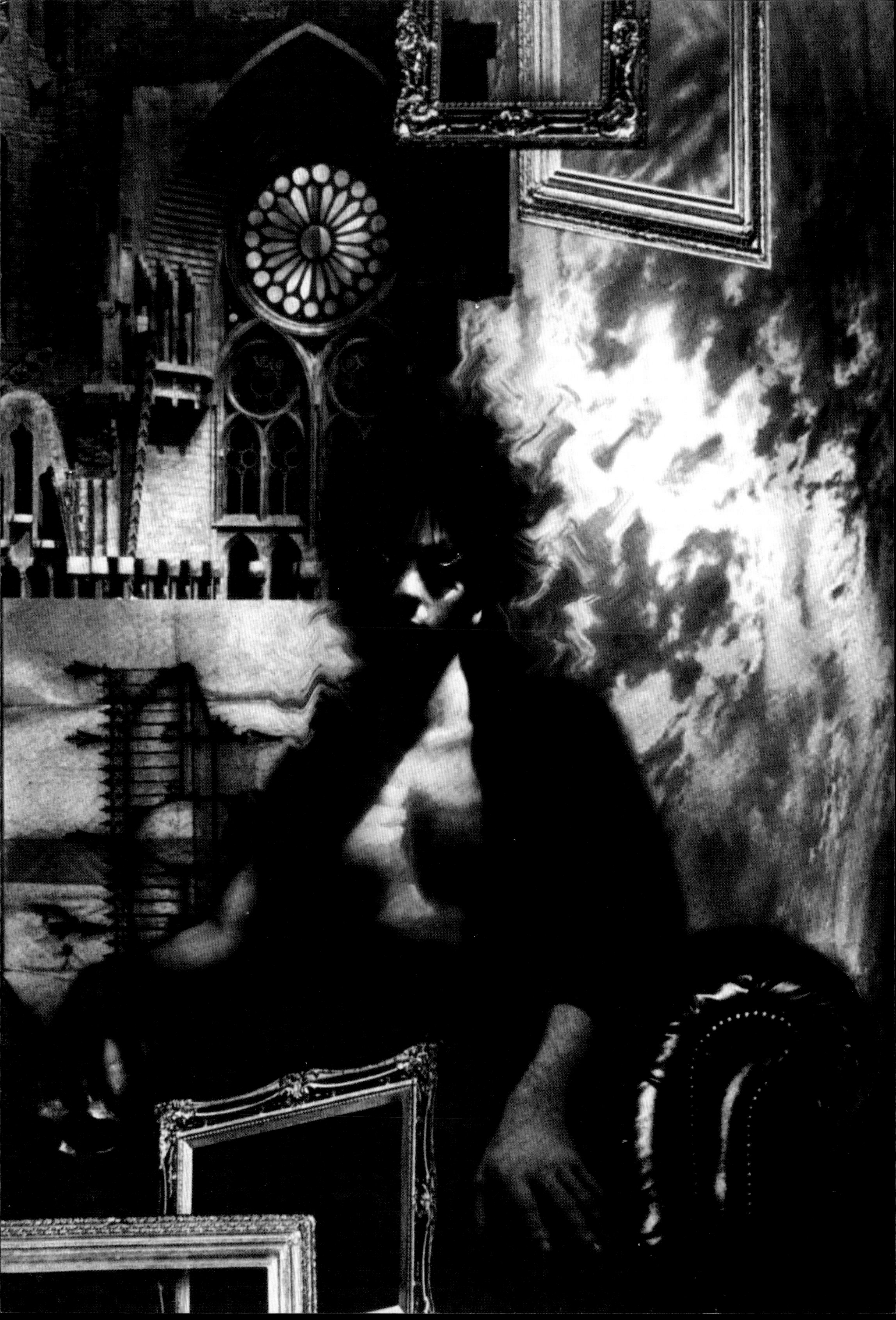

INTRODUCTION

BY NEIL GAIMAN

ACCORDING TO AN OLD NEW YORK FOLKTALE, ALISA KWITNEY APPEARS IN A BATHROOM MIRROR TO PEOPLE IN THE FINAL STAGES OF DELIRIUM TREMENS, AND PLEADS WITH THEM TO MEND THEIR WAYS. IN ANOTHER VERSION OF THE SAME STORY SHE CAN BE INDUCED (BY THREATENING TO BREAK THE MIRROR) TO REVEAL WINNING LOTTERY TICKET NUMBERS. (BIOGRAPHIES – *SEASON OF MISTS*)

If I have a concern over *The Sandman,* the 2,000-page story I was able to tell between 1988 and 1996, it is that the things that have come after it – the toys (whether plastic and articulated or soft and cuddly), the posters, the clothes, the calendars and candles, the companion volume, and even the slim book of quotations, along with the various spin-offs and such – will try people's patience and goodwill, and that a book like this will be perceived, not unreasonably, as something that's being used to flog the greasy patch on the driveway where once, long ago, a dead horse used to lie.

The ten volumes of *The Sandman* are what they are, after all, and that's the end of it.

But many people have not heard of *Sandman.* (You may find this hard to believe, or you may be one of the people I'm talking about and thus find this statement pretty obvious.) I think it's probably fair to say, if one considers the whole population of the world, that most people haven't heard of *Sandman.* Which means that there are people out there who would like it and do not even know it exists. It is good to give them pointers, road maps, ways in.

Everybody has to start somewhere, after all. I discovered J.R.R. Tolkien through a book of oddments called *The Tolkien Reader;* found Gilbert and Sullivan through a

PAGE 6 The cover of *The Sandman* no. 16, which also happens to be a photograph of Mr. Gaiman. Artwork by Dave McKean.

children's book — an illustrated *Children's Mikado*; discovered Charles Schulz through *Happiness Is a Warm Puppy* and America in a panel in a Mort Weisinger–era *Superman* comic. There is no wrong way to reach something. There is no wrong path to a place you need to visit.

If you've never been here before, if you've never encountered Morpheus, or Matthew the Raven, or Death, then this book is a fine place for you to become acquainted. If you and the *Sandman* stories are old friends, then I suspect there are oddments and secrets in here that even you may be surprised to find.

But I like to think that a book like this can do a little more than simply serve as an introduction and a gloss. After all, there is a magic to art when taken out of context. It's a magic that exists in quotations. There are things we've seen so often we no longer see them at all, and books like this can grant those Warhol moments when we get to see something everyday from another direction or in another context. Pulled from their familiar settings, images change and are made new. Our eyes are opened.

Many talented artists worked on *The Sandman*. Many more talented artists have come since, to paint a favorite character or snatch a moment of magic. You'll find many of them in this book, which is an introduction to *Sandman*, and a discussion of *Sandman*, and a gallery of art from *Sandman* — some of it familiar, some of it obscure. It's a way of seeing *Sandman*, and it is brought to you by Alisa Kwitney.

Alisa Kwitney was *Sandman*'s third assistant editor. (She was preceded by Art Young and Tom Peyer. After her came, momentarily, Lisa Aufenanger, then afterward and forever, no matter how grand her current title, Shelly Bond, née Roeberg.) Karen Berger was the editor, who is concerned with the grand scheme of things. The assistant editor is the person who makes sure that the script is in on time and that it goes to the artist, that the art goes to be lettered, that the author gets a photocopy of the art to review. This meant that the people I talked to on a day-to-day basis were the assistant editors.

Alisa and I were friends from day one — partly, I think, because Alisa was a writer herself. When she got the job at DC Comics she was the author of a seriously funny book called *Till the Fat Lady Sings*, and was also, as I later discovered, the daughter of an excellent writer (Robert Sheckley, the fabulist and satirist). She knew the peculiar ways of writers, and she wanted to know how things worked.

Alisa would phone me up and ask me pertinent questions. Perhaps she'd want to know what to say for the solicitation copy about an issue I hadn't yet written (once I didn't know, and simply made one up on the spot, and then spent the next few weeks madly reading everything I could about revolutionary France in order to write the story). When we were done talking about work we'd talk about writing, and she'd listen, and several times in the years to come she would surprise me by remembering something sensible I'd said that I had told her in passing and promptly forgotten.

She's not been my editor for a very long time. For that matter it's been over five years since I stopped writing an episode of *Sandman* every month. (Although I've spent eight months telling interesting stories of Dream and his family for a volume called *Endless Nights*, celebrating ten years of DC Comics' VERTIGO imprint.)

These days, having assistant-edited and then edited, raised two children and a cat, Alisa is writing novels once more, so even now some of the most fun conversations I have begin with Alisa phoning me up and saying, "Look, I really have to get rid of a body . . . ", or "What do you do when you're halfway through a book and your main character hasn't turned up yet?"

She knows words, she has a fine eye for pictures, and she certainly knows her *Sandman*. You're in safe hands.

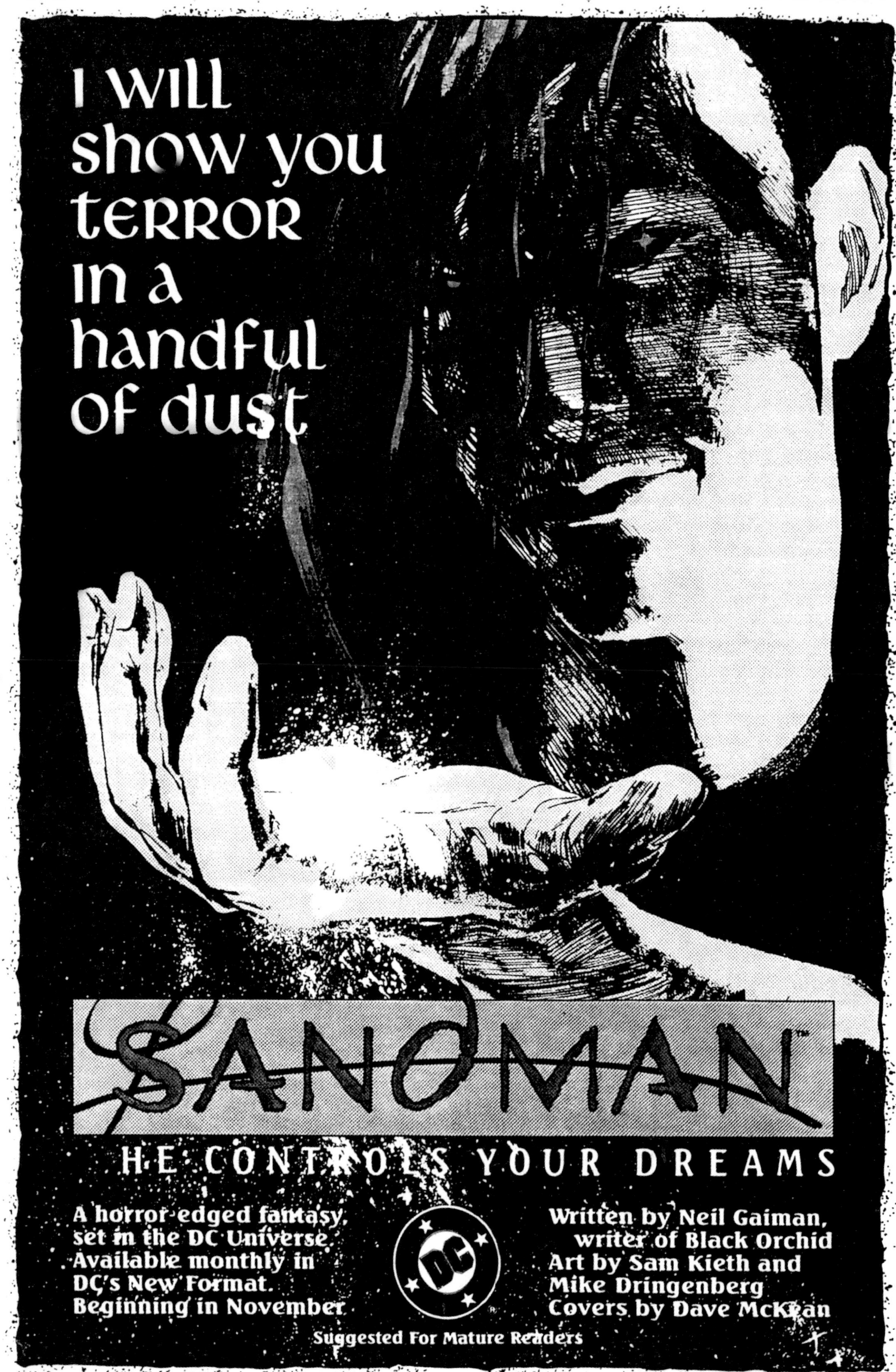
I will show you terror in a handful of dust
SANDMAN™
HE CONTROLS YOUR DREAMS
A horror-edged fantasy, set in the DC Universe. Available monthly in DC's New Format. Beginning in November
Written by Neil Gaiman, writer of Black Orchid
Art by Sam Kieth and Mike Dringenberg
Covers by Dave McKean
Suggested For Mature Readers

CHAPTER 1

THE SANDMAN 101

The Sandman library consists of ten story arcs – penned by best-selling and critically acclaimed author Neil Gaiman – that tell the saga of the Sandman, who is also known as Morpheus and Dream. The Sandman is the solitary, autocratic, complex ruler of the Dreaming – the realm of our collective unconscious. Some of the Dreaming, constructed long ago from the myths of entire cultures, is quite solid; some of it is as new and impermanent as the memory of the waitress who forgot to bring you cream. And sometimes it turns out that your waitress is really an ancient myth from another culture, which can complicate things enormously.

The Sandman may be king in the Dreaming, and possess immense power in our own waking world, but he is also a member of a family of siblings who rival him in strength and influence and . . . well, who sometimes just plain rival him, as siblings will. The seven siblings, who are older than the gods of ancient Egypt and Greece, but have kept up with modern fashions in dress and intrigue, are Destiny, Desire, Despair, Destruction, Delirium, Dream . . . and Death. Together, they are known as the Endless.

As you might expect from a family of archetypes, the Endless are both characters and concepts, and the tale of the Sandman's rise and fall is both the story of an individual's journey and the recounting of a mythic cycle, done with deftness and grace and a deceptive lightness of touch.

PAGE 10 This promotional poster for *The Sandman* from 1988 unleashed the character on an unsuspecting public. Artwork by Sam Kieth and Mike Dringenberg.

BELOW   Cover, *Preludes & Nocturnes* (reprinting *Sandman* nos. 1–8; introduction by F. Paul Wilson/Karen Berger).   BOTTOM   Cover, *Dream Country* (nos. 17–20; introduction by Steve Erickson).   PAGE 13   Cover, *The Doll's House* (nos. 9–16; introduction by Clive Barker). Artwork by Dave McKean.

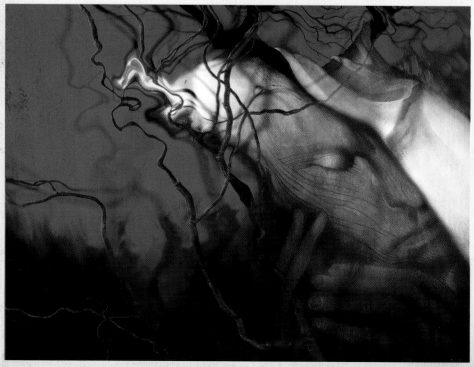

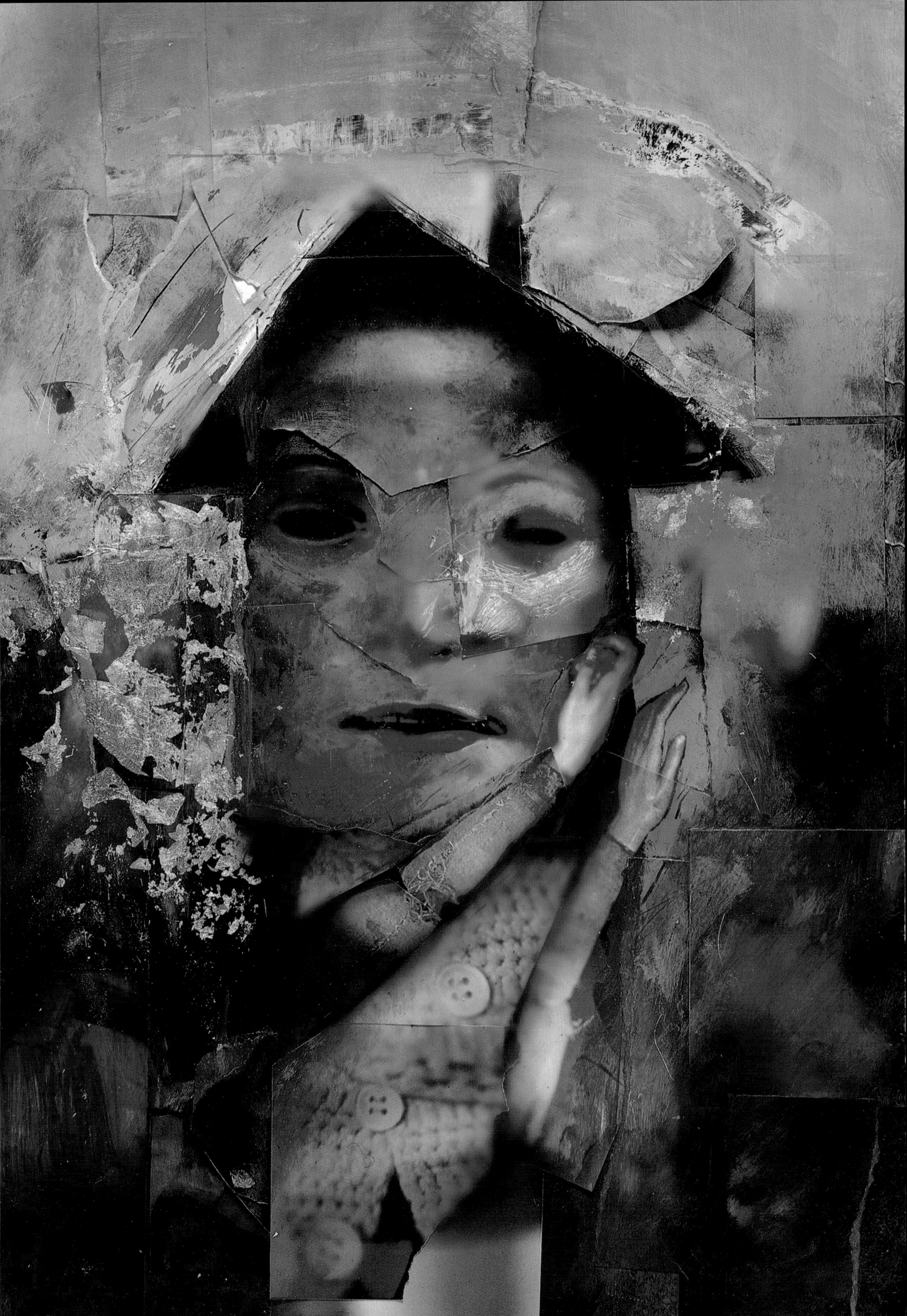

BELOW Cover, *Fables & Reflections* (nos. 29–31, 38–40, 50, *The Sandman Special*, a ten-page short story from *Vertigo Preview;* introduction by Gene Wolfe). PAGE 15 Cover, *Season of Mists* (nos. 21–28; introduction by Harlan Ellison). Artwork by Dave McKean.

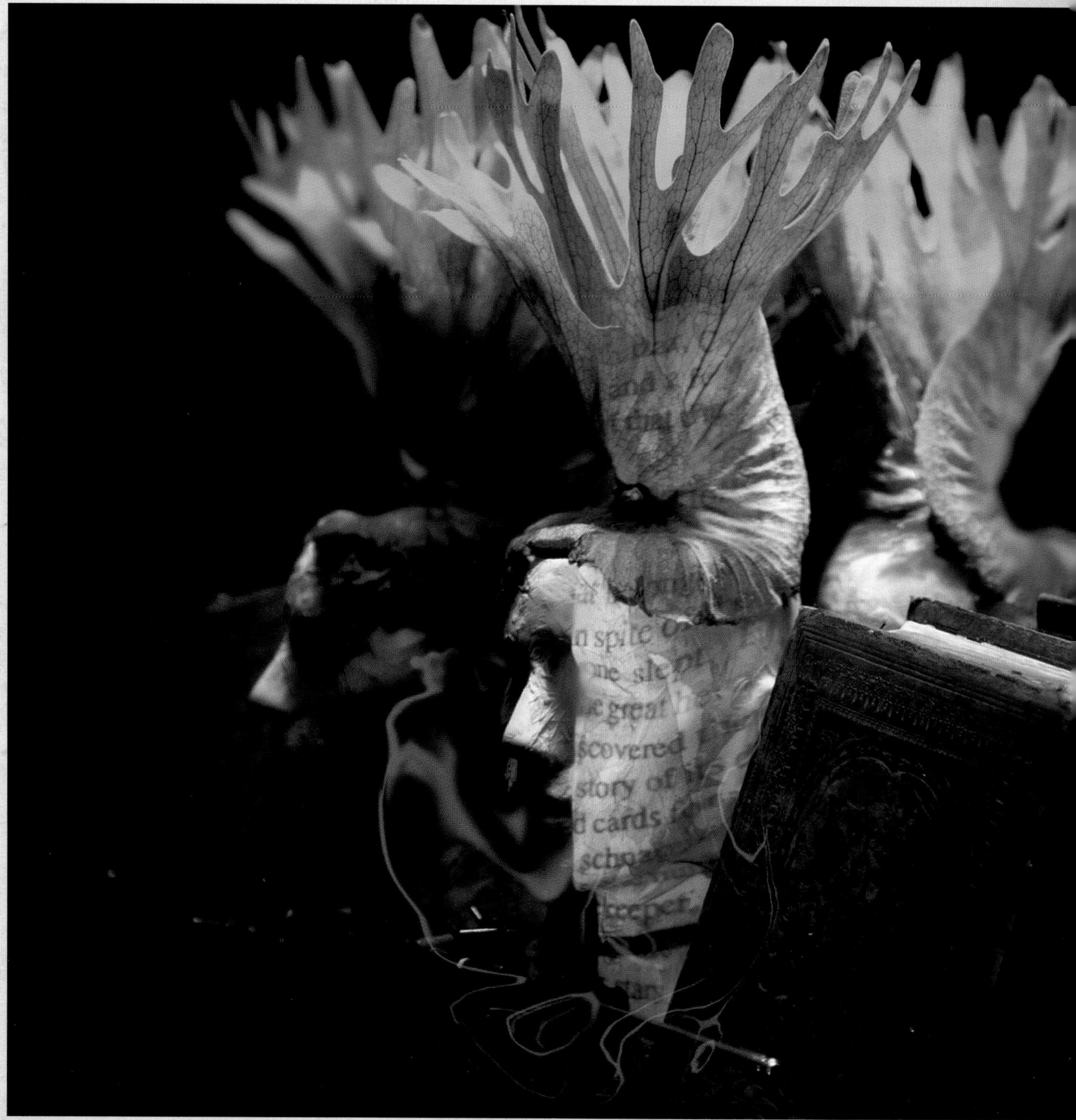

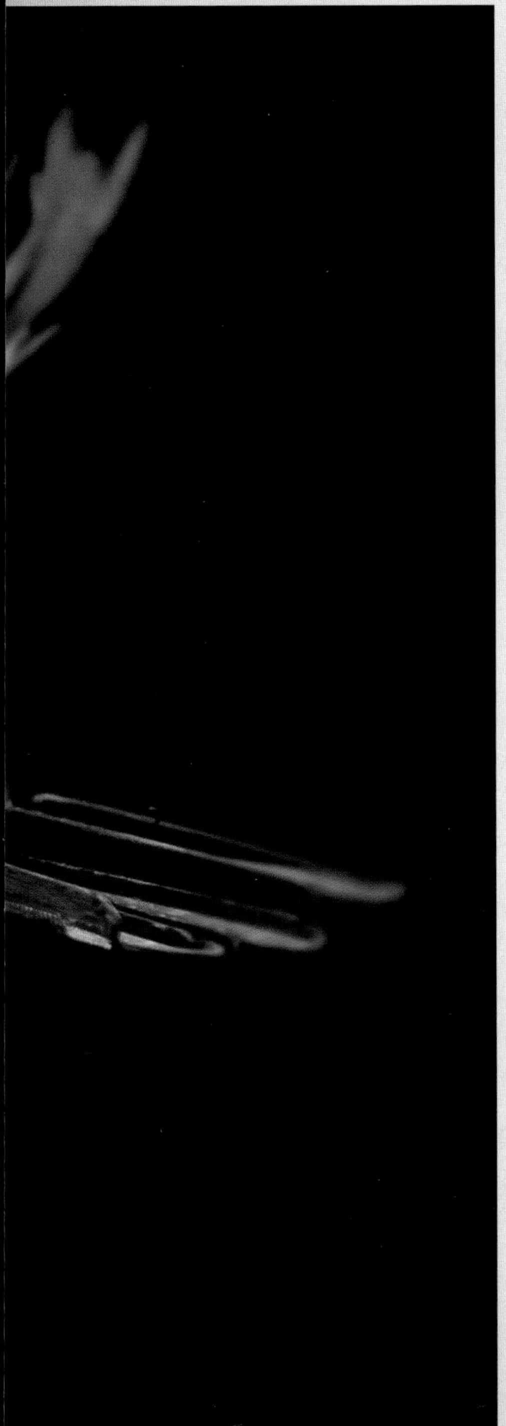

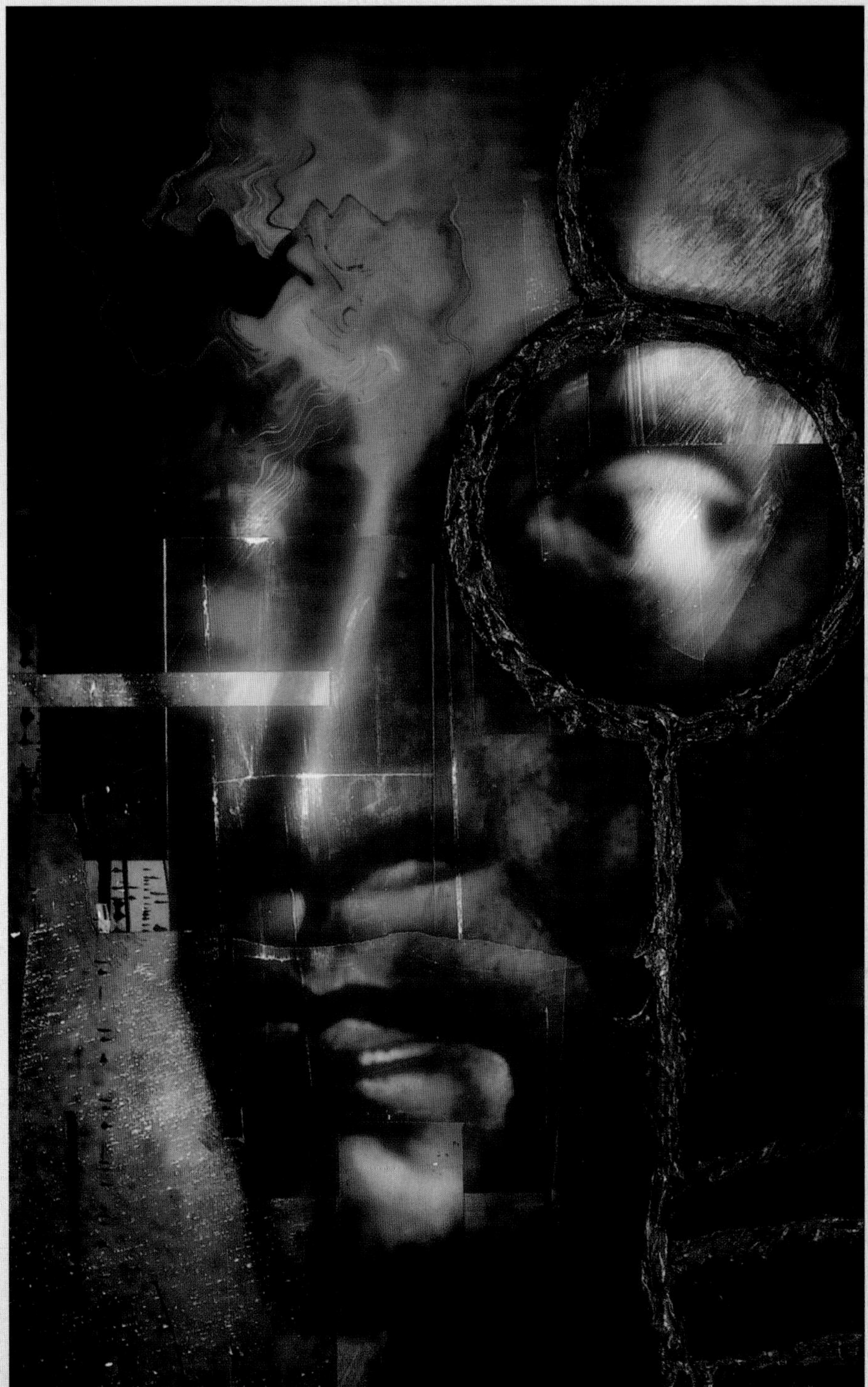

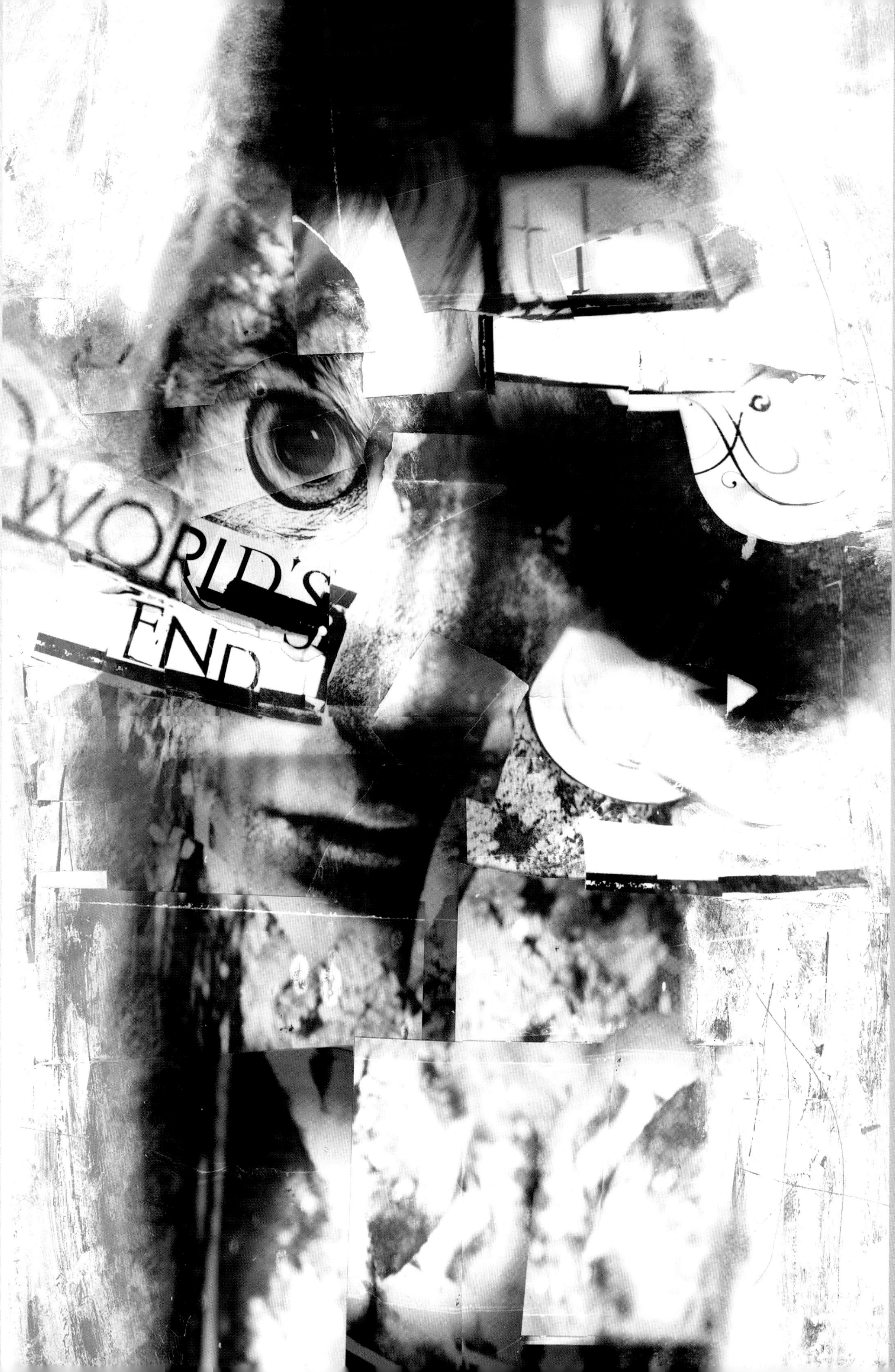
WORLD'S
END

PAGE 16   Cover, *Worlds' End* (nos. 51–56; introduction by Stephen King).   BELOW   *Brief Lives* (nos. 41–49; introduction by Peter Straub). Artwork by Dave McKean.

BELOW LEFT Cover, *A Game of You* (nos. 32–37; introduction by Samuel R. Delany). BELOW RIGHT Cover, *The Kindly Ones* (nos. 57–69, an eight-page story from *Vertigo Jam*). PAGE 19 Cover, *The Wake* (nos. 70–75; introduction by Mikal Gilmore). Artwork by Dave McKean.

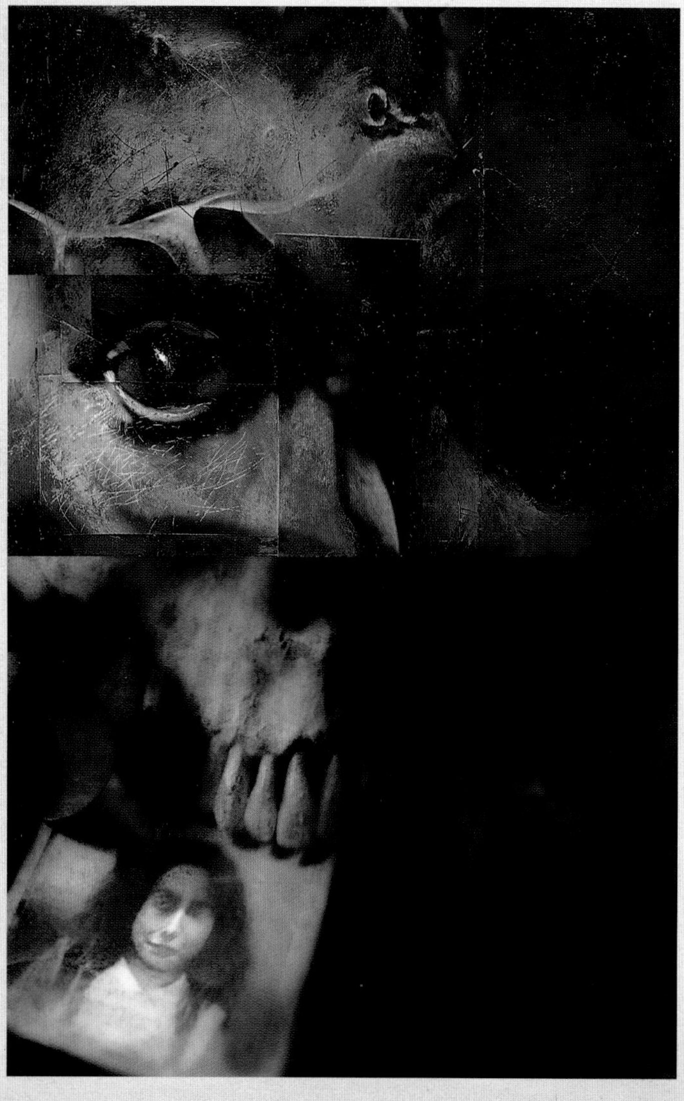

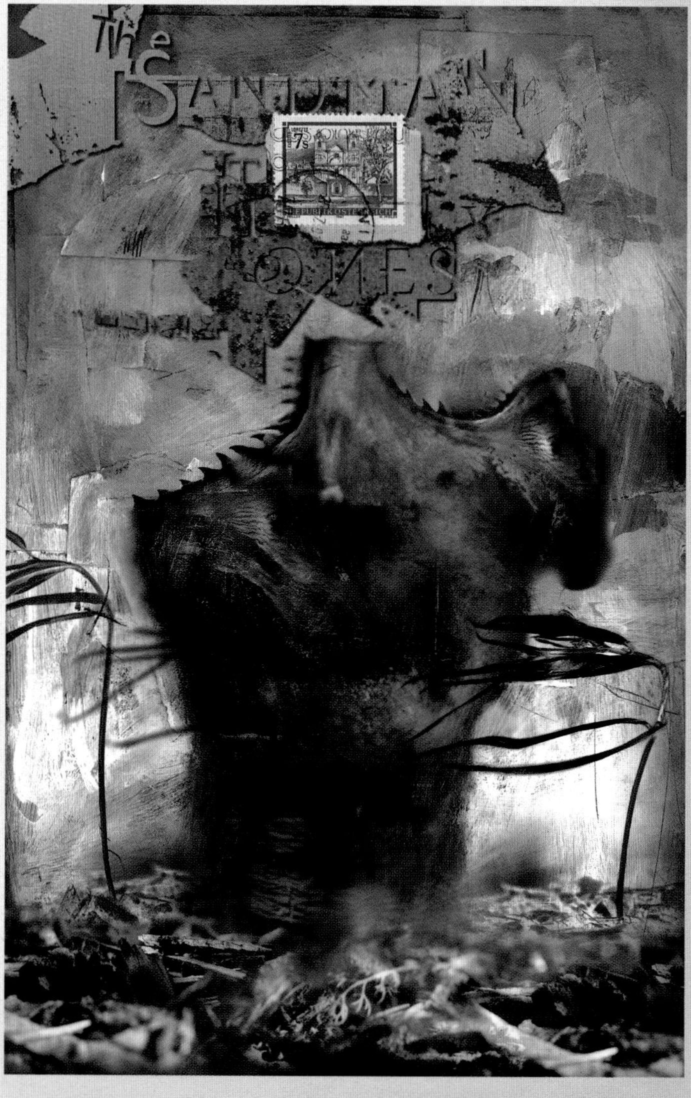
The
ONES

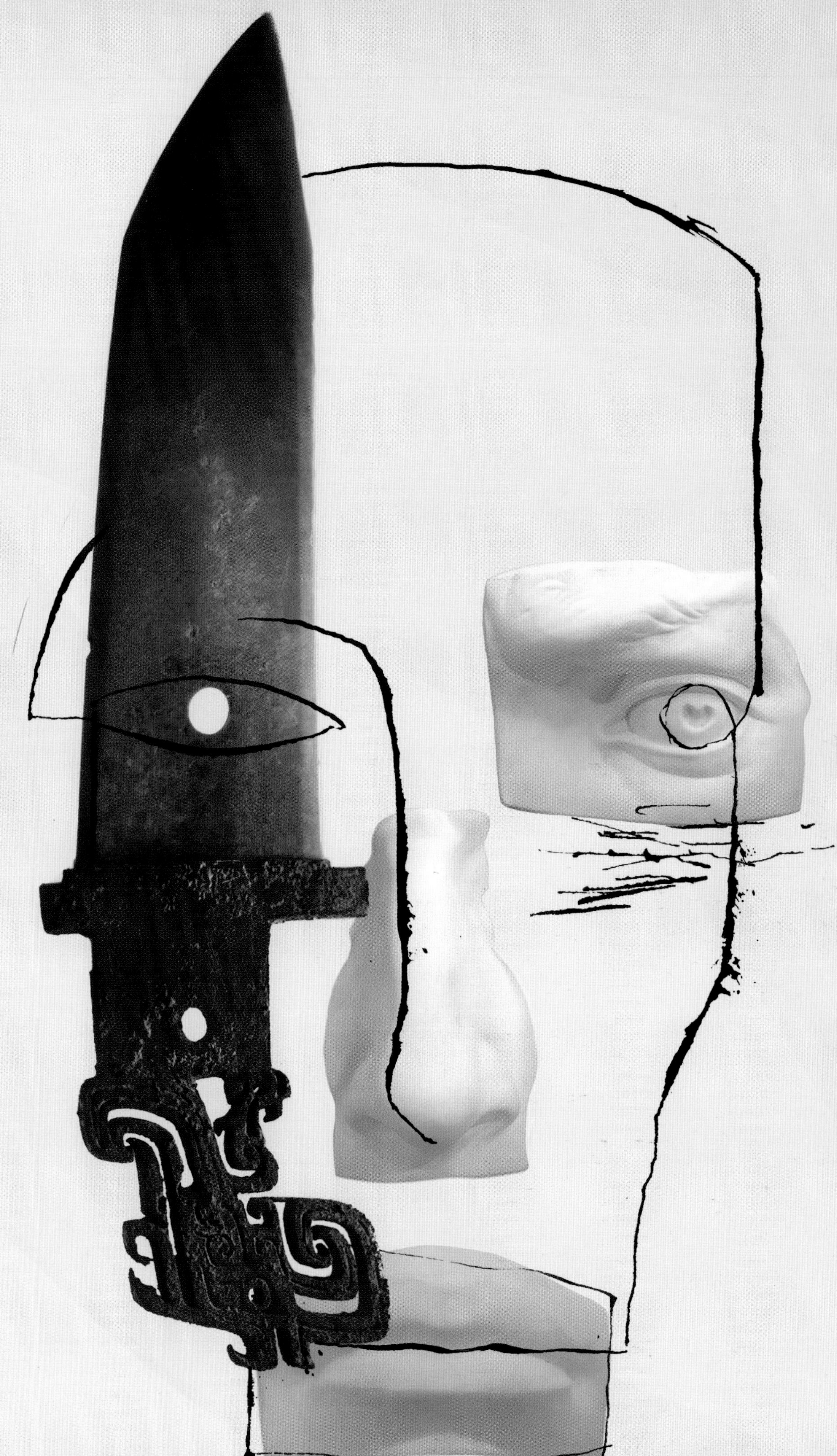

BELOW Early Sandman character models. Artwork by Leigh Baulch.

Within the two thousand pages of *The Sandman*, caliphs and presidents and angels struggle with the vocation of rulership. And there are other strands and motifs besides, woven through the many storylines: themes of sibling rivalry and passion turned to revenge, themes of the dangerous nature of gifts, particularly the gift of creativity, as well as recurrent meditations on the power of women, the nature of vision, and the distinctions between Dream and Death.

But first, a warning: Enter the realm of *The Sandman* and you may never want to leave. It's the kind of story that maintains its hold on the imagination over time. In the decade and a half since the book's inception, and over ten years after it helped launch VERTIGO, DC's imprint of comics for mature readers, *The Sandman* continues to fascinate its legion of old fans and to enthrall new ones.

But maybe you've just picked up this book because the cover caught your eye. You don't read comic books. You've graduated to books without pictures, thank you very much.

Well, just because you've shown no prior interest in comic books is no proof against getting addicted to this one. *The Sandman* manages to bridge the gap between comic

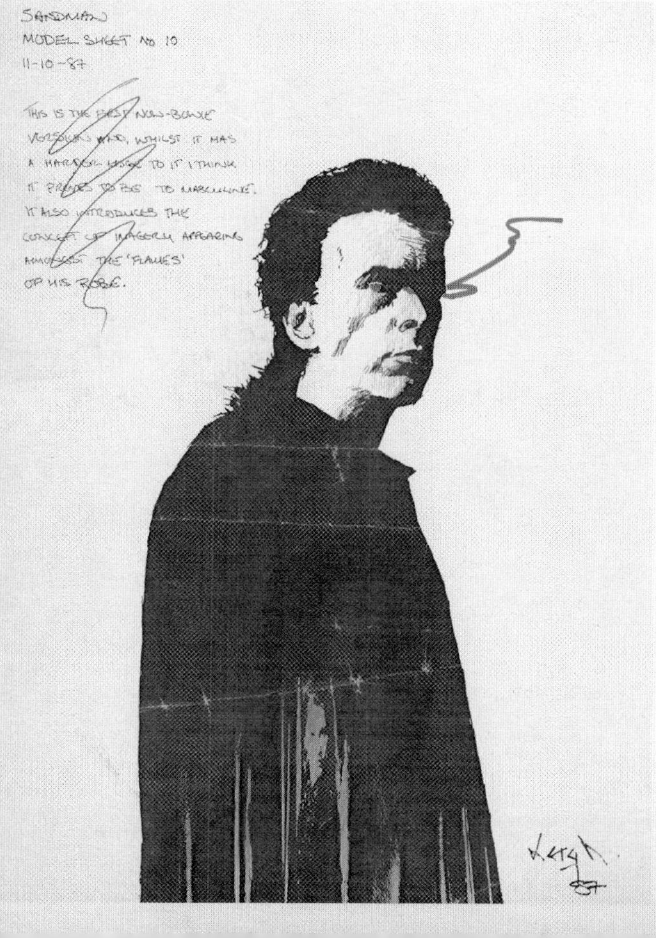
SANDMAN
MODEL SHEET No 10
11-10-87

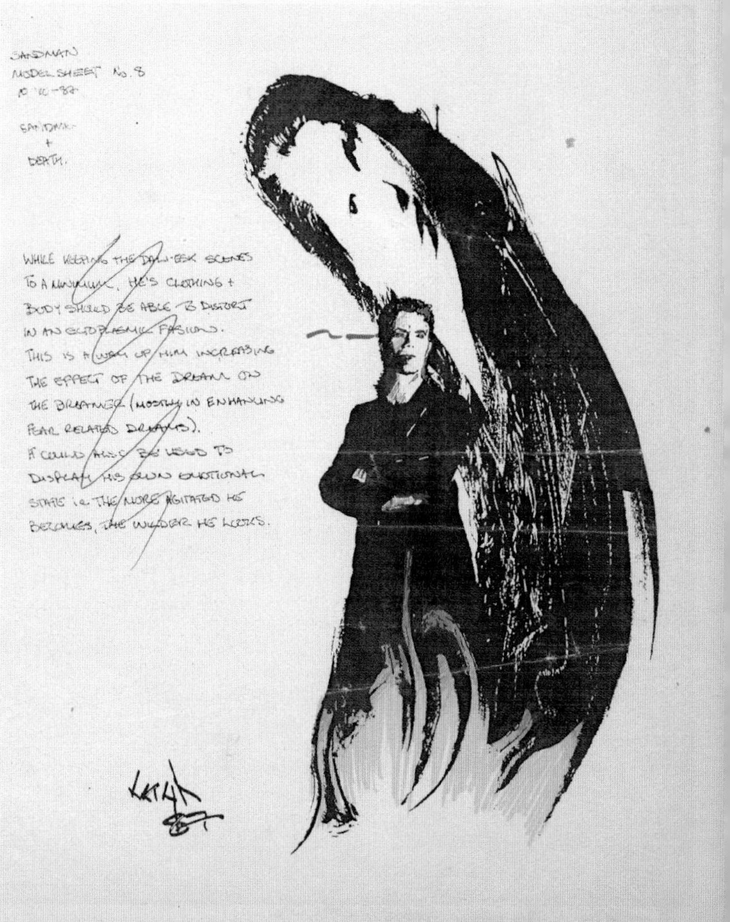
SANDMAN
MODEL SHEET No. 8
SANDMAN
+
DEATH.

BELOW A Dave McKean concept sketch for Morpheus.

books and prose. It has garnered praise, awards, and, most important, readers from both worlds, and its collected library has won a place in bookstores alongside classic novels of fantasy and horror.

And all this has been achieved in a medium that is generally considered to be the literary and artistic equivalent of a Twinkie. Not to cast aspersions on Twinkies, which have a certain reassuringly bland appeal, but *The Sandman* satisfies a very different appetite. It's a book for people who don't equate visual storytelling with a dumbed-down version of a classic.

Sandman stories assume a certain level of sophistication on the part of their audience. You won't find any comic book footnotes to explain the multitude of arcane historical, mythological, literary, and comic book references. It is possible to read and enjoy volume V, *A Game of You*, without knowing about DC's run of Bizarro Superman stories or about Thessalian witches, because although these lovely, clever bits are woven into the fiction, their use is never arbitrary; the stories are never clever for the sake of being clever.

BELOW The Sandman takes Rose Walker for a ride in *The Doll's House*. Artwork by Mike Dringenberg and Sam Kieth for Malcolm Jones III. (As Neil remembers it, Sam was pulled in to help out while Malcolm was away on holiday.) Robbie Busch, colorist.

The fact that *The Sandman* is geared toward a thinking audience is reinforced by the distinctive style of its covers. Traditionally, comic book covers depict scenes, while prose book covers suggest themes. Dave McKean broke fifty-odd years of comic book precedent with his provocatively nonliteral covers that change their look from story arc to story arc, invoking themes and symbols that augment our understanding of the story that follows.

Complex and intriguing, the look of *The Sandman's* covers is a commentary on the series itself.

Yet, despite its uniqueness and profundity, *The Sandman* cannot be completely compared to words-only fiction. A story conceived and created in comic book form is a very different animal than a story comprised of straight prose.

For example, in a novel, the choice of font might not be considered an issue of major importance, but in a comic book or graphic novel, all the visual details matter enormously, and great care is taken with the way the words look.

It has been said that God is in the details: Well, in the intricately imagined realm of the Sandman, the gods are in the details. Or, to put it another way, much of *The Sandman*'s complexity lies in the interplay of image and text, and in the nuances of visual as well as thematic motifs. In a scene early on in the series, a character called Rose Walker asks the Sandman: "Say, whoever you are. Do you know what Freud said about dreams of flying? It means you're really dreaming about having sex."

The Sandman, flying through a dreaming sky, looks down on the young woman in his arms and replies, "Indeed? Tell me, then, what does it mean when you dream about having sex?"

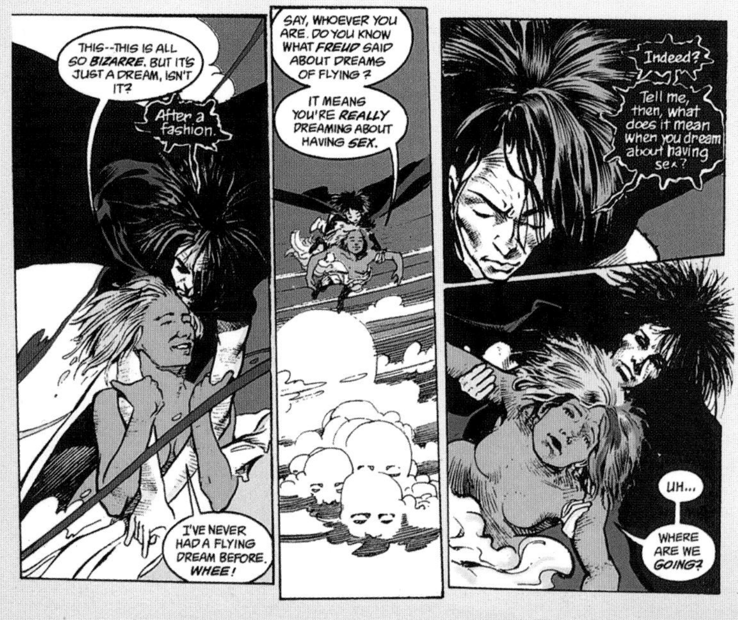
THIS--THIS IS ALL SO BIZARRE. BUT IT'S JUST A DREAM, ISN'T IT?
After a fashion.
I'VE NEVER HAD A FLYING DREAM BEFORE. WHEE!
SAY, WHOEVER YOU ARE. DO YOU KNOW WHAT FREUD SAID ABOUT DREAMS OF FLYING?
IT MEANS YOU'RE REALLY DREAMING ABOUT HAVING SEX.
Indeed?
Tell me, then, what does it mean when you dream about having sex?
UH...
WHERE ARE WE GOING?

It is a moment that acknowledges the simple, iconic truth of comic books and fly-ing superheroes and the more ambiguous truth of dreams and symbols and subtext. It is also a moment that owes as much of its erotic, ironic punch to the image as to the word.

"In most word-only short fiction, both mainstream and genre, there is sometimes a sense of self-awareness and a feeling that the work is meaningful . . . but there is hardly ever a sense of humor," writes Stephen King in his introduction to the *Worlds' End* trade paperback. "In words-and-pictures fiction — comics books, in other words — there's usu-ally a *lot* of humor . . . but no sense of self-awareness, no feeling that the work needs to be taken seriously on its own terms . . . that it has merit as art." Neil Gaiman's *Sandman* stories, King concludes, contain both elements — a sense of the absurd and a sense of weight and meaning, "and the result is works with the clarity of fairy tales and the sub-versive undertone of top-drawer modern fiction."

Of course, there will always be those who distrust the idea of pictures along with their words, much as toddlers distrust peas with their carrots. For them, *The Sandman* can be one big scary gumbo, spiced as it is with the flavors of African legend and Bizarro Superman, G. K. Chesterton and the hobgoblins of Shakespearean England.

Speaking of which, those hobgoblins have managed to cause a fair bit of modern mischief. Back in 1991, at the Thirteenth Annual World Fantasy Convention, there was some consternation when the award for the year's best short story went to "A Midsummer Night's Dream," a single-issue story of the Sandman. Rules were subse-quently changed to keep the bad fairies from attending future affairs, but the dam-age had been done: Word was getting out that there's nothing inherently shallow about the comics medium.

"As soon as the academic critics get off their butts and realize it's okay to admire a mere comic book, you'll see dissertations, books, annotations galore on *The Sandman*, and then on the great comics writers — Alan Moore, Frank Miller, Will Eisner . . . " writes academic critic Frank McConnell in the Introduction to *The Kindly Ones*. While no one has a Ph.D. in *The Sandman* yet, there are definitely dissertations being done on the subject.

The Sandman contains a whole, complex mythography of its own devising, but this alone doesn't make it special. As Harlan Ellison states in his introduction to the *Season of Mists* trade paperback, every fantasist builds a new universe each time he or she writes a story. But what Gaiman has done, says Ellison, is do it splendidly, "so splendidly that it raises the high-water mark and puts more sunlight in the world."

Well, maybe not sunlight. To my mind, *The Sandman* works a darker magic, in the shadow places where childhood fantasies about superheroes bleed into half-remembered tales of old gods and private demons. If *The Sandman* feels familiar, it's probably because these stories touch on ancient truths. *The Sandman*'s world is a Jungian realm of our collective subconscious, where the psychology of the individual bleeds into the landscape of a thousand folk and fairy tales. Here, every decisive

BELOW The first page of Neil's response to VERTIGO editor Karen Berger's editorial letter, in which she commented on his original proposal (in the days before the laser printer).

Dear Karen,

OK. Let's go over your questions:

1) What does our lead character do to show you 'fear in a handful of dust?' It's a number of things -- you've correctly pointed to a couple -- the majesty of his character, the fact that he is Lord of Nightmares. I suppose, though, that for me, the third factor is his inhumanity. He is the Lord of his realm, and, as he will say at some point, "Not fair? Of course it's not fair. There is no fairness and no justice here. There's just me." He can plunge you into nightmares, or into dreams, but often gradually, so that the person being plunged (and the reader) hardly know what's happening at first.

He is scary. He inspires awe, and he can inspire fear. Also, in dreams, he changes shape. He could be a black cat with eyes of flame, or a shadow, or a house, or...

2) Bits of humanity early on. Yes, definitely. But this is a gradual process. I want to see flashes of humanity. I also want, to some degree, to alternate viewpoints in stories, so in some we see him as worried, lost, confused, because we're seeing it from his viewpoint; in others he's mysterious, apparently all-knowing, mysterious etc, because we're seeing him from other people's points of view.

3) Yes, there'll be flashes of humanity in the Cain and Abel sequence -- if only because they're weirder than he is.

4) Good dreams for people in need of them? Well, I had planned for seeing a couple of aspects of this in the Constantine story, then doing that kind of thing more in the Dr Destiny trilogy.

5)I obviously didn't make myself clear (my fault) about his trappings. You can take away a calculator from someone without taking away their ability to do arithmetic. You may slow them up a lot, they may be rusty, there may even be ways to do calculations they've forgotten how to do without a calculator, but that doesn't mean they are magically helpless without one.

Specifically: The dream sand bag. The Sandman can obtain sand from dreams and materialise it into the world. He can imbue any sand or dust, real or from dreams, with the power to send people to sleep. This takes time and concentration, though. The Bag is a short-cut. It is always full of dream-sand, already imbued with dream properties.

The helm: This may well have specific properties of its own, but its chief use is simply that of recognition. Wearing it, he is formally to be recognised as the Lord of the Night World, whether he is visiting Hell, or other worlds or dimensions.

BELOW Leigh Baulch's cover for the original proposal for *The Sandman*.

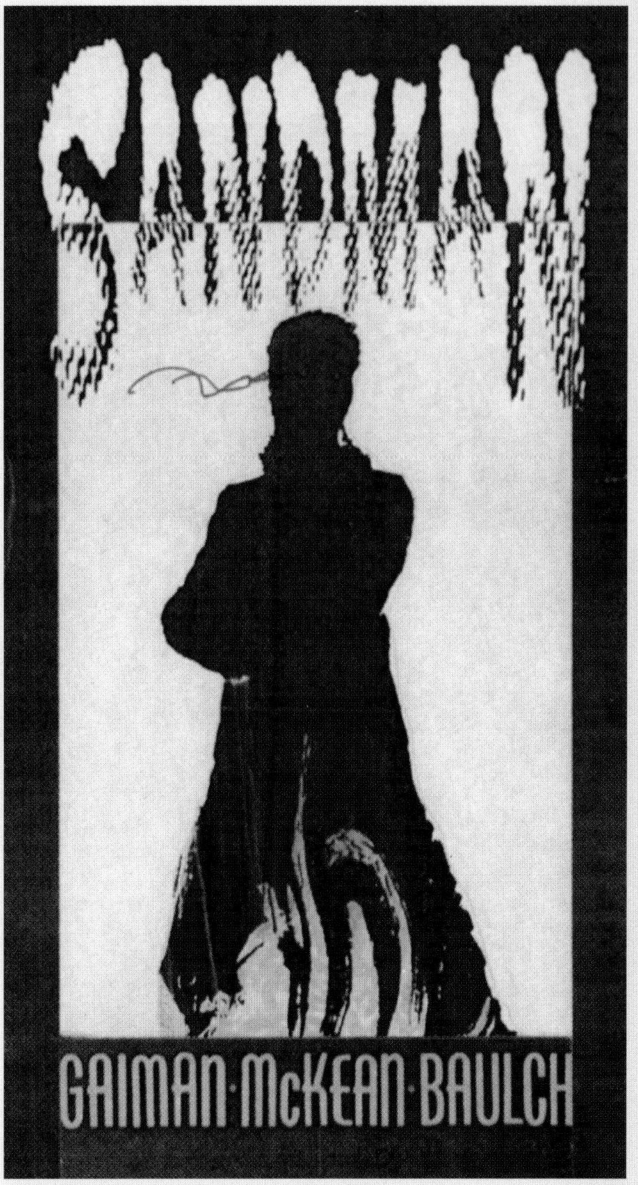
SANDMAN
GAIMAN·McKEAN·BAULCH

action, every bond broken or forged, casts ripples of far-reaching consequence, and that's part of what gives *The Sandman* such longevity.

Over the past decade, the sales of the ten collected trade paperbacks have never dipped. Any new Neil Gaiman *Sandman* project is awaited today with even more anticipation than it might have been eight years ago, in the heyday of the series, and the ever-increasing supply of *Sandman*-related publications, such as this one, speaks to the ever-present demand for more tales of the prince of stories.

Ten years ago, when I first interviewed for a job at DC comics, I was given the first couple of issues of *The Sandman.* Not knowing whether or not I would get the position, I rushed out to a comic book store and bought the rest of the issues. Something about the stories thrilled me in a way I hadn't been thrilled since the age of eleven, back when comics were still a subversive treat I hid from my grandparents. I felt that I was in the hands of a master storyteller who would fulfill his promise to take me places splendid and strange, the half-remembered, half-invented landscape of dreams.

PAGE 27 Original pencils, partly inked, by Sam Keith, for the splash panel of "Imperfect Hosts" from *Preludes & Nocturnes*.

I did get the gig as Karen Berger's assistant editor and basically I haven't stopped reading *The Sandman* since. But always in bits and pieces — searching for a minor character with star potential for a spin-off, trying to find the perfect quote for a line of copy, or just getting lost in a story for a few minutes.

Then, in preparing to write this book, I read the complete series from beginning to end for the first time. I was struck by the way in which this deft intermingling of fantasy, horror, myth, and literature, with its dazzling array of narrative and artistic styles, stands together as a cohesive whole.

So, yes, more of my waking life has been spent on *The Sandman* than is probably healthy. But like myths and fairy tales and great literature, it's the kind of story that grows in the retelling, revealing its secrets without ever losing its mystery or power.

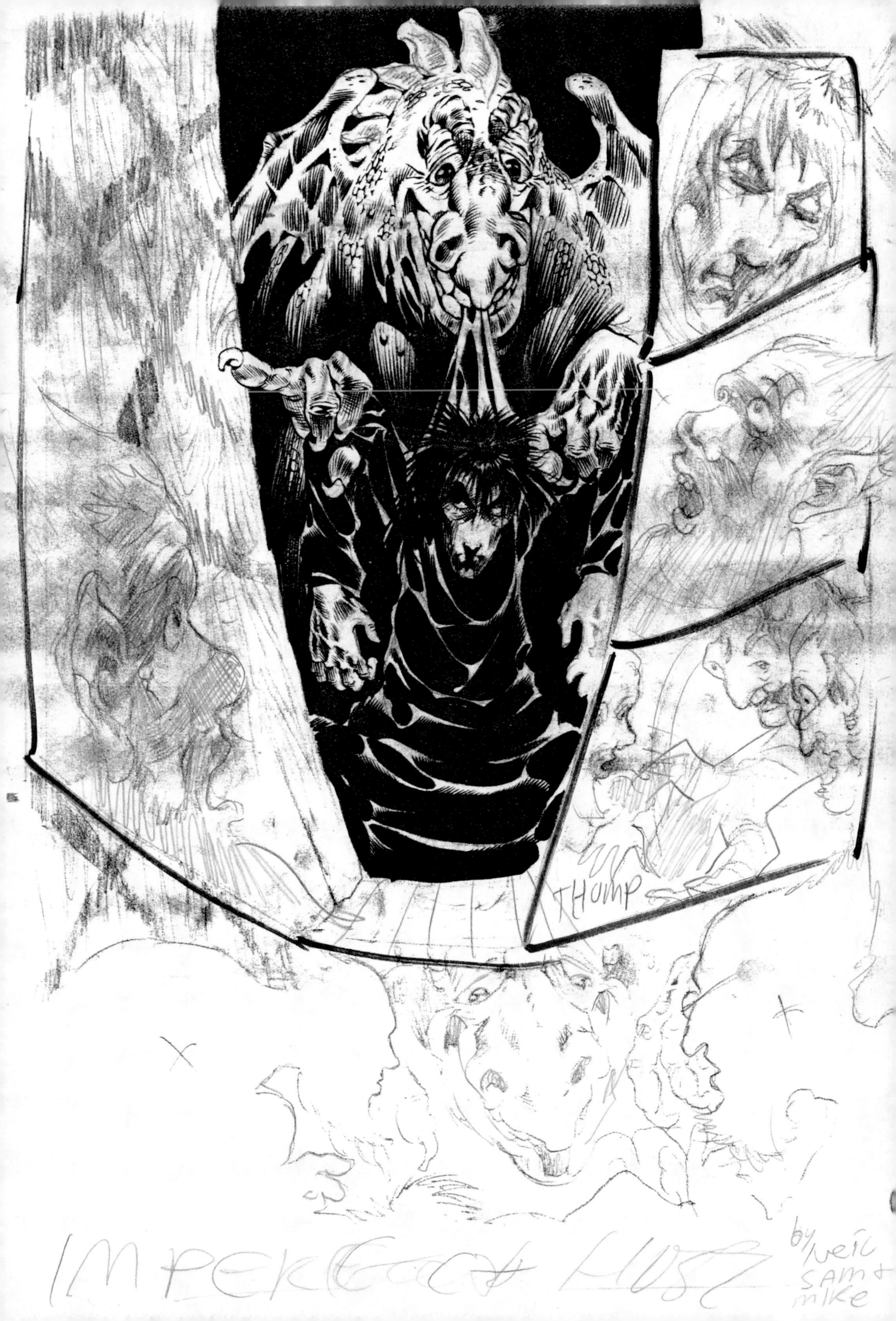
THUMP
by Neil SAM + Mike

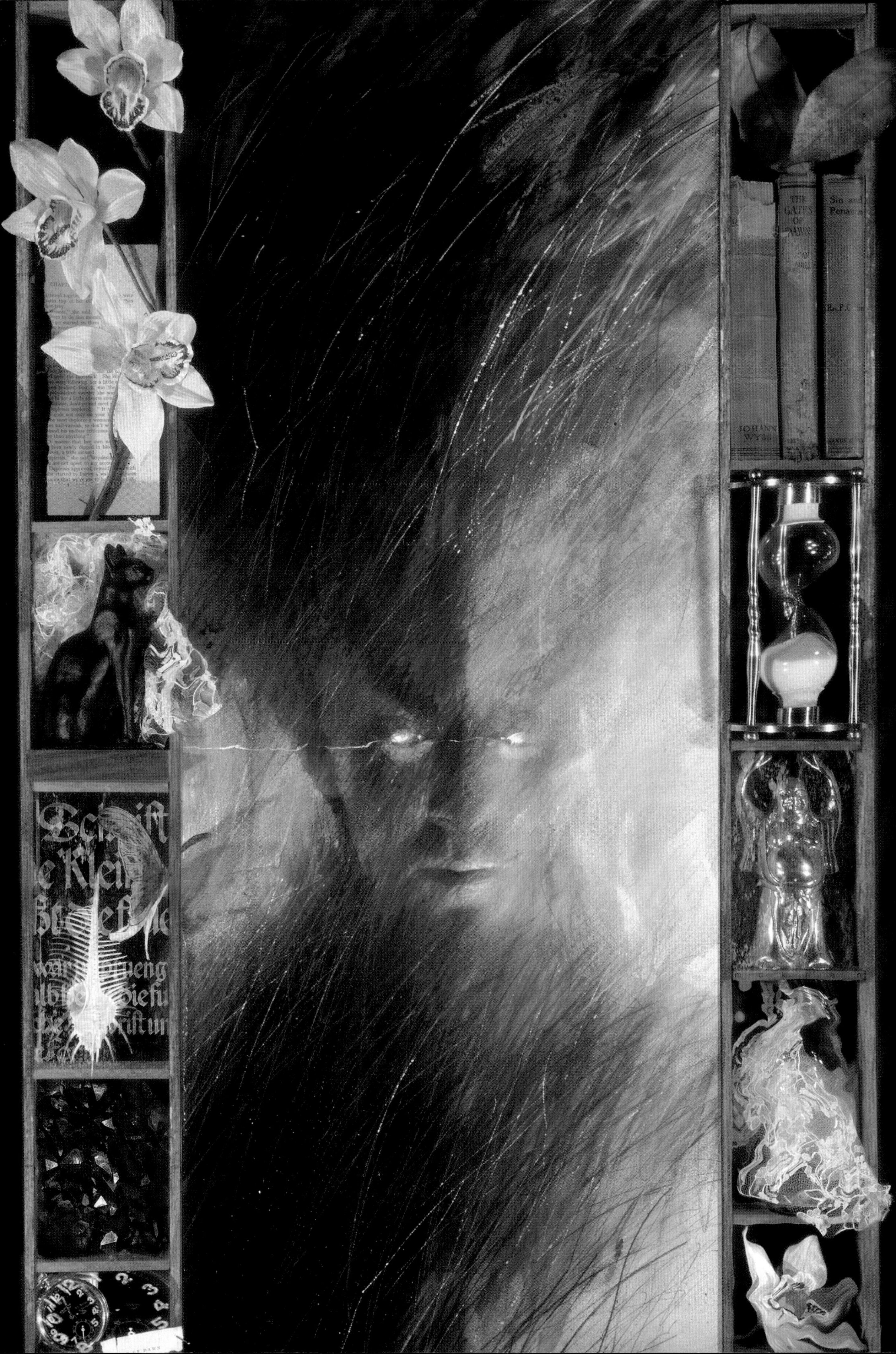

CHAPTER 2

PRELUDES & NOCTURNES

IN WHICH THE DREAM KING ESCAPES FROM CAPTIVITY, RECLAIMS HIS KINGDOM, AND FEEDS PIGEONS IN A NEW YORK CITY PARK WITH HIS OLDER SISTER.

One of Neil Gaiman's single most brilliant imaginings is this: Mr. Sandman is not Mr. Happy. No, the Dream King is not a cheery fellow who will sprinkle sleep dust in your eyes and send you a dream. Instead, he is a dark, enigmatic figure, gaunt, brooding, and somber. His duty weighs heavily on him: Like a tortured rock star or a reluctant king, he has the look of a loner forced into a very public role. Give him a scythe, and he would look like a portrait of the Grim Reaper as a young man.

And like all great literary inventions it has the ring of truth of something always known but previously unacknowledged. This is why your dreams are not usually the dreams of candyland and happily-ever-after. This is why you wake up sweating, unsettled, the sheets in a tangle around your legs. Dream of the Endless family is a spooky bastard. And, like all gracefully dangerous things, more than a little bit sexy, too.

"ONE OF THE THINGS YOU NEVER HAD IN COMICS WAS FAMILY. YOU DIDN'T HAVE SIBLING RELATIONSHIPS, AND ALL THAT THAT IMPLIED — RIVALRIES, ALLIANCES — ALL THAT YOU GET IN LARGE FAMILIES." —NEIL GAIMAN ON CREATING THE ENDLESS.

The flip side of this invention is just as brilliant, or maybe more so: Dream has a sister, and that sister is Death. And she is perky. She's also pretty, piquant, bright, and sunny as any classic Hollywood gamine. She is the eternal "It" girl, youthful, poised, slender as a gazelle, impossibly sweet and surprisingly wise, cast in the role of a lifetime. Of all of our lifetimes.

PAGE 28 Cover, *The Sandman* no.1. Artwork by Dave McKean.

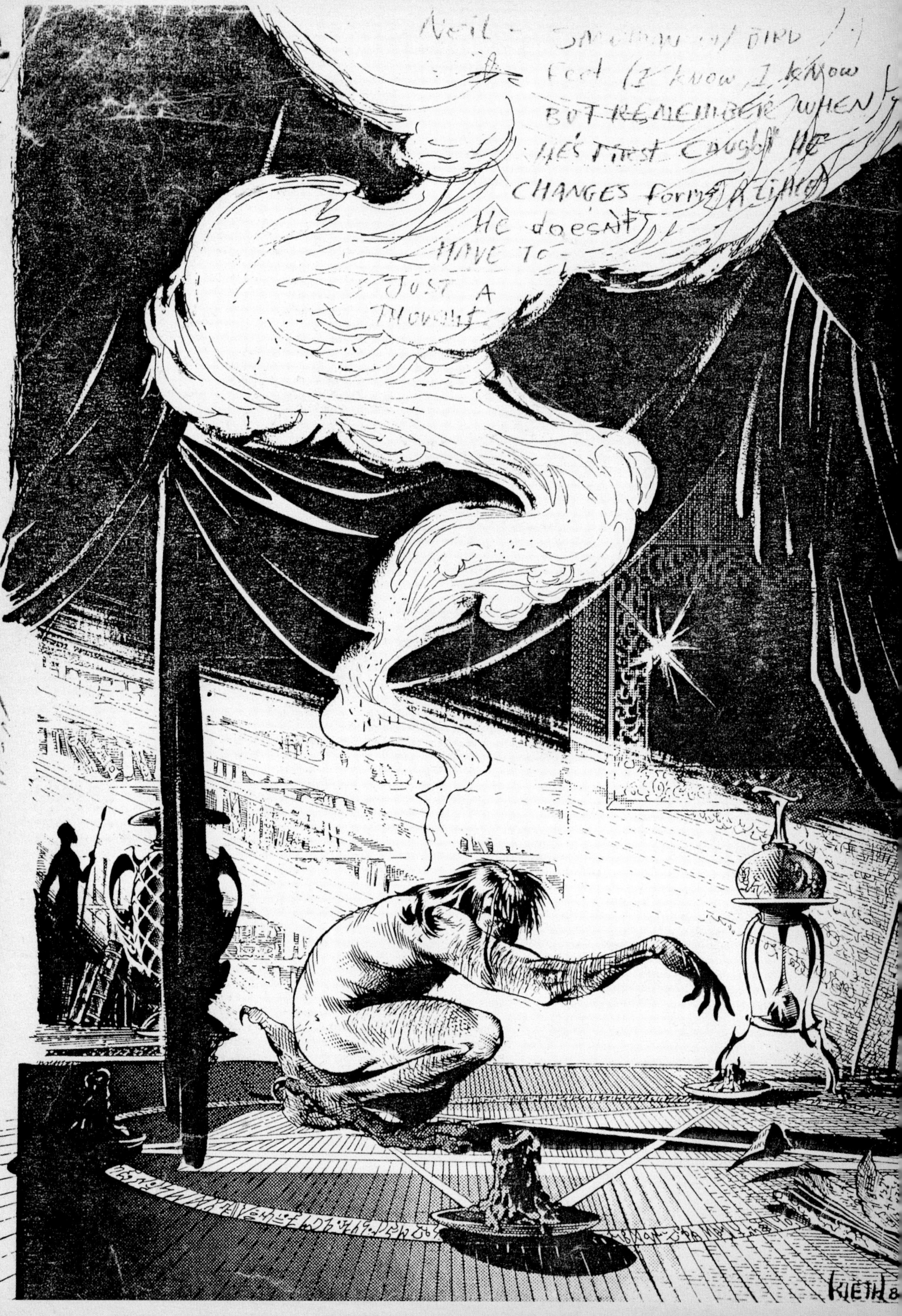
Neil - SANDMAN w/ BIRD
feet (I know I know
BUT REMEMBER WHEN
HE'S FIRST CAUGHT HE
CHANGES forms A LITTLE
He doesn't
HAVE TO -
JUST A
THOUGHT
KIETH

PAGE 30 A Sam Kieth Sandman sample. BELOW LEFT Neil's first sketch, and the second drawing ever, of Death from the cover of his thumbnail comic for *The Sandman* no. 8. BELOW RIGHT Dave McKean's cover for *The Sandman* no. 8, "The Sound of Her Wings," in which Death is introduced.

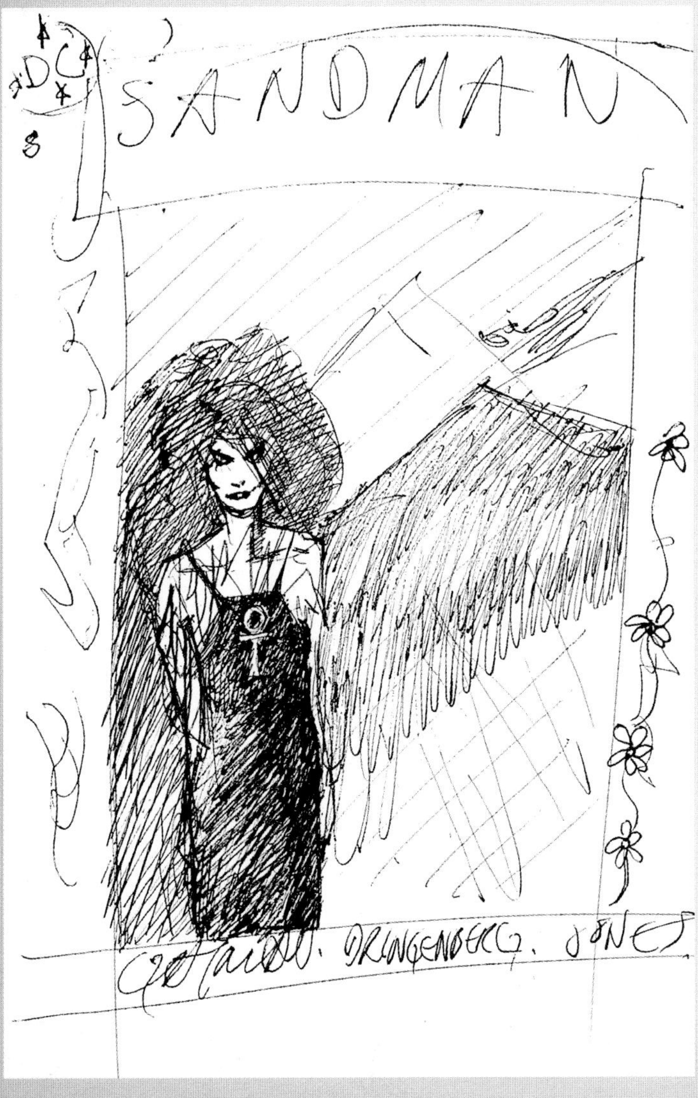
SANDMAN

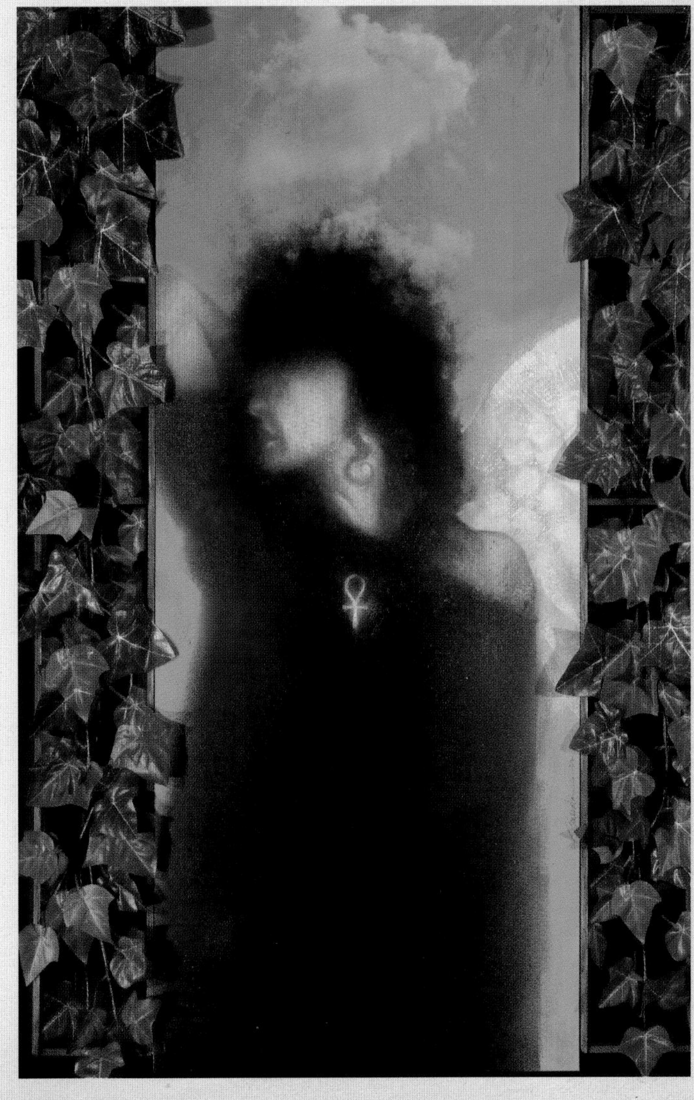

BELOW Death's first appearance, *"The Sound of Her Wings."* Artwork by Mike Dringenberg and Malcolm Jones III. Robbie Busch, colorist. BOTTOM Artwork by Mike Dringenberg and Malcolm Jones III. Robbie Busch, colorist. PAGE 33 Death's sensible attitude made her the perfect character to inform readers about safer sex in this 1994 comic handout. (The free volume first appeared as an insert to pre-VERTIGO titles in late 1992.) Artwork by Dave McKean.

Many great stories have a compelling brother-sister pairing at their core. Isis and Osiris. Hansel and Gretel. Donny and Marie. All right, so only some of these examples work. But with Dream and Death, this pairing of opposites operates on many different levels. Dream's gloom and Death's carefree attitude play off each other. Here is Hamlet's soliloquy incarnate, except it's not the sleep of Death we need fear: It's the other guy. It's Dream.

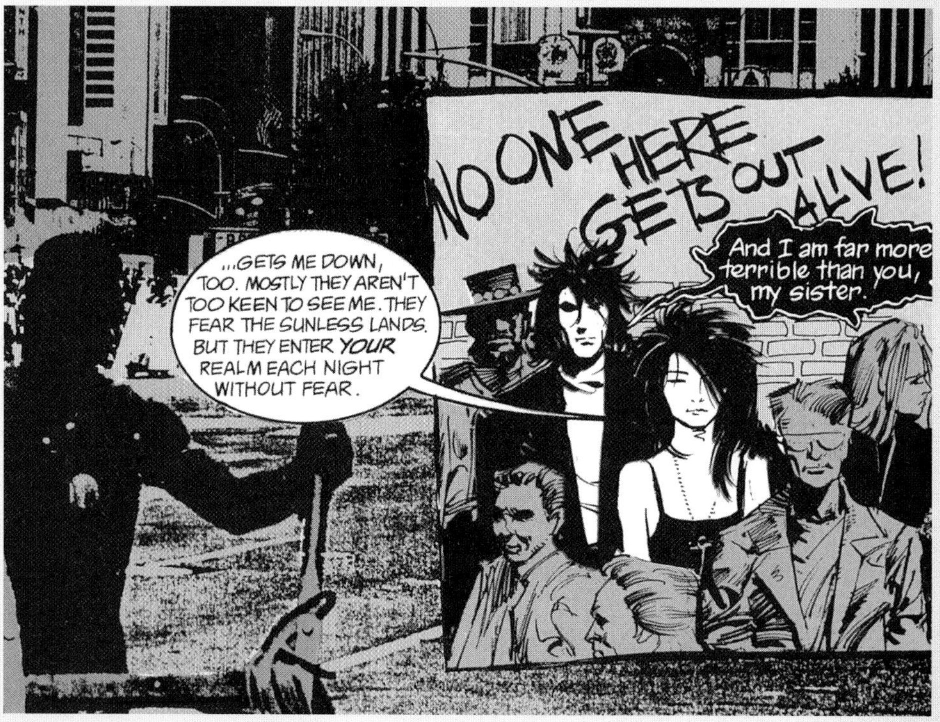
NO ONE HERE GETS OUT ALIVE!
...GETS ME DOWN, TOO. MOSTLY THEY AREN'T TOO KEEN TO SEE ME. THEY FEAR THE SUNLESS LANDS. BUT THEY ENTER YOUR REALM EACH NIGHT WITHOUT FEAR.
And I am far more terrible than you, my sister.

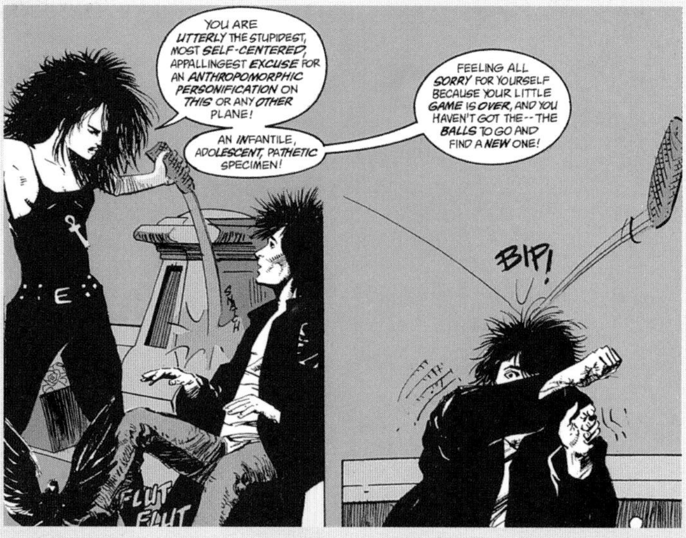
YOU ARE UTTERLY THE STUPIDEST, MOST SELF-CENTERED, APPALLINGEST EXCUSE FOR AN ANTHROPOMORPHIC PERSONIFICATION ON THIS OR ANY OTHER PLANE!
AN INFANTILE, ADOLESCENT, PATHETIC SPECIMEN!
FEELING ALL SORRY FOR YOURSELF BECAUSE YOUR LITTLE GAME IS OVER, AND YOU HAVEN'T GOT THE-- THE BALLS TO GO AND FIND A NEW ONE!
BIP!
FLUT FLUT

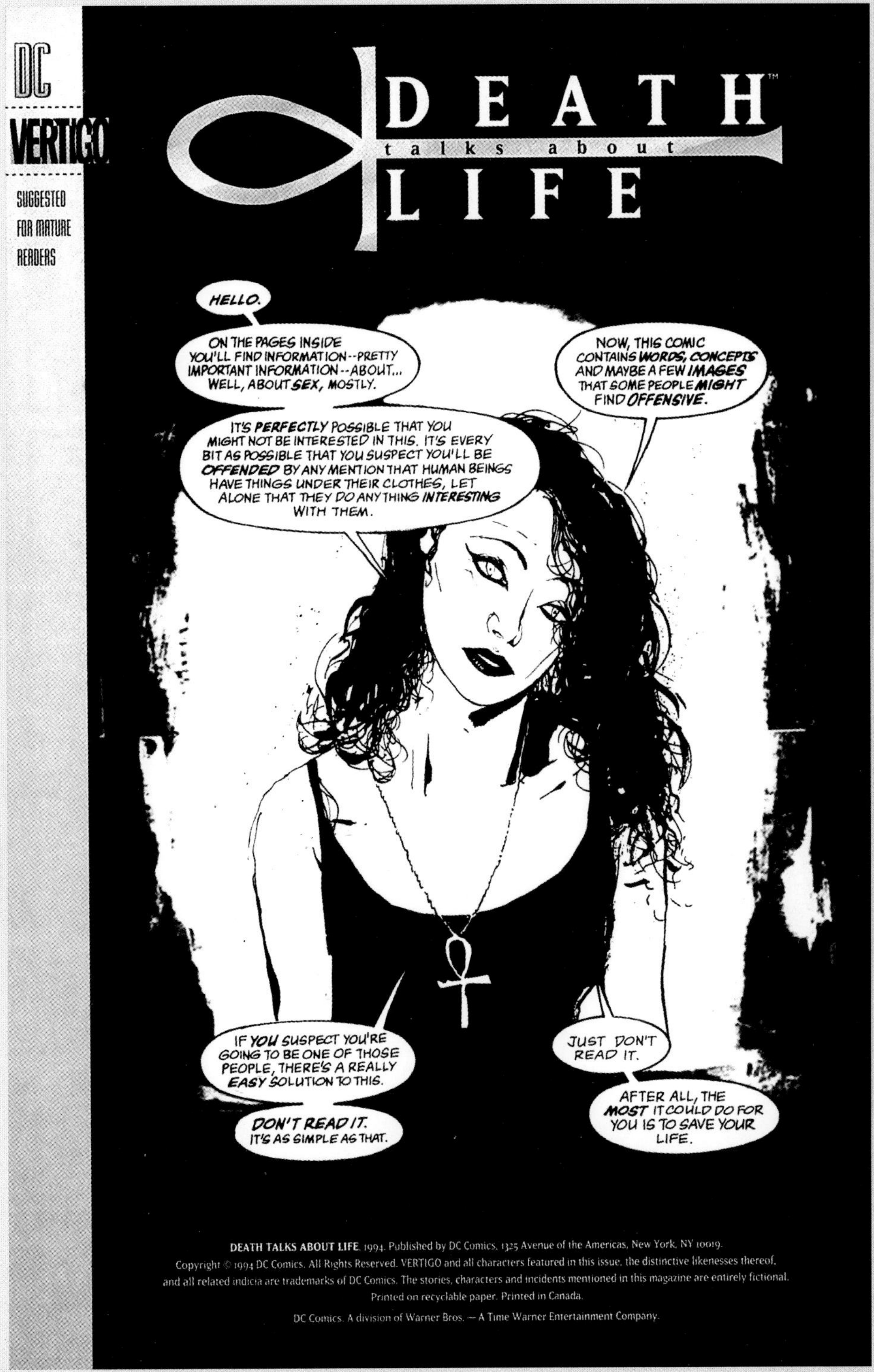
DC
VERTIGO
SUGGESTED FOR MATURE READERS
DEATH talks about LIFE
HELLO.
ON THE PAGES INSIDE YOU'LL FIND INFORMATION--PRETTY IMPORTANT INFORMATION--ABOUT... WELL, ABOUT SEX, MOSTLY.
NOW, THIS COMIC CONTAINS WORDS, CONCEPTS AND MAYBE A FEW IMAGES THAT SOME PEOPLE MIGHT FIND OFFENSIVE.
IT'S PERFECTLY POSSIBLE THAT YOU MIGHT NOT BE INTERESTED IN THIS. IT'S EVERY BIT AS POSSIBLE THAT YOU SUSPECT YOU'LL BE OFFENDED BY ANY MENTION THAT HUMAN BEINGS HAVE THINGS UNDER THEIR CLOTHES, LET ALONE THAT THEY DO ANYTHING INTERESTING WITH THEM.
IF YOU SUSPECT YOU'RE GOING TO BE ONE OF THOSE PEOPLE, THERE'S A REALLY EASY SOLUTION TO THIS.
DON'T READ IT. IT'S AS SIMPLE AS THAT.
JUST DON'T READ IT.
AFTER ALL, THE MOST IT COULD DO FOR YOU IS TO SAVE YOUR LIFE.
DEATH TALKS ABOUT LIFE. 1994. Published by DC Comics, 1325 Avenue of the Americas, New York, NY 10019.
Copyright © 1994 DC Comics. All Rights Reserved. VERTIGO and all characters featured in this issue, the distinctive likenesses thereof, and all related indicia are trademarks of DC Comics. The stories, characters and incidents mentioned in this magazine are entirely fictional.
Printed on recyclable paper. Printed in Canada.
DC Comics. A division of Warner Bros. — A Time Warner Entertainment Company.

But lest we get too carried away with literary pairings, Death and Dream are also typical siblings. They bicker. They criticize. And, in Dream's case, they sulk. Until Death beans him on the head, that is.

The basic mythology of *The Sandman* is set up in *Preludes & Nocturnes*, the trade paperback collection of the first eight issues of the series.

This is the first and most straightforward of the major storylines, a quintessential quest for objects of great magical value. In it, we find the Sandman in the classic position of a hero down on his luck. He is a ruler who has been held prisoner and made a slave, and as we follow his quest to restore himself to his rightful place, we watch his persona reforming. Weak and vulnerable at the beginning, he becomes more and more regal, arrogant, and aloof. It will be halfway through the series before we again see the Sandman made vulnerable, but for now there is real pleasure in watching a dethroned king win his kingdom back through the use of his wits. It's like observing a victim of

BELOW Cain and Abel as they appeared during Alan Moore's run on *Swamp Thing*. Artwork by Ron Randall.
PAGE 35 Neil shows an early appreciation for dreams in his first assignment for DC Comics, *Black Orchid*. Artwork by Dave McKean.

starvation returning to health, and Morpheus has been starved of all the things that nourish him. He has been starved of dreams.

The Sandman's kingdom, the Dreaming, has also suffered in his absence, and many of his subjects have fled into the waking world, where they do not belong. But Cain and Abel, the caretakers of the Houses of Mystery and Secrets, remain, as does Lucien the librarian. Cain and Abel are old narrators from 1970s horror comics titled, aptly enough, *The House of Mystery* and *The House of Secrets;* Lucien originally hosted a book called *Tales of Ghost Castle.*

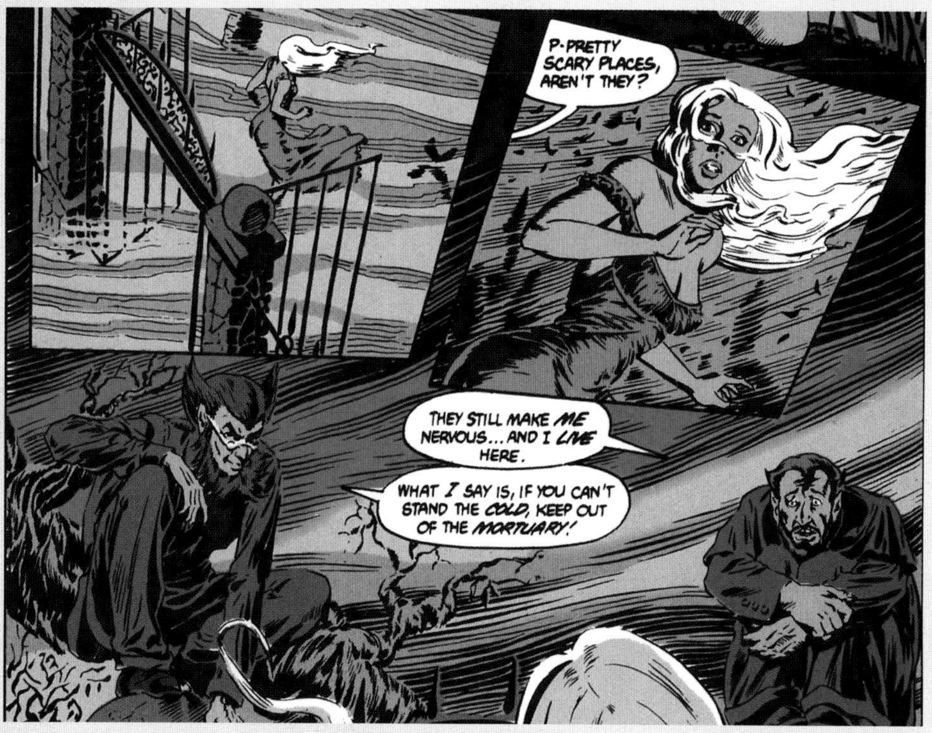
P-PRETTY SCARY PLACES, AREN'T THEY?
THEY STILL MAKE ME NERVOUS... AND I LIVE HERE.
WHAT I SAY IS, IF YOU CAN'T STAND THE COLD, KEEP OUT OF THE MORTUARY!

Cain and Abel are also familiar to readers of *Swamp Thing*. In the early '80s, writer Alan Moore's work on *Swamp Thing* changed the course of comics history, as his dark, rich, subtly shaded stories revealed the level of characterization, emotion, and even poetry that could be achieved in the medium. Naturally, DC went hunting in England for more writers of Alan's ilk, and it was on one of these shopping expeditions that Neil Gaiman and Dave McKean got their first DC assignment, *Black Orchid*, a lovely eco-terror tale featuring a long-forgotten plant lady from the annals of DC.

"Neil had sent me a short *Swamp Thing* story," recalls Karen Berger, "and politely pestered me for a year before I actually met him in England. It wasn't a case of instant recognition. I knew he was good, but it wasn't until *The Sandman* that I saw the scope and breadth of his writing ability."

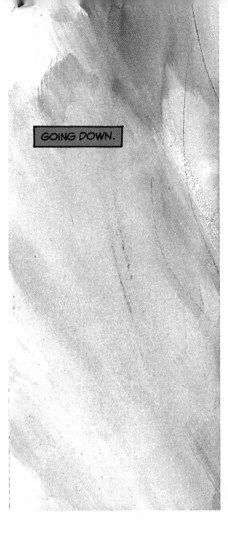

GOING DOWN.

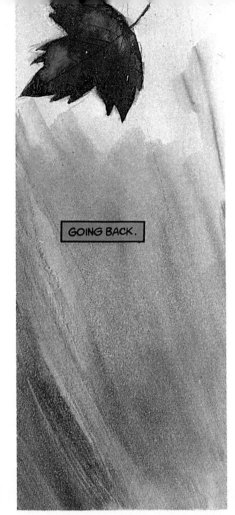

GOING BACK.

FALLING.

IN DREAMS WE FIND ONLY CONTRADICTIONS.

I TUMBLE INTO THE PAST, AWASH IN ANOTHER'S MEMORIES.

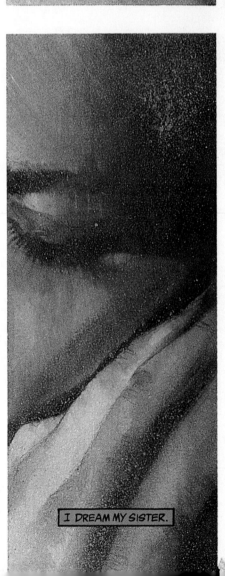

I DREAM MY SISTER.

BELOW The Sandman from the 1940s, Wesley Dodd, appears in *The Sandman*'s first issue. Artwork by Sam Kieth and Mike Dringenberg. Robbie Busch, colorist. PAGE 37 *Sandman Midnight Theatre,* written by Neil Gaiman and plotted by Matt Wagner, was the first and only meeting between the Sandman of the 1940s and Neil's Dream King. Artist Teddy Kristiansen, who supplied the images for the prestige format comic, executed this haunting piece as well.

The Sandman was not Neil's first choice of a character to star in a monthly series. Neil had a fondness for the brooding, solitary, mysterious Phantom Stranger – a wielder of magic who first appeared in the 1950s. Despite the character's longevity he remained somewhat obscure. DC also felt that the Stranger's passive nature was too much a vehicle for other people's stories, and the idea was rejected.

So Neil would end up inventing another character, the Sandman, or, rather, reinventing. (There was a 1940s character by the same name and a second incarnation in the 1970s. The latter also appears in Neil's series and figures into *Sandman* mythology.)

THE UNIVERSE KNOWS SOMEONE IS MISSING, AND SLOWLY IT ATTEMPTS TO REPLACE HIM.
WESLEY DODDS'S NIGHTMARES HAVE STOPPED SINCE HE STARTED GOING OUT AT NIGHT.
HE PUTS EVIL PEOPLE TO SLEEP WITH GAS, THEN SPRINKLES SAND ON THEM, LEAVES THEM FOR THE POLICE TO FIND IN THE MORNING...
THE IDEA CAME TO HIM IN HIS SLEEP.
HE DOESN'T DREAM ABOUT THE MAN IN THE STRANGE HELMET ANYMORE. NO MORE BURNING EYES.
EVERYTHING'S ALL RIGHT.
WESLEY DODDS SLEEPS THE SLEEP OF THE JUST.
18
30

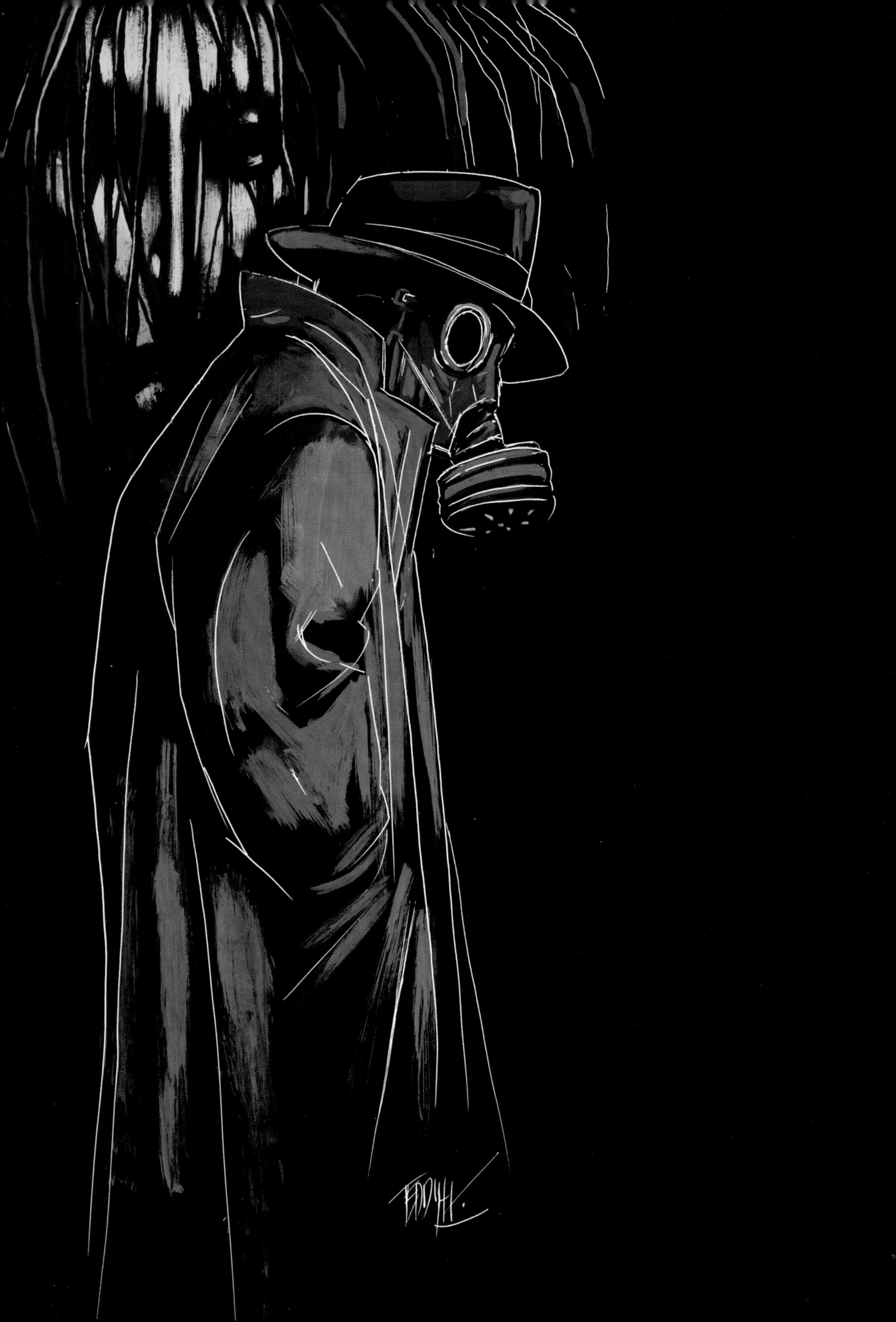

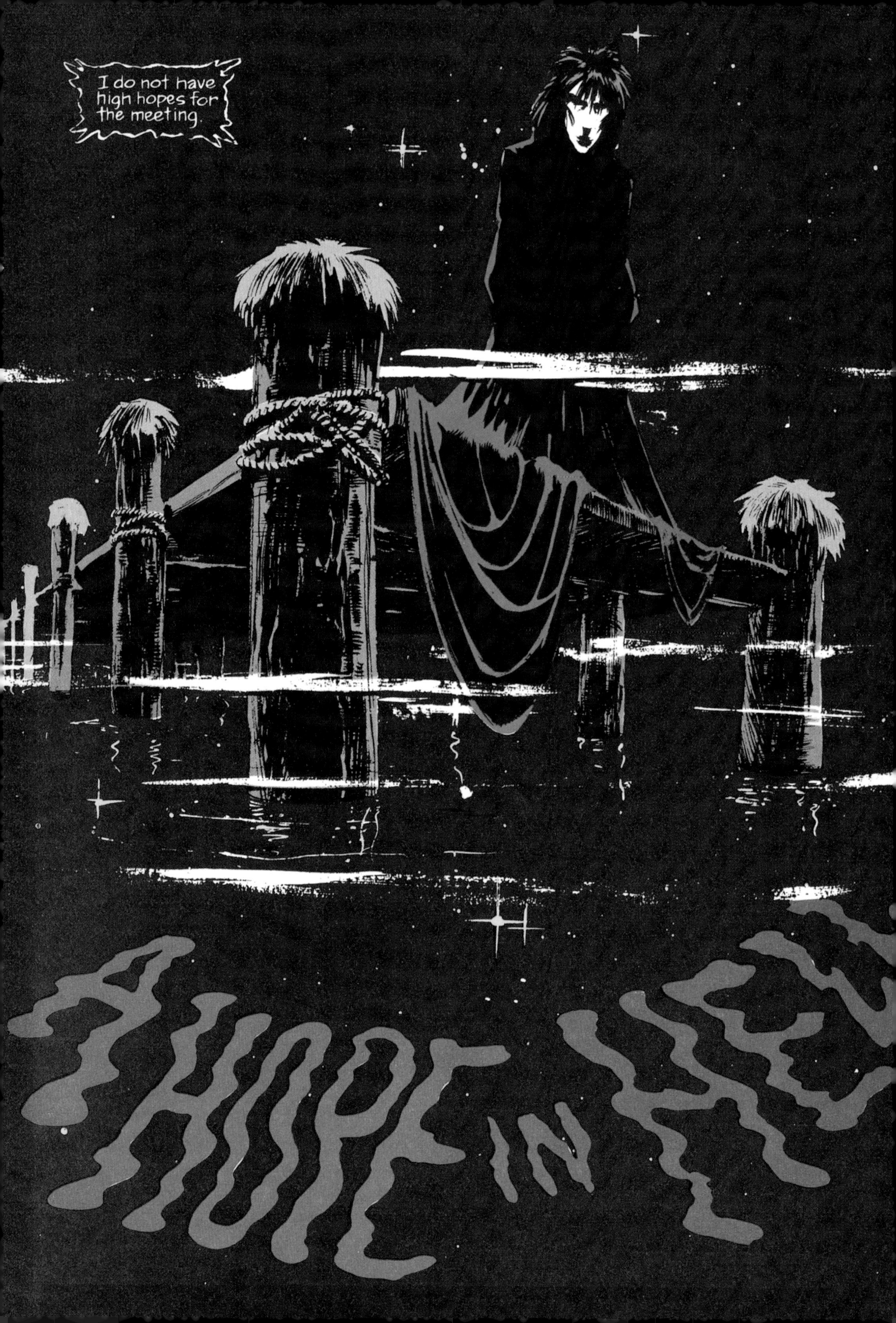
I do not have high hopes for the meeting.
A HOPE IN

PAGE 38 *Sam Kieth's version of the character, inked by Mike Dringenberg. Robbie Busch, colorist.* BELOW *Several Sandman doodles done in margins and on scraps by Neil while he was working on the initial proposal in 1987. These sketches are a few of the many that Neil drew as studies on the Sandman's visage. "I was trying to experiment with different ways Morpheus might look; the myriad forms and shapes that his face might take," says Neil.*

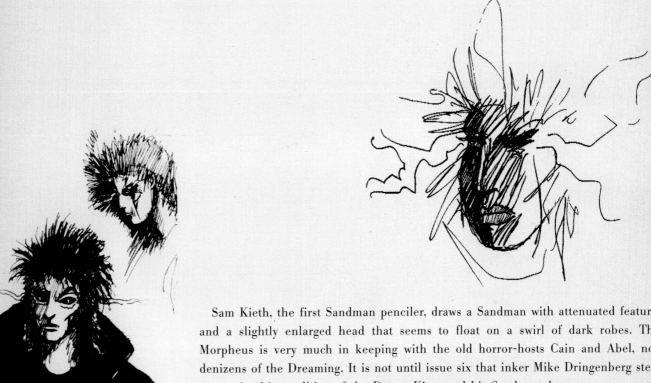

Sam Kieth, the first Sandman penciler, draws a Sandman with attenuated features and a slightly enlarged head that seems to float on a swirl of dark robes. This Morpheus is very much in keeping with the old horror-hosts Cain and Abel, now denizens of the Dreaming. It is not until issue six that inker Mike Dringenberg steps up to give his rendition of the Dream King, and his Sandman does not appear until the very last panel of the very last page. But already we can see a difference in tone. Neil Gaiman is not just a good writer, he is a good *comics* writer, which means he knows how to write to an artist's strengths. With Dringenberg, Neil's ability to create a darkly erotic undertone becomes apparent for the first time. Dringenberg's Sandman has none of Kieth's gnomish charm. Instead, he is deadly serious and deadly beautiful. He still has the dark cloak, but sometimes he exchanges it for black jeans and a T-shirt, and he is no longer a huge head and a frail body. Dringenberg shows us a Sandman who sprawls with the muscular grace of a young man, and in issue eight — the quiet, poignant meditation on mortality that crystallized *The Sandman*'s promise and made everyone sit up and take notice — Dringenberg helps create a creature never before seen in mainstream comics, Dream's sister, Death.

Even now, over a decade later, sexy comic book females tend to come in one size only: busty and curvy. But Dringenberg didn't just contribute a face for Death and a few props; he showed real vision when he invested this thin, wild-haired Goth-girl with a face that reflects winsome intelligence and utterly confident charm.

It is this quiet meeting between two siblings that marks the first major turning point in *The Sandman*. Neil knew that he'd already done what everyone expected him to do with his character — sent him on an adventure filled with danger, horror, and the promise of reward. Now he had the audience in hand enough to show what this character could really do.

BELOW AND PAGE 41 From "The Sound of Her Wings." Artwork by Mike Dringenberg and Malcolm Jones III. Robbie Busch, colorist.

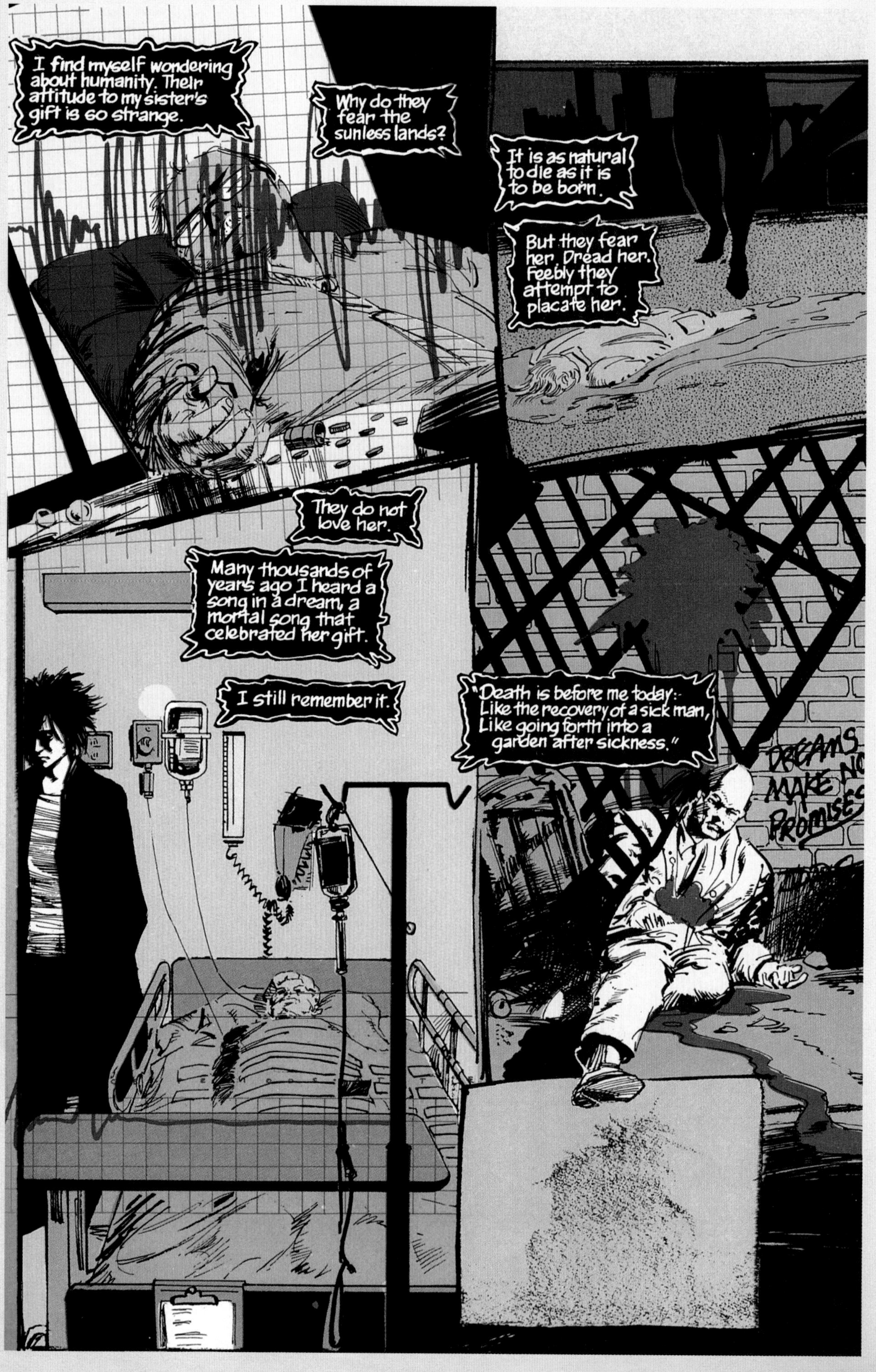
I find myself wondering about humanity. Their attitude to my sister's gift is so strange.
Why do they fear the sunless lands?
It is as natural to die as it is to be born.
But they fear her. Dread her. Feebly they attempt to placate her.
They do not love her.
Many thousands of years ago I heard a song in a dream, a mortal song that celebrated her gift.
I still remember it.
"Death is before me today: Like the recovery of a sick man, Like going forth into a garden after sickness."
DREAMS MAKE NO PROMISES

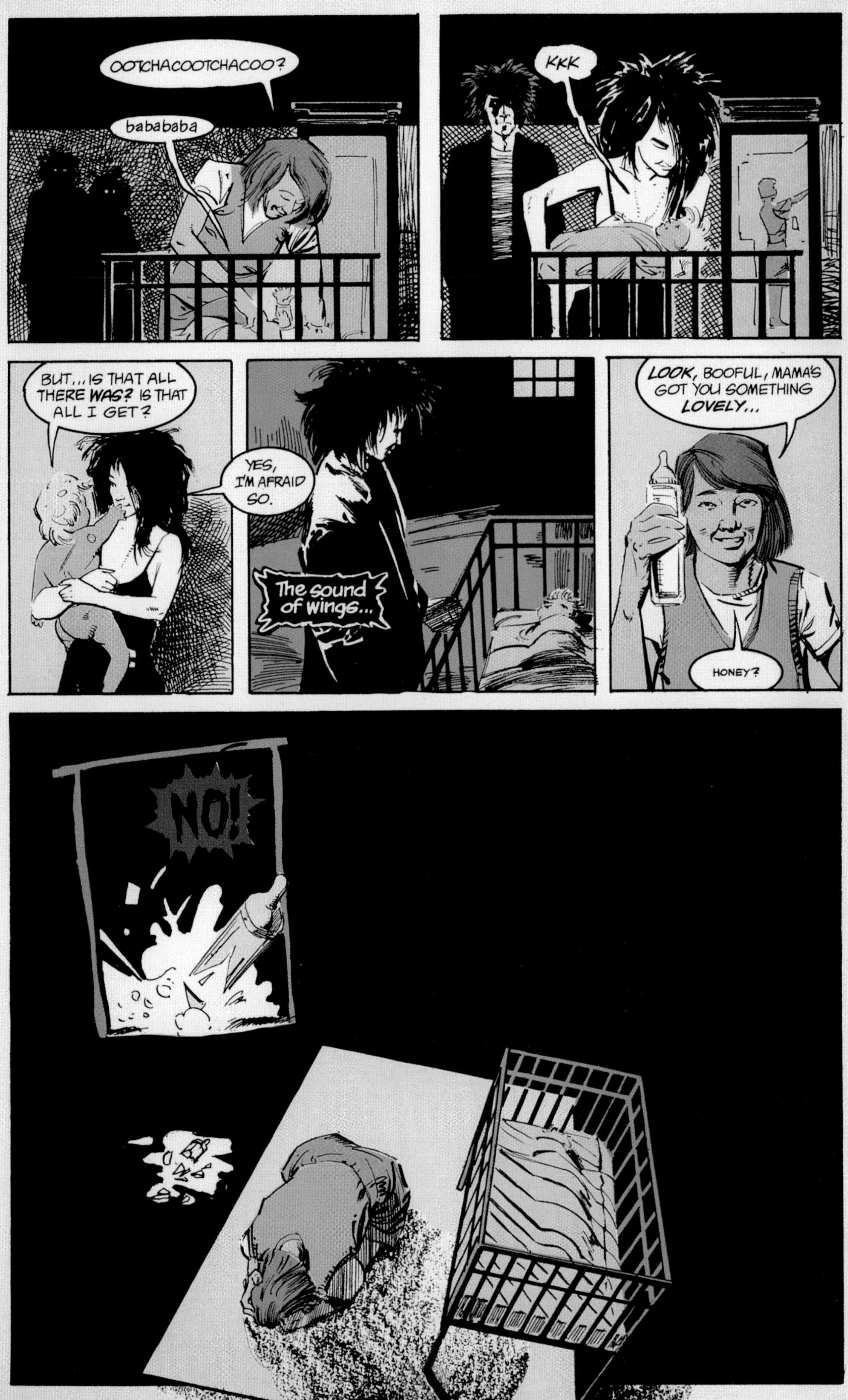
OOTCHACOOTCHACOO?
babababa
KKK
BUT... IS THAT ALL THERE WAS? IS THAT ALL I GET?
YES, I'M AFRAID SO.
The sound of wings...
LOOK, BOOFUL, MAMA'S GOT YOU SOMETHING LOVELY...
HONEY?
NO!

BELOW From the original *Witching Hour* comic. Artwork by the legendary Alex Toth.

Yet, looking back on the first seven issues, there are unexpected treasures to be found. From the beginning, Neil introduces themes that will be explored again and again throughout the series. The basic arc of this first storyline seems like a fairy tale: The displaced hero must fight his way back to reclaim his kingdom. But, as we learn later on in the series, we are really in the paradigm of classical mythology, not folk tale, because the actions Morpheus takes to secure his throne ultimately lead to his destruction – ironically, in order to safeguard his kingdom.

One excellent example of how *The Sandman* seeds its beginning with hints of the end occurs in issue two, "Imperfect Hosts." It is here that we meet the three witches from DC's old *Witching Hour* comic, Cynthia, Mildred, and Mordred, who appear as an incarnation of the Triple Goddess, the three who are one: maiden, mother, and crone.

In three short pages, we are told how very many names the ladies possess: the Hecateae, Queen of Witches; The Fates (Clotho, Lachesis, and Atropos); the Furies (Tisiphone, Alecto, and Magaera); and the Irish Morrigan. Morpheus flatteringly calls them the Graces.

We meet this mutable triad of female power in an issue that deals with vengeance and rules, and it is as if we are hearing an overture to an opera, exploring for the first time motifs that will be played in countless, exquisite variations throughout the series.

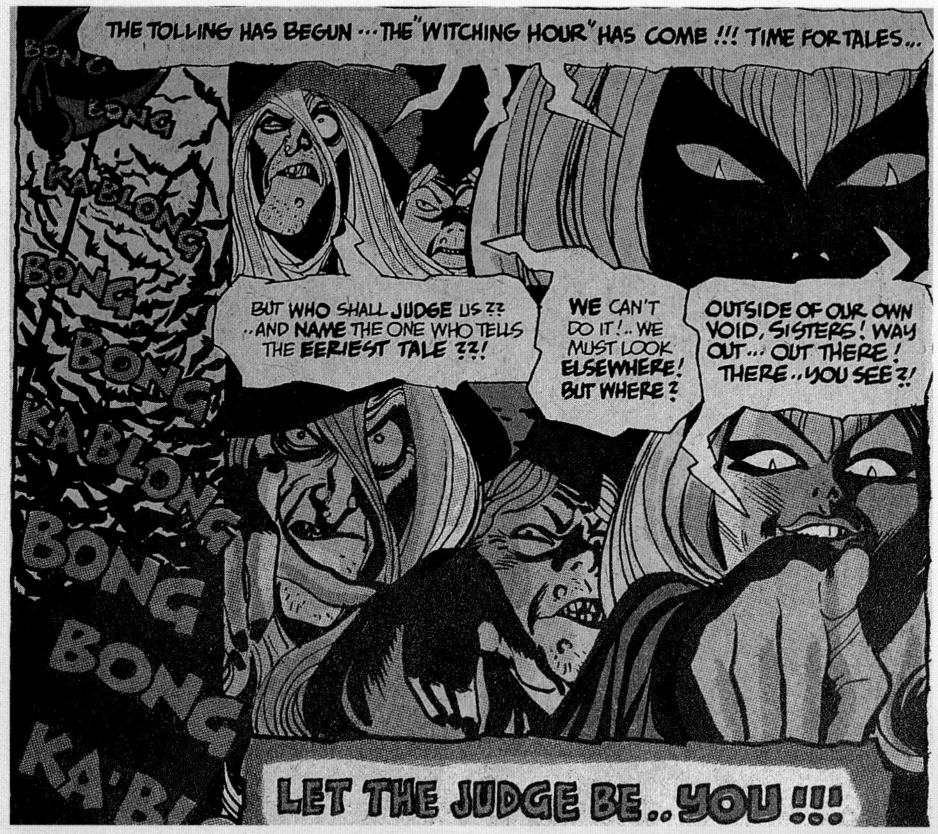
THE TOLLING HAS BEGUN ... THE "WITCHING HOUR" HAS COME !!! TIME FOR TALES...
BONG
BONG
KABLONG
BONG
BONG
KABLONG
BONG
BONG
BONG
BUT WHO SHALL JUDGE US ?? ..AND NAME THE ONE WHO TELLS THE EERIEST TALE ??!
WE CAN'T DO IT! .. WE MUST LOOK ELSEWHERE! BUT WHERE?
OUTSIDE OF OUR OWN VOID, SISTERS! WAY OUT... OUT THERE! THERE..YOU SEE?!
LET THE JUDGE BE.. YOU !!!

BELOW The version of the Three Witches that appeared in Alisa Kwitney's and James Robinson's *Witchcraft* from *The Sandman* trading-card series. Artwork by Michael Zulli.

Along with duty and mercy, these themes are woven throughout *The Sandman* saga until they are gathered together at the end by — who else? The Fates, the spinner, the measurer, and the cutter of the threads of existence.

"I BEGAN WITH TRYING TO FIGURE OUT WHO DREAM IS, WHAT DREAM IS, AND FIGURED DREAM IS THE BROTHER OF DEATH — IT'S A CLASSIC LINE. AND I WAS THINKING OF THE OLD DC CHARACTER DESTINY — WHAT I LIKED THE MOST ABOUT HIM WAS THAT NOBODY KNEW ANYTHING ABOUT HIM. HE WAS THIS GUY WITH A BOOK AND A CLOAK AND SEEMED TO BE AS POWERFUL AS ANYONE IN THE DC UNIVERSE WHEN HE WANTED TO BE. IN THIS ONE STORY I REMEMBER READING, SUPERMAN WAS GOING TO THE EDGE OF THE UNIVERSE, AND WHEN HE GOT THERE DESTINY WAS STANDING WITH HIS BOOK AND TOLD HIM, 'FURTHER THAN THIS YOU CANNOT GO.'

  SO THEN I HAD DREAM, DEATH AND DESTINY, THE THREE DS, AND I HAD THE AGES. THEY WERE A FAMILY, BECAUSE DESTINY HAD TO BE THE OLDEST, AND THEN CAME DEATH, BECAUSE ONCE YOU HAVE THE FIRST LIVING THING YOU HAVE TO HAVE DEATH. AND THEN YOU HAVE DREAM. AND THEN I WANTED TO DO THE YOUNGER ONES. SEVEN IS SUCH A GOOD NUMBER TO HAVE IN A FAMILY. IT SETS UP A PATTERN." — NEIL GAIMAN

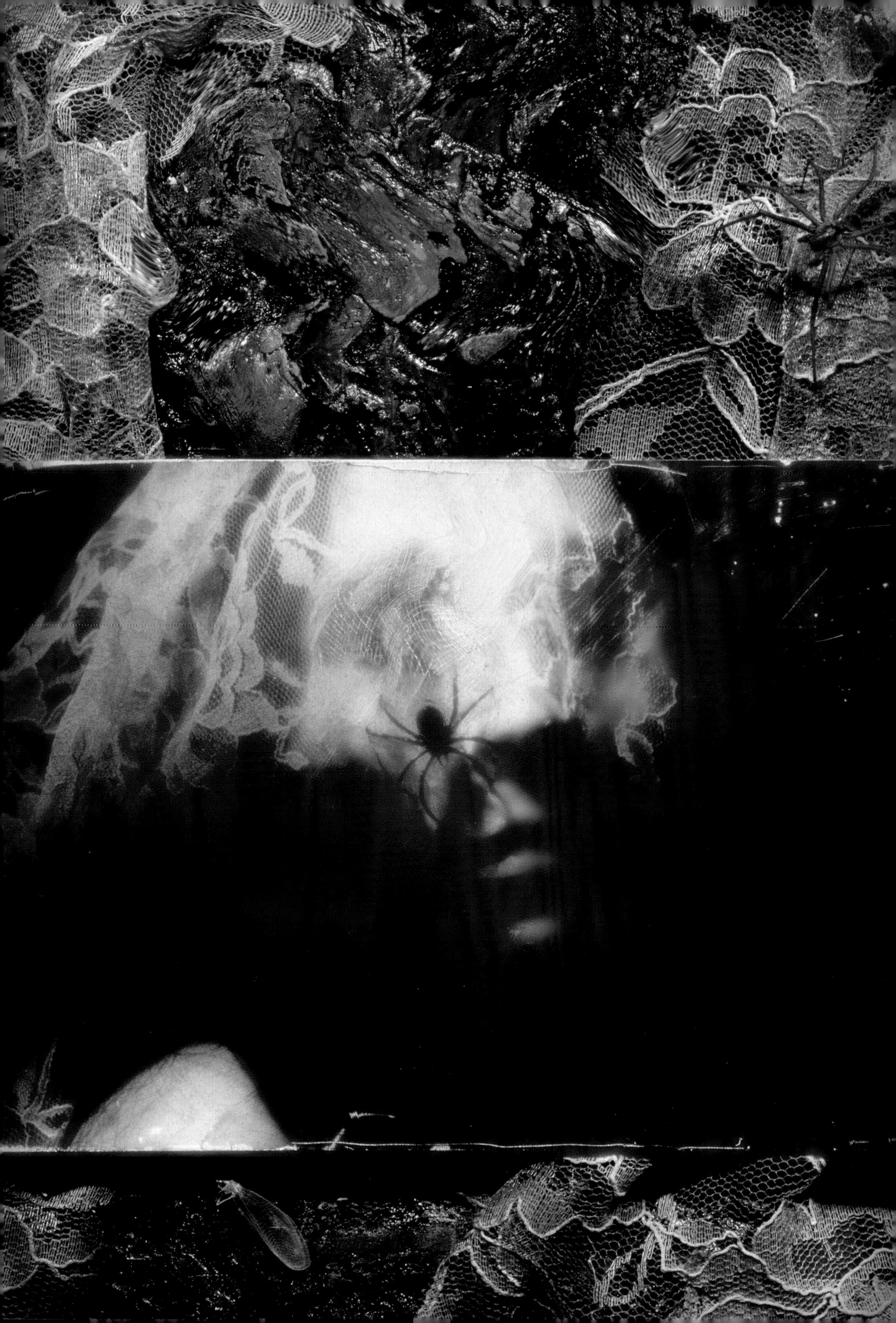

CHAPTER 3

THE DOLL'S HOUSE

IN WHICH ROSE WALKER FINDS MORE THAN SHE BARGAINED FOR, WE VISIT A SERIAL KILLER'S CONVENTION, ARE REINTRODUCED TO THE SANDMAN FROM THE 1970S, AND DISCOVER THAT DESIRE LIKES TO PLAY GAMES.

The next collected trade paperback, *The Doll's House*, is a clear demonstration of Neil's increasing confidence and command as a storyteller. Having begun his series with a more or less straightforward tale of the hero's quest, Neil establishes a new pattern with his next issue. Radically changing tone and setting, Neil writes a powerful stand-alone issue that precedes a longer storyline as well as comments upon it.

"Tales in the Sand," a prologue to *The Doll's House*, is the first Sandman story to showcase Neil's ability to capture the flavor of a specific kind of story (in this case, an African folktale about one of Sandman's tragic mortal loves), and it hints again at the ongoing theme of male vs. female magics and realities.

From this point on, *The Sandman* alternates between short, self-contained stories and longer storylines. But more connects the disparate sequences than is immediately apparent: Again and again, themes, objects, and background characters that make brief appearances in one tale reappear center stage later on.

"Tales in the Sand" marks another kind of turning point as well. For a while, *The Sandman*'s artistic team seemed firmly in place, but it was during the time this issue was in development that this, too, began to change.

Like many marriages and most rock bands, there were tensions beneath the surface. Mike Dringenberg, who had invested Morpheus with a brooding, masculine beauty and Death with her signature punk gamine look, had trouble keeping to the rigorous monthly schedule.

PAGE 44 Cover, *The Sandman* no. 15. Artwork by Dave McKean. PAGES 46–47 This is an unusual spread in that, as Neil Gaiman points out, "it is the only time in 2,000 pages that we see the Sandman laugh." Artwork by Chris Bachalo and Malcolm Jones III. Robbie Busch, colorist.

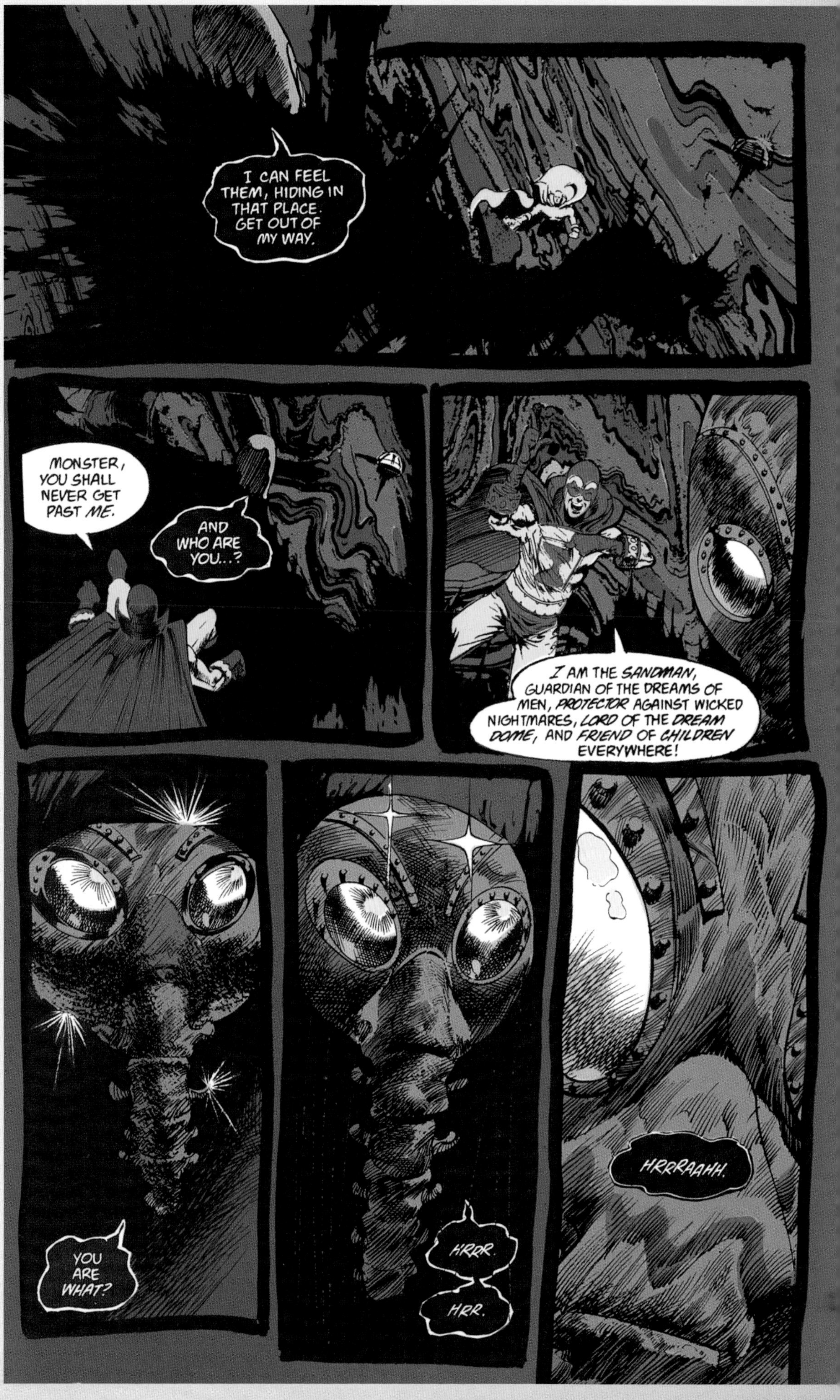
I CAN FEEL THEM, HIDING IN THAT PLACE. GET OUT OF MY WAY.
MONSTER, YOU SHALL NEVER GET PAST ME.
AND WHO ARE YOU...?
I AM THE SANDMAN, GUARDIAN OF THE DREAMS OF MEN, PROTECTOR AGAINST WICKED NIGHTMARES, LORD OF THE DREAM DOME, AND FRIEND OF CHILDREN EVERYWHERE!
YOU ARE WHAT?
HRRR.
HRR.
HRRRAAHH.

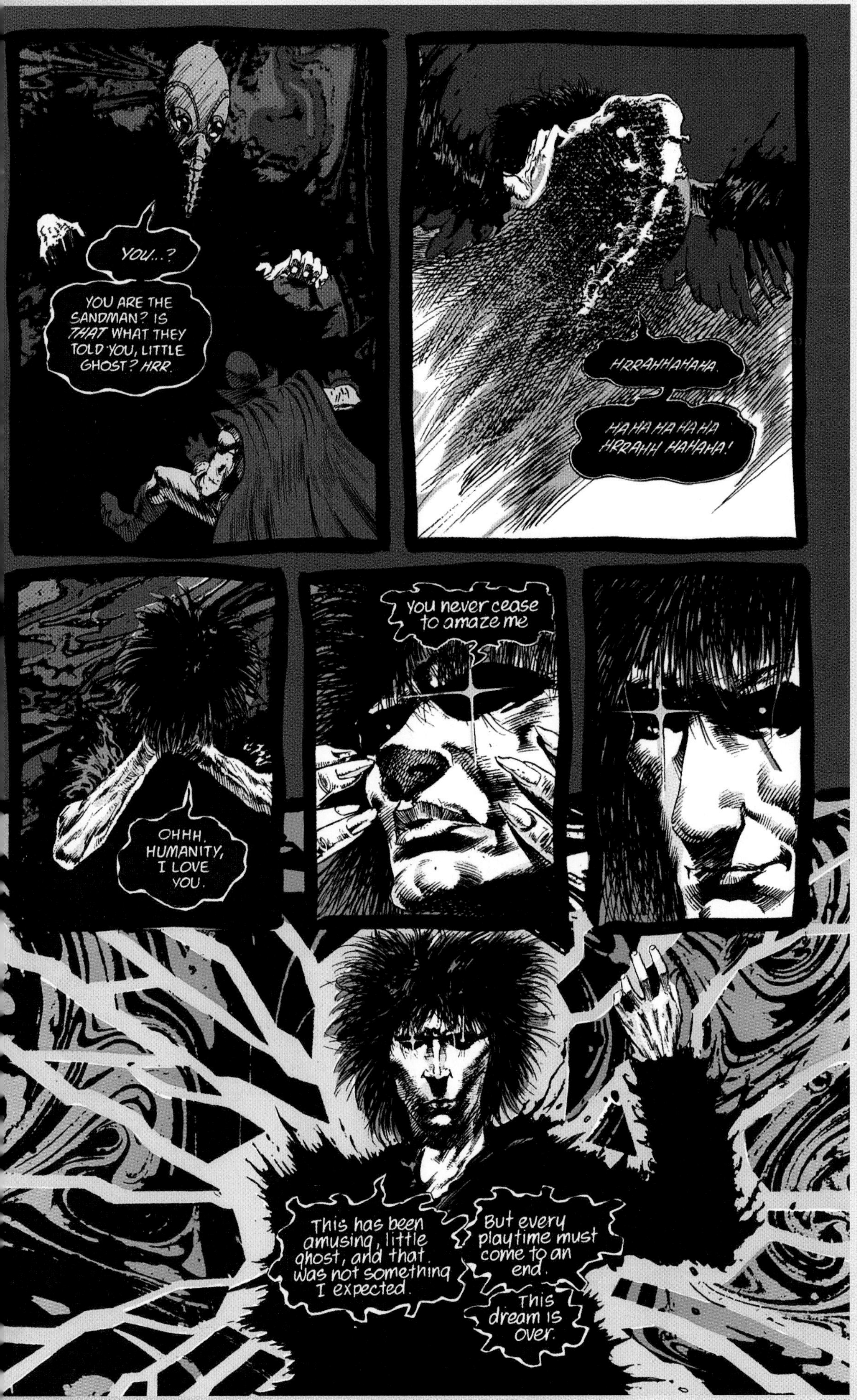
YOU...?
YOU ARE THE SANDMAN? IS *THAT* WHAT THEY TOLD YOU, LITTLE GHOST? *HRR.*
HRRAHHAHAHA.
HA HA HA HA HA HRRAHH HAHAHA!
OHHH. HUMANITY, I LOVE YOU.
you never cease to amaze me
This has been amusing, little ghost, and that was not something I expected.
But every playtime must come to an end.
This dream is over.

BELOW The Sandman confronts Lyta Hall for the first time. Artwork by Chris Bachalo and Malcolm Jones III. Robbie Busch, colorist.

As Dringenberg began work on the longer storyline of *The Doll's House*, Karen Berger tagged fledgling artist Chris Bachalo, who would become an industry star in his own right, to pencil another stand-alone issue. Chris filled in with the issue entitled, "Playing House."

In this issue, we meet Hector Hall, an earlier, gold-and-red-garbed incarnation of the Sandman. Hector, it turns out, has been dead for the past two years, living in the dreams of a very special child. Hector believes himself to be the Sandman because Brute and Glob, two escapees from the Dreaming, have been deluding him into being a puppet king.

The Sandman emotionlessly consigns Hector Hall to his sister's realm ("You belong with the dead, little ghost.") He handles Hector's grief-stricken wife, Lyta, with equal

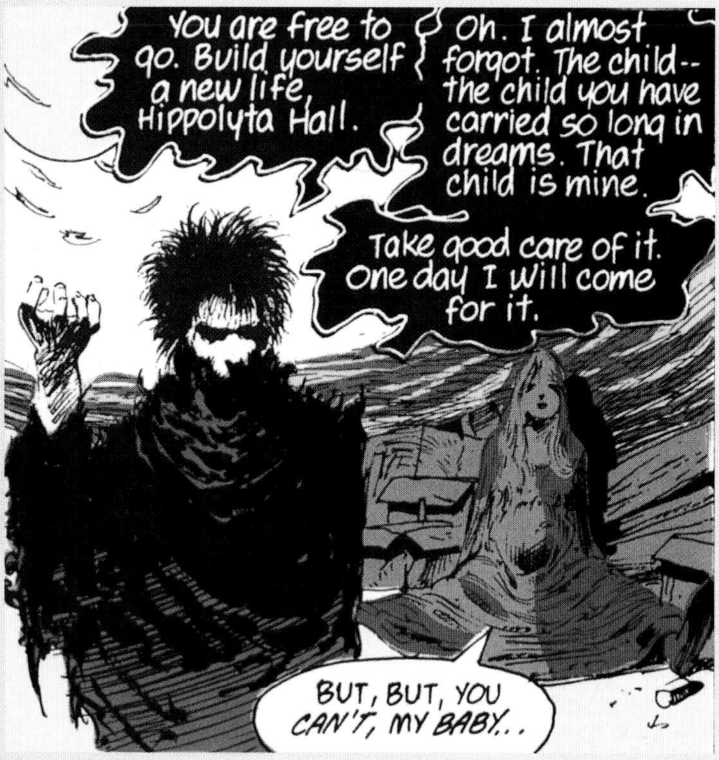
You are free to go. Build yourself a new life, Hippolyta Hall.
Oh. I almost forgot. The child-- the child you have carried so long in dreams. That child is mine.
Take good care of it. One day I will come for it.
BUT, BUT, YOU CAN'T, MY BABY. . .

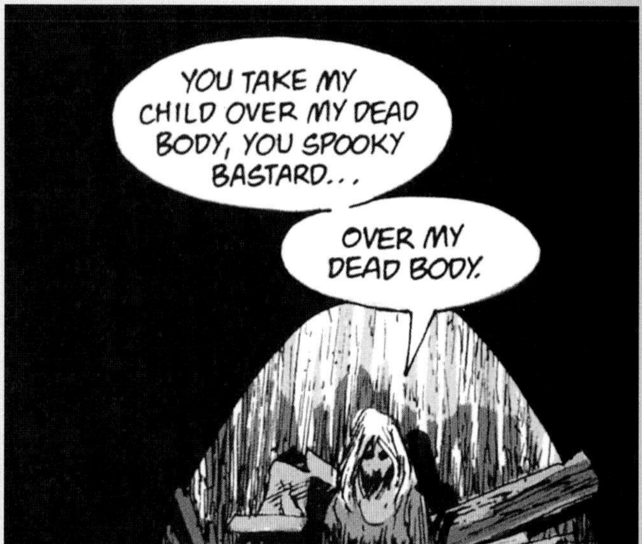
YOU TAKE MY CHILD OVER MY DEAD BODY, YOU SPOOKY BASTARD. . .
OVER MY DEAD BODY.

sangfroid. But when he tells her to rebuild her life, he turns his back on her before dealing the cruelest blow of all. The child she has carried so long in dreams, Morpheus says, is his. And one day he will come for it.

Depicting Lyta with her legs spread wide, one panel focusing on the V of her body below her swollen belly, Chris captures something of the awkward power of pregnancy. By repeating this pose in the last panel, with Lyta now highlighted against a black background, we are also shown another level of meaning: This is a birth of something dark and powerful. This is the birth of hatred so profound that it will set in motion a series of events leading to Morpheus's eventual demise.

BELOW Hob argues that death is not inevitable. Artwork by Michael Zulli and Steve Parkhouse. Robbie Busch, colorist.

And, of course, there is a powerful irony at work, because on some level Morpheus must intuit that what he is doing is self-destructive. How else could he know that the child in Lyta's belly will eventually become the next Sandman, as he cryptically implies?

The next artist to do a fill-in issue, Michael Zulli, would go on to become a major contributor to the series. Zulli's exquisitely detailed pencil style is not as apparent in "Men of Good Fortune" as it would become in later issues, but his ability to re-create authentic historical detail is showcased here. Once again, Neil wisely writes to his artist's strengths.

In "Men of Good Fortune," we meet Hob, a nice, regular fellow having a drink at the local pub where someone is telling a certain Geoffrey that nobody wants "filthy tales about pilgrims." Chaucer fans may even hazard a guess as to the date being late fourteenth century (1389 is the actual date Neil had in mind). Hob, who is mortal, does not want to die, which is pretty typical of mortals, but he also does not believe that death is inevitable, which is not so common.

Y'ARE A FOOL, HOB. DEATH COMES TO EVERY MAN. THIRTY YEARS, IF HE ESCAPE THE PLAGUE, OR THE FLUX, OR THE FRENCH. SIXTY YEARS, WITH FORTUNE, AND IF GOD IS WILLING.
THEN THEY PUT YOU IN THE GROUND, TO AWAIT THE DAY OF JUDGEMENT.
THERE YOU GO-- PROVES MY POINT. ALL I'M SAYING IS THIS.
NOBODY HAS TO DIE.

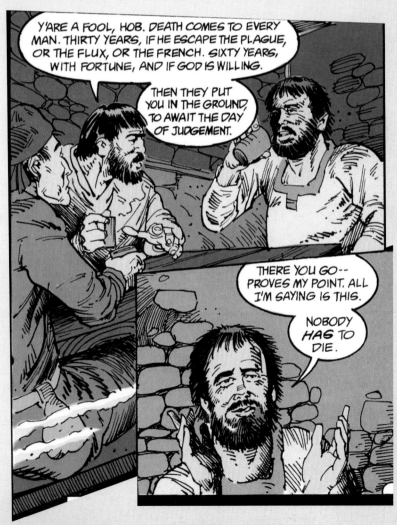

BELOW Artwork by Michael Zulli and Steve Parkhouse. Robbie Busch, colorist.

Morpheus has been dragged to the pub by his sister Death, who clearly wishes for her brother to understand humans a bit better – to "see them on *their* terms," instead of his. Overhearing Hob's pronouncement, Morpheus exchanges a look with his sister, and the lovely composition of these three panels shows us the Sandman in his frame and Death in hers, and between them, a background of oblivious mortals. This is a clear suggestion of three realities, and is followed by not one but two panels of the Sandman smiling – not a grin, but a small, amused smile – as he tells Hob that he will not die and arranges to meet him a hundred years later in the same tavern.

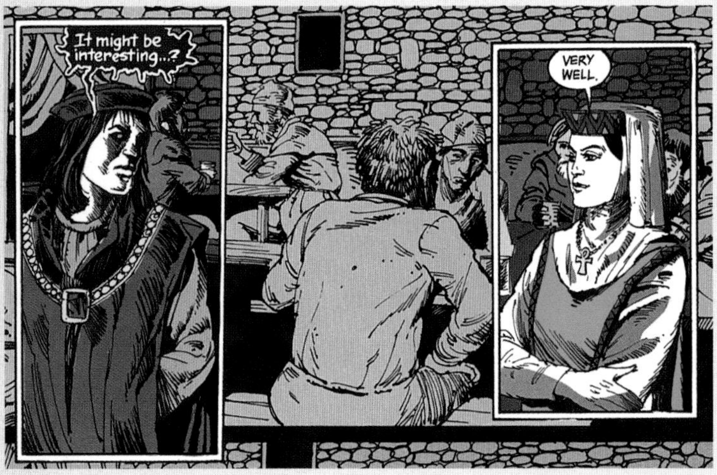
It might be interesting...?
VERY WELL.

This remarkable issue covers a lot of ground, hinting at the award-winning "A Midsummer Night's Dream" issue to come, laying the groundwork for the Sandman's partnership with a down-on-his-luck William Shakespeare, and introducing two sharp and streetwise characters, Mad Hettie and Lady Johanna Constantine. But the most important development here is an interior one: This issue marks a key turning point in character development as the Sandman comes to acknowledge the bond of friendship between himself and Hob Gadling.

The extent of Morpheus's developing consciousness of the connection between himself and humankind really becomes clear in the final chapters of *The Doll's House*, which begin with a convention of serial killers and culminate in Morpheus's confrontation with his androgynous sibling, Desire. In "Collectors," a story that can be read as a commentary on the bond between author and audience, the Sandman becomes aware of the consequences of cutting oneself off from the very people collaborating in the enterprise – you become petty; you become warped; you become lesser.

One of the big, unwritten rules of comics is do not insult the fans. Comics, like science fiction, has a tradition of a fervent, highly educated, detail-oriented fan base, who will happily go to conventions and debate the minutiae of invented worlds. But Neil, himself both a comic book and science fiction fan, never resorts to satire in his use of the convention; instead, he allows room for irony, but it is a shared irony, not the kind that creates a wedge between author and reader.

BELOW Neil's original sketches of the Corinthian from his thumbnail comics, and Dave Gibbon's version of the character from the *Sandman* trading-card series.

One major milestone that deserves mentioning here: It is in *The Doll's House* that new readers first become fully aware that the Sandman and his sister Death are part of a larger mythological structure. Or, to put it another way, this is where we learn the archetypal siblings are part of a family, and the family has a name: the Endless. But more about them later.

Another highlight in *The Doll's House:* Matthew the Raven, in the story "Moving In." We do see a raven in the second story of *Preludes & Nocturnes,* but it is probably Jessamy (there is always a raven in the Dreaming, but it is not always the same raven). Matthew the Raven was formerly Matt Cable, a key player in the *Swamp Thing* saga. Fans of both series may recall Matt died in *Swamp Thing* issue 83, right around the time *The Sandman*'s issue 4 or 5 was released.

The Corinthian

The Sandman was an unfailingly sympathetic character in the beginning of the series — for who can fail to sympathize with a prisoner who has lost everything? By the end of this second long storyline, he is a far more nuanced creation — arrogant, cold, and clearly judgmental, but just as clearly capable of change. Morpheus, because he is in the process of changing, allows a mortal to insult him, apologizes to a mortal, and even admits that he made a mistake (when he created the first Corinthian, a Nightmare with razor-toothed eyes).

Of all the Endless, Dream seems the most human because he changes incrementally, the way we do. Delight may change by transforming into Delirium, and Desire may meddle most directly in human affairs, while Destruction and Death appear to be the fondest of mortal customs. But it is Dream who gets in over his head, who struggles to do what is right, who makes mistakes and becomes aware that the only way to right the wrong is to make a sacrifice.

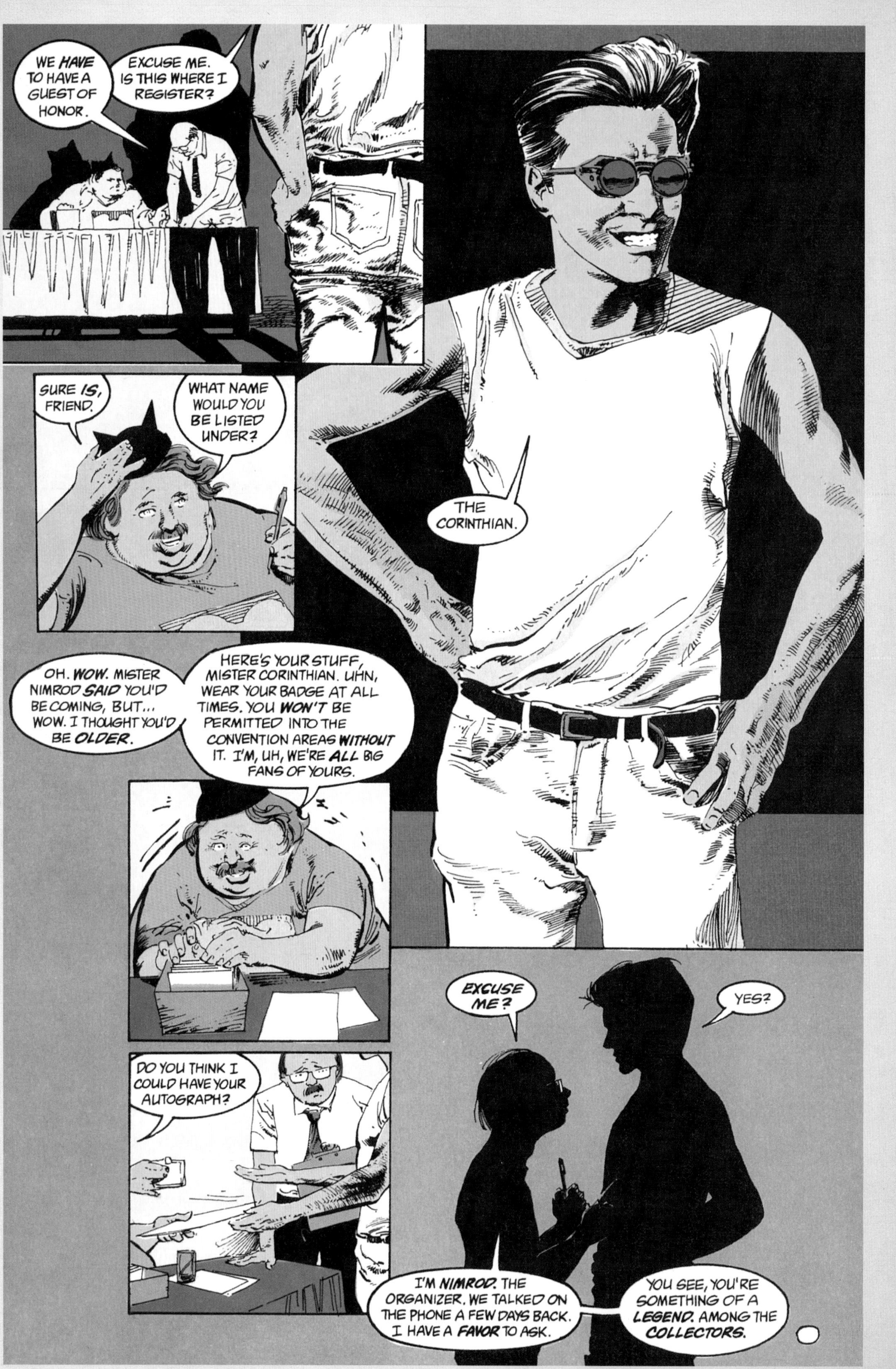
WE HAVE TO HAVE A GUEST OF HONOR.
EXCUSE ME. IS THIS WHERE I REGISTER?
SURE IS, FRIEND.
WHAT NAME WOULD YOU BE LISTED UNDER?
THE CORINTHIAN.
OH. WOW. MISTER NIMROD SAID YOU'D BE COMING, BUT... WOW. I THOUGHT YOU'D BE OLDER.
HERE'S YOUR STUFF, MISTER CORINTHIAN. UHN, WEAR YOUR BADGE AT ALL TIMES. YOU WON'T BE PERMITTED INTO THE CONVENTION AREAS WITHOUT IT. I'M, UH, WE'RE ALL BIG FANS OF YOURS.
DO YOU THINK I COULD HAVE YOUR AUTOGRAPH?
EXCUSE ME?
YES?
I'M NIMROD. THE ORGANIZER. WE TALKED ON THE PHONE A FEW DAYS BACK. I HAVE A FAVOR TO ASK.
YOU SEE, YOU'RE SOMETHING OF A LEGEND. AMONG THE COLLECTORS.

PAGE 52 Everybody's favorite villain, the Corinthian, makes his debut in his trademark dark glasses (which, unlike Neil Gaiman's trademark dark glasses, conceal not eyes but mouths). Artwork by Mike Dringenberg and Malcolm Jones III. Robbie Busch, colorist. BELOW LEFT In a speech he gives Desire (who can appear as male or female, and yet is neither male nor female) the Sandman reveals that "we of the Endless are the servants of the living – we are not their masters." Artwork by Mike Dringenberg and Malcolm Jones III. Robbie Busch, colorist. BELOW RIGHT Matthew is first named in *The Sandman* no. 11. Artwork by Mike Dringenberg and Malcolm Jones III. Robbie Busch, colorist.

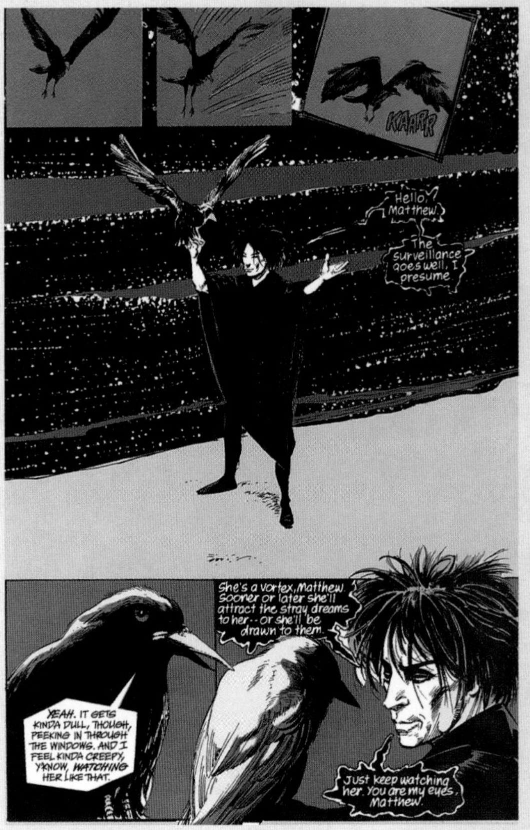
KAARR
Hello, Matthew.
The surveillance goes well, I presume.
She's a vortex, Matthew. Sooner or later she'll attract the stray dreams to her--or she'll be drawn to them.
YEAH. IT GETS KINDA DULL, THOUGH, PEEKING IN THROUGH THE WINDOWS. AND I FEEL KINDA CREEPY, Y'KNOW, WATCHING HER LIKE THAT.
Just keep watching her. You are my eyes, Matthew.

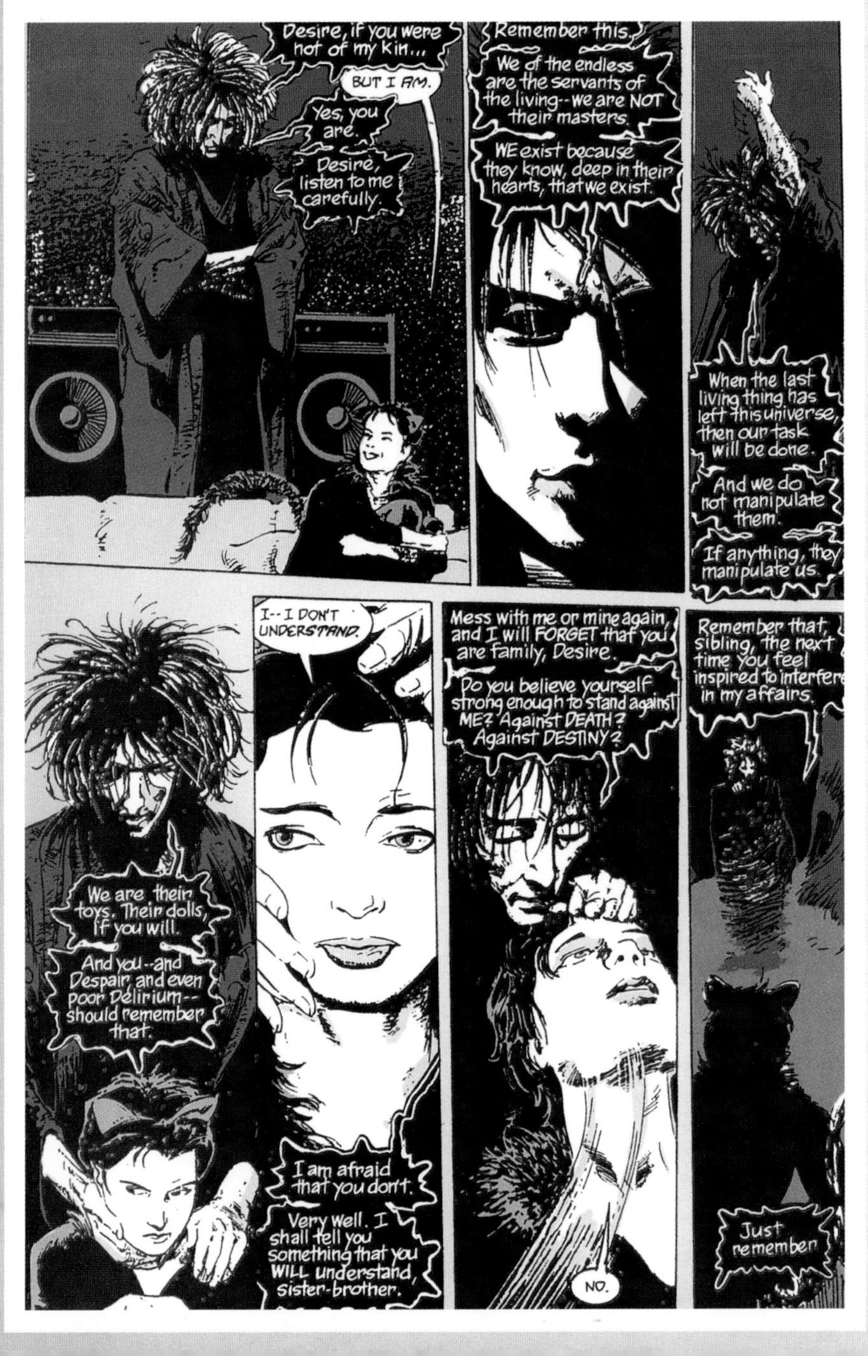
Desire, if you were not of my Kin...
BUT I AM.
Yes, you are.
Desire, listen to me carefully.
Remember this.
We of the endless are the servants of the living--we are NOT their masters.
WE exist because they know, deep in their hearts, that we exist.
When the last living thing has left this universe, then our task will be done.
And we do not manipulate them.
If anything, they manipulate us.
We are their toys. Their dolls, if you will.
And you--and Despair, and even poor Delirium--should remember that.
I--I DON'T UNDERSTAND.
I am afraid that you don't.
Very well. I shall tell you something that you WILL understand, sister-brother.
Mess with me or mine again, and I will FORGET that you are family, Desire.
Do you believe yourself strong enough to stand against ME? Against DEATH? Against DESTINY?
NO.
Remember that, sibling, the next time you feel inspired to interfere in my affairs.
Just remember.

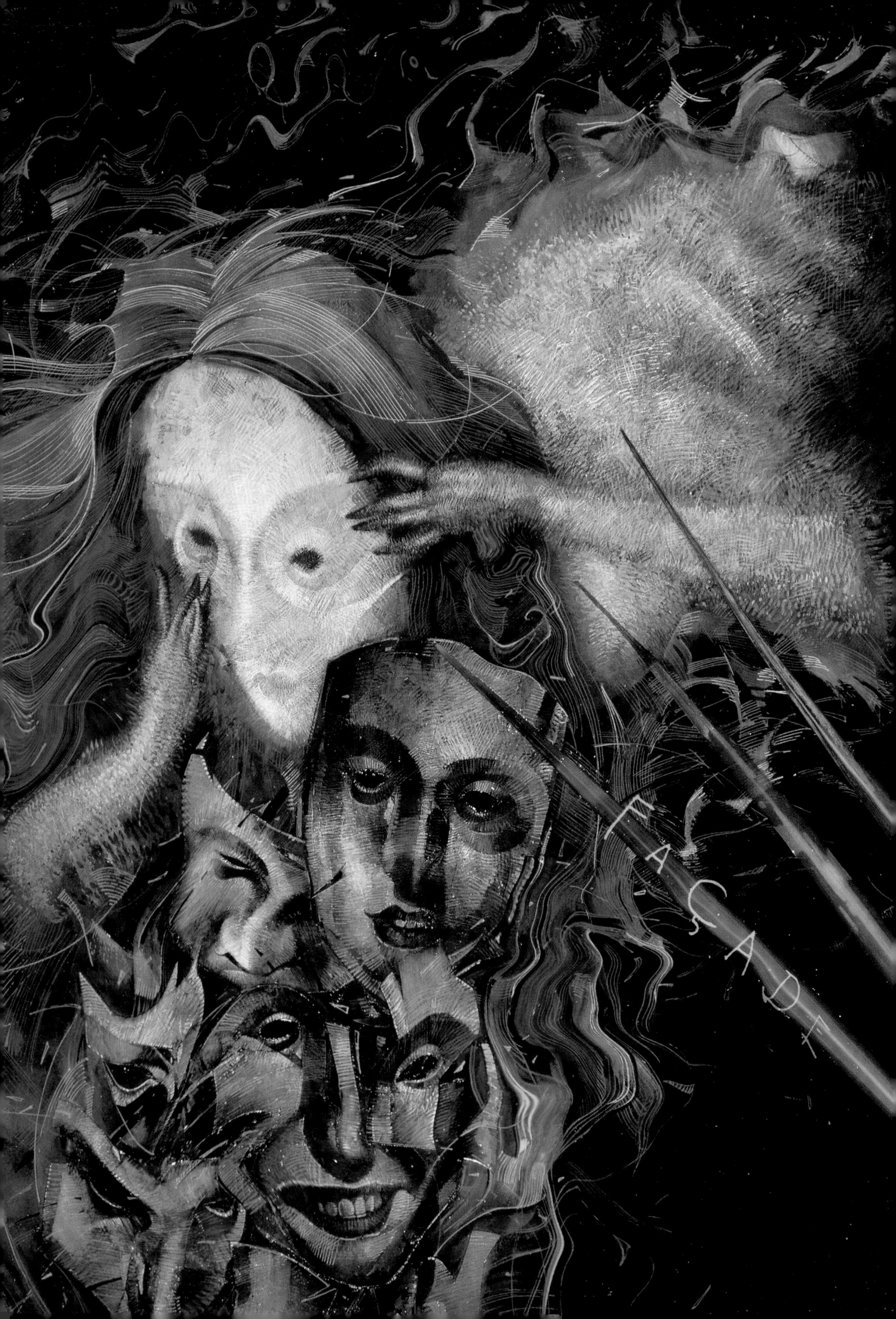
FAÇADE

CHAPTER 4

DREAM COUNTRY

IN WHICH WE LEARN WHAT CATS DREAM ABOUT, AND WHO HELPED WILL ALONG WITH THE STORY WHEN HE WROTE *A MIDSUMMER NIGHT'S DREAM.*

The Sandman is not a god any more than he is a superhero. But he shares common themes with gods and superheroes, and has been known to spend time with both on occasion.

In *Dream Country,* while mining the quintessentially American mythology of flying heroes in funny masks, Neil Gaiman reminds us that once upon a time we all believed in heroes who combined elements of the carnal and the divine. With the short issues in this collection, Neil demonstrates the full range of his talent for channeling the voices of the world's ancient storytellers, and it is at this point in the series that some of the best single-issue stories were written. Many of the artists who appear here for the first time reappear later on in the series.

In 1990, as Neil began to take creative advantage of having more than one artist to write for on *The Sandman,* he also went to work on *The Books of Magic* – a miniseries painted by four separate artists, including John Bolton, Scott Hampton, Charles Vess, and Paul Johnson. Predating the *Harry Potter* phenomenon by quite a few years, this series tells the story of a young, bespectacled English boy named Timothy Hunter who has to choose whether or not he desires a life of magic. *The Books of Magic* later became a monthly series, for which Neil acted as a consultant.

Meanwhile, artist Kelley Jones came on board *The Sandman,* bringing a new vision. Kelley's protean Sandman, all folds and shadows and long muscles unseen in any modern

PAGE 54 Dave McKean's reworking of the cover of *The Sandman* no. 20.

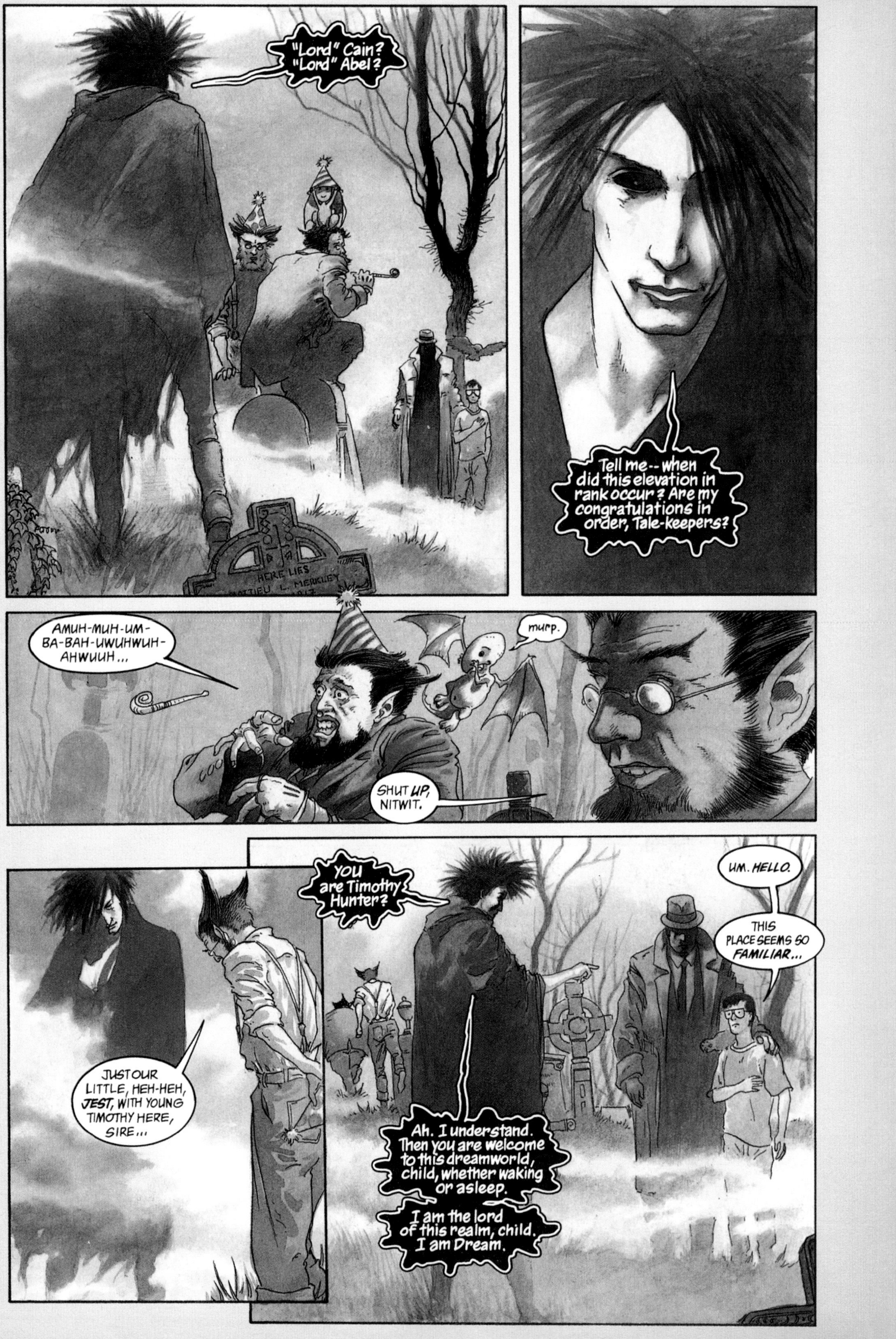
"Lord" Cain? "Lord" Abel?
HERE LIES
Tell me-- when did this elevation in rank occur? Are my congratulations in order, Tale-keepers?
AMUH-MUH-UM-BA-BAH-UWUHWUH-AHWUUH...
murp.
SHUT UP, NITWIT.
YOU are Timothy Hunter?
UM. HELLO.
THIS PLACE SEEMS SO FAMILIAR...
JUST OUR LITTLE, HEH-HEH, JEST, WITH YOUNG TIMOTHY HERE, SIRE...
Ah. I understand. Then you are welcome to this dreamworld, child, whether waking or asleep.
I am the lord of this realm, child. I am Dream.

PAGE 56 *The Books of Magic*'s Tim Hunter visits the Dreaming. Artwork by Charles Vess over pencils by Mike Dringenberg. BELOW From "Calliope." Artwork by Kelley Jones and Malcolm Jones III. Robbie Busch, colorist.

anatomy book, evoked a late Gothic sensibility: The fanciful musculature makes humans look like mythic creatures and mythic creatures appear oddly human.

In a series known for its consistent quality, it is hard to pick out particular feats of artistry. Nevertheless, "Calliope," Kelley and Neil's first collaboration, is one of *The Sandman*'s shining moments, and a particular favorite of writers everywhere. It is essentially a horror story that provides a very disturbing answer to the classic question: Where do writers get their ideas?

Neil – who once said that new writers all worry if they have it and more experienced writers all worry if they've lost it – manages to create a chilling story that appears at first to stand quite alone. For readers who are familiar with the entire series, however, there are cleverly planted clues – such as the introduction of the muses as maiden, mother and crone, and the mention of a son born to Oneiros, the Greek name for the Dream King. But what makes this story memorable is the rendering of a mythical creature as a real and grief-stricken woman, and the depiction of magic as something that takes an emotional toll.

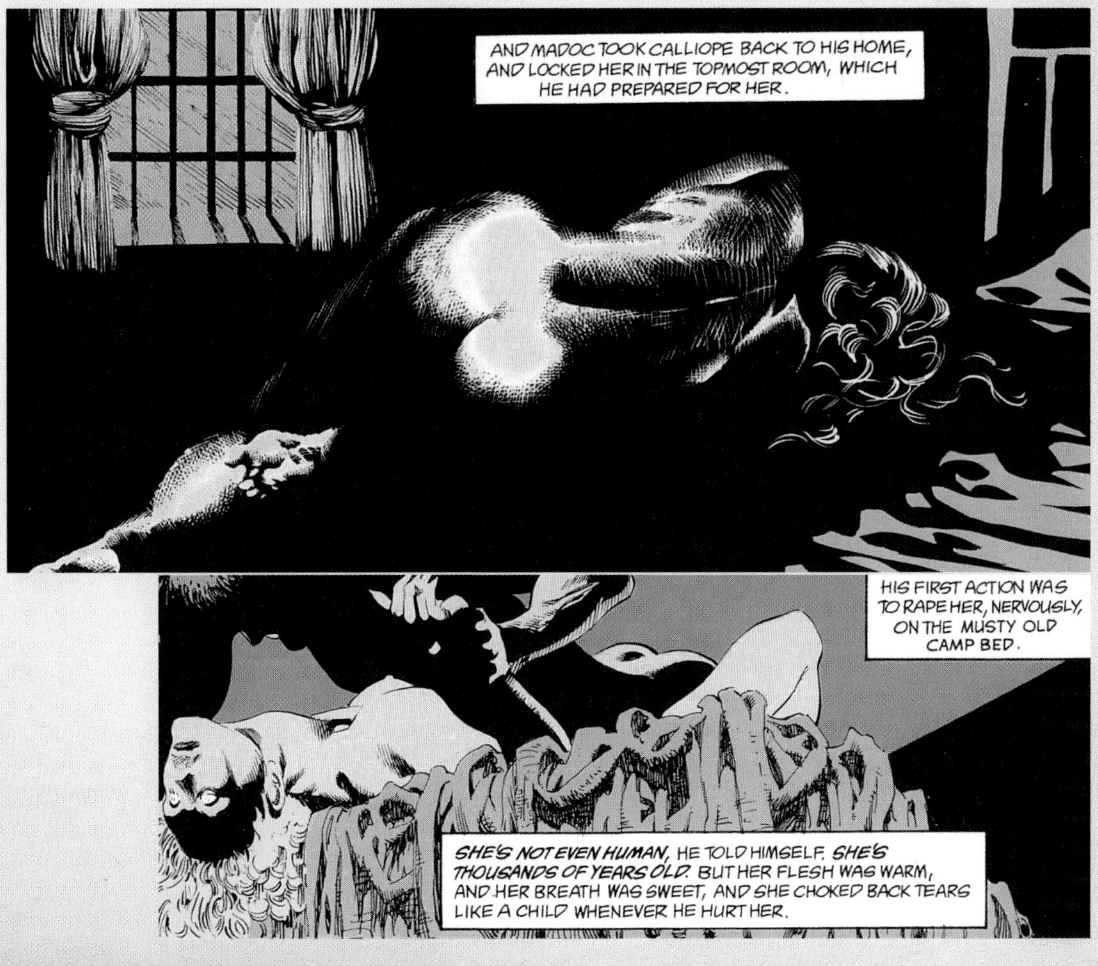
AND MADOC TOOK CALLIOPE BACK TO HIS HOME, AND LOCKED HER IN THE TOPMOST ROOM, WHICH HE HAD PREPARED FOR HER.
HIS FIRST ACTION WAS TO RAPE HER, NERVOUSLY, ON THE MUSTY OLD CAMP BED.
SHE'S NOT EVEN HUMAN, HE TOLD HIMSELF. SHE'S THOUSANDS OF YEARS OLD. BUT HER FLESH WAS WARM, AND HER BREATH WAS SWEET, AND SHE CHOKED BACK TEARS LIKE A CHILD WHENEVER HE HURT HER.

PAGES 58–59 You'll notice, in the series of panels on this page, that the middle panel is blank. That same panel, in the otherwise identical artwork on page 59, is occupied by an, errrr . . . , interestingly drawn Morpheus. According to Neil, the letterer who worked on the German edition of *Dream Country* doodled this piece into the originally blank panel. Upon going to press, the publisher, assuming that it was part of the artwork, took great care to make sure that it reproduced "properly." Artwork by Kelley Jones and Malcolm Jones III. Robbie Busch, colorist.

"WHEN YOU GET TO SOMETHING LIKE ORPHEUS [THE SON OF MORPHEUS AND CALLIOPE] I CHEAT A CERTAIN AMOUNT. WHAT WAS CALLIOPE? SHE CERTAINLY WASN'T HUMAN. SHE WAS A MUSE, AND I TENDED TO THINK THAT BECAUSE SHE WAS NOT MORTAL, IT WAS AN AWFUL LOT EASIER FOR HER TO GIVE BIRTH AND HAVE A RELATIVELY UNDOOMED RELATIONSHIP WITH MORPHEUS (ANOTHER IMMORTAL). RELATIVELY. IN TERMS OF HOW MUCH DOOM PER SQUARE INCH A RELATIONSHIP WITH MORPHEUS ENTAILS." — NEIL GAIMAN, ON THE ENDLESS AS LOVERS AND PARENTS.

IT'S SO HARD TO THINK...
...MORPHEUS? ...ORPHEUS?...ONE OF THOSE...
YOU CAN TAKE IT WITH YOU TO THE HOSPITAL, RICHARD.
SHE'S GONE, YOU SEE. AND IT'S ALL GONE WITH HER. EVERYTHING. ALL OF THEM, ALL THE DREAMS...
NO... I CAN'T REMEMBER. I'VE LOST IT...
IT'S GONE.
I'VE GOT NO IDEA ANY MORE.
NO IDEA AT ALL.

The collected trade paperback of *Dream Country* reprinted part of Neil's original "Calliope" script, with details such as Neil's instruction to the artist to "try to get across the rape, and the horror and dominance, fairly subtly, doing all the work in the reader's head . . . we can see Calliope's left arm and hand, palm upward, laying flat on the floor. Coming down from above is Rick's arm; his hand is clamped around her wrist, holding it down to the ground. That's all we can see."

Kelley worked with Neil on another stand-alone issue, "A Dream of a Thousand Cats," a deceptively charming and wholly unsentimental story about consensual reality. The pair's increasing rapport would lead to the selection of Kelley as the artist for the next long storyline, *Season of Mists*

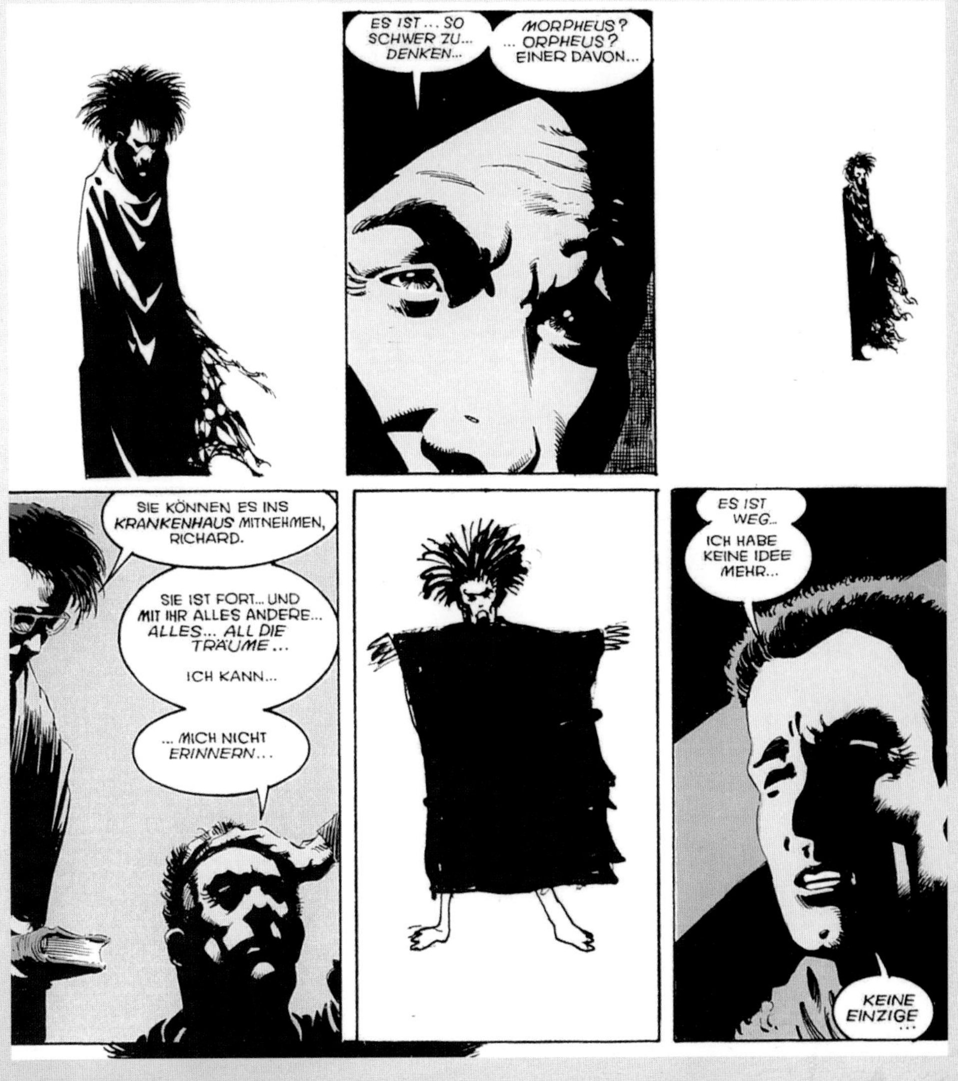
ES IST ... SO SCHWER ZU... DENKEN...
MORPHEUS? ... ORPHEUS? EINER DAVON...
SIE KÖNNEN ES INS KRANKENHAUS MITNEHMEN, RICHARD.
SIE IST FORT... UND MIT IHR ALLES ANDERE... ALLES... ALL DIE TRÄUME...
ICH KANN...
... MICH NICHT ERINNERN...
ES IST WEG...
ICH HABE KEINE IDEE MEHR...
KEINE EINZIGE...

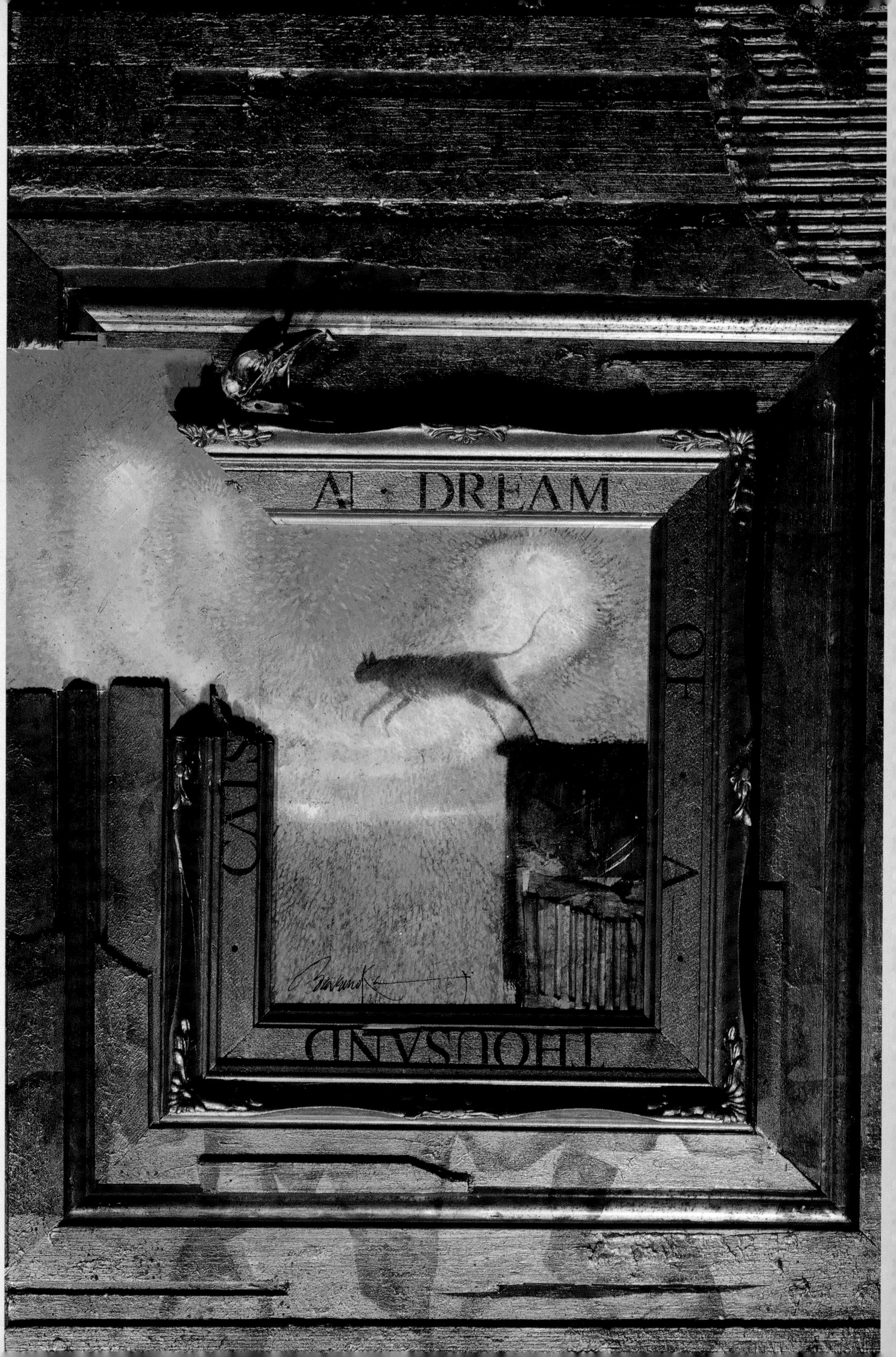
A · DREAM
OF
A
THOUSAND
CATS

PAGE 60 The cover for "A Dream of a Thousand Cats." Artwork by Dave McKean. BELOW LEFT The title page of "A Midsummer Night's Dream." Artwork by Charles Vess. Steve Oliff, colorist. BELOW RIGHT Morpheus ponders his action in conversation with Titania during "A Midsummer Night's Dream." Artwork by Charles Vess. Steve Oliff, colorist.

It was Charles Vess, however, who was chosen to illustrate "A Midsummer Night's Dream," the award-winning story that relates the events leading up to the mythical faeries' abandonment of our plane of reality.

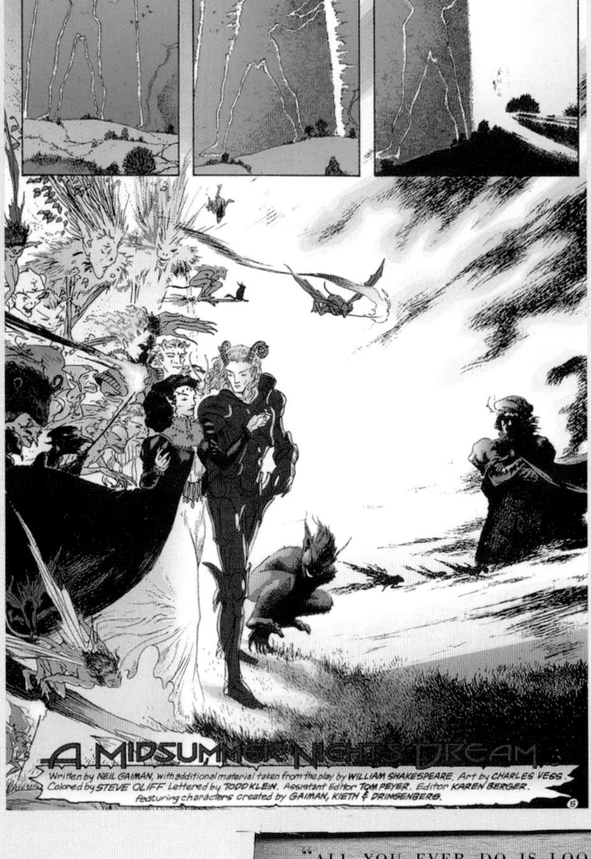
Written by NEIL GAIMAN, with additional material taken from the play by WILLIAM SHAKESPEARE. Art by CHARLES VESS.
Colored by STEVE OLIFF. Lettered by TODD KLEIN. Assistant Editor TOM PEYER. Editor KAREN BERGER.
featuring characters created by GAIMAN, KIETH & DRINGENBERG.

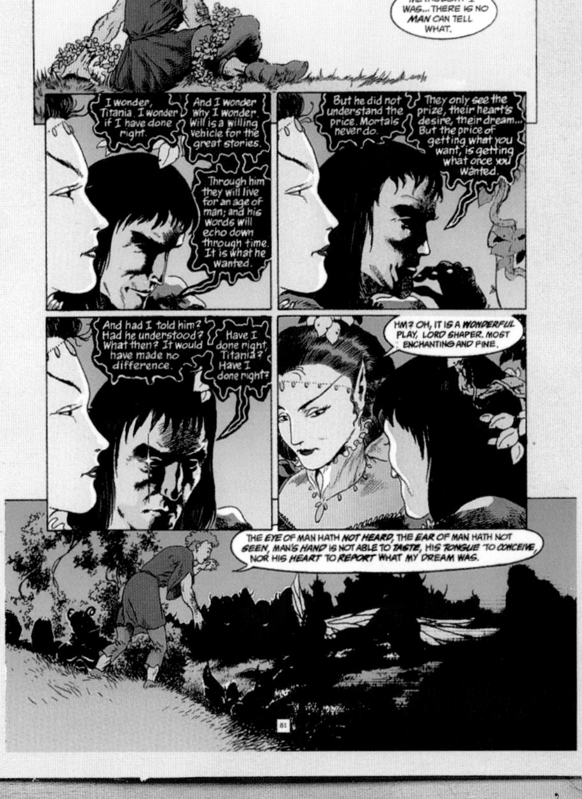
I HAVE HAD... A MOST RARE VISION.
I HAVE HAD A DREAM... PAST THE WIT OF MAN TO SAY WHAT WIT IT WAS.
MAN IS BUT AN... ASS... IF HE GO ABOUT TO EXPOUND THIS DREAM.
METHOUGHT I WAS... THERE IS NO MAN CAN TELL WHAT.
I wonder, Titania. I wonder if I have done right.
And I wonder why I wonder. Will is a willing vehicle for the great stories.
Through him they will live for an age of man; and his words will echo down through time. It is what he wanted.
But he did not understand the price. Mortals never do.
They only see the prize, their heart's desire, their dream... But the price of getting what you want, is getting what once you wanted.
And had I told him? Had he understood? What then? It would have made no difference.
Have I done right, Titania? Have I done right?
HM? OH, IT IS A WONDERFUL PLAY, LORD SHAPER. MOST ENCHANTING AND FINE.
THE EYE OF MAN HATH NOT HEARD, THE EAR OF MAN HATH NOT SEEN, MAN'S HAND IS NOT ABLE TO TASTE, HIS TONGUE TO CONCEIVE, NOR HIS HEART TO REPORT WHAT MY DREAM WAS.

"ALL YOU EVER DO IS LOOK UP THINGS IN OLD BOOKS AND STEAL OTHER PEOPLE'S IDEAS AND MAKE THINGS UP!" —ATTRIBUTED TO HOLLY GAIMAN, AGE SEVEN OR EIGHT.

"ALL THOU EVER DURST IS LOOK THINGS UP IN OLD BOOKS AND STEAL THE TALES OF OTHERS AND INVENT LIES!" —ATTRIBUTED TO JUDITH SHAKESPEARE, AGE NINE OR TEN.

Vess's delicate, elegant, darkly classical style draws attention to details and nuances: the hints of a romance, now over, between Morpheus and Titania as they watch a play depicting the faerie queen's infidelities; the successful playwright's obliviousness to his son's emotional state, which we will soon discover parallels the Sandman's relationship with his own son ("It seems to me that I heard this tale sung once, in old Greece, by a boy with a lyre," says Titania, a nugget that resonates for readers on their second or third pass through the series).

This happy pairing of talents – Neil's gift for reinventing classic myths, Charles Vess's gift for rendering the graceful danger of enchanted forests and fairy markets – led to the two reuniting to create *Neil Gaiman and Charles Vess's Stardust*, an illustrated novel about the fair folk.

Colleen Doran became the series' first female artist when she penciled "Façade" (also the first issue in which Sandman does not appear at all). This is Death's first solo issue, and although the title primarily refers to the main character's metaphysical condition, there is also a sense of uncovering the fiercely pragmatic layer of steel beneath Death's determinedly cheerful surface. Colleen would return to lend her artistic talent – and her face – to another terrifyingly pragmatic character, the witch Thessaly in *A Game of You*.

By the end of *Dream Country*, *The Sandman* had reinvented itself as a comic in which the titular character could appear for pages – or for one page, one panel, or even not at all.

When he did take the stage, the Dream King had shown that he did not, like most comic book heroes, always wear the same costume or even the same face. He might appear as an African prince, as a Medieval gentleman, even as a tomcat. But like Elvis and pizza, the Sandman is instantly recognizable in each of his incarnations. Whether you encounter Mike Dringenberg's brooding young Dream King, still debating whether or not to release his

PAGE 62 A sampling of *Neil Gaiman and Charles Vess's Stardust's* ethereal beauty. Artwork by Charles Vess.
BELOW Death grants the Element Girl her boon in "Façade." Artwork by Colleen Doran and Malcolm Jones III. Steve Oliff, colorist.

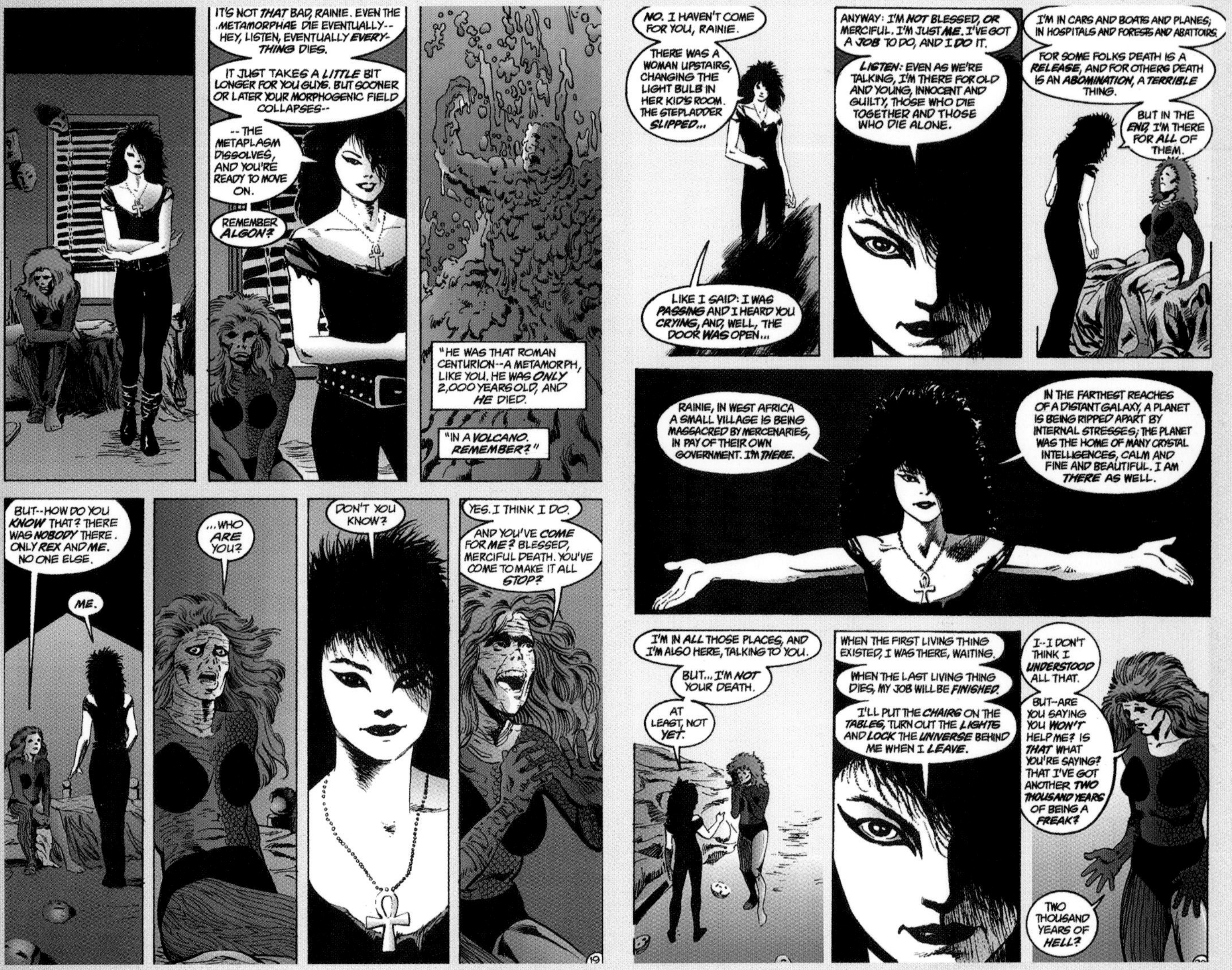
IT'S NOT THAT BAD, RAINIE. EVEN THE METAMORPHAE DIE EVENTUALLY-- HEY, LISTEN, EVENTUALLY EVERY-THING DIES.
IT JUST TAKES A LITTLE BIT LONGER FOR YOU GUYS. BUT SOONER OR LATER YOUR MORPHOGENIC FIELD COLLAPSES--
--THE METAPLASM DISSOLVES, AND YOU'RE READY TO MOVE ON.
REMEMBER ALGON?
"HE WAS THAT ROMAN CENTURION--A METAMORPH, LIKE YOU. HE WAS ONLY 2,000 YEARS OLD, AND HE DIED.
"IN A VOLCANO. REMEMBER?"
BUT--HOW DO YOU KNOW THAT? THERE WAS NOBODY THERE. ONLY REX AND ME. NO ONE ELSE.
ME.
...WHO ARE YOU?
DON'T YOU KNOW?
YES. I THINK I DO.
AND YOU'VE COME FOR ME? BLESSED, MERCIFUL DEATH. YOU'VE COME TO MAKE IT ALL STOP?
NO. I HAVEN'T COME FOR YOU, RAINIE.
THERE WAS A WOMAN UPSTAIRS, CHANGING THE LIGHT BULB IN HER KID'S ROOM. THE STEPLADDER SLIPPED...
LIKE I SAID: I WAS PASSING AND I HEARD YOU CRYING, AND, WELL, THE DOOR WAS OPEN...
ANYWAY: I'M NOT BLESSED, OR MERCIFUL. I'M JUST ME. I'VE GOT A JOB TO DO, AND I DO IT.
LISTEN: EVEN AS WE'RE TALKING, I'M THERE FOR OLD AND YOUNG, INNOCENT AND GUILTY, THOSE WHO DIE TOGETHER AND THOSE WHO DIE ALONE.
I'M IN CARS AND BOATS AND PLANES; IN HOSPITALS AND FORESTS AND ABATTOIRS.
FOR SOME FOLKS DEATH IS A RELEASE, AND FOR OTHERS DEATH IS AN ABOMINATION, A TERRIBLE THING.
BUT IN THE END, I'M THERE FOR ALL OF THEM.
RAINIE, IN WEST AFRICA A SMALL VILLAGE IS BEING MASSACRED BY MERCENARIES, IN PAY OF THEIR OWN GOVERNMENT. I'M THERE.
IN THE FARTHEST REACHES OF A DISTANT GALAXY, A PLANET IS BEING RIPPED APART BY INTERNAL STRESSES; THE PLANET WAS THE HOME OF MANY CRYSTAL INTELLIGENCES, CALM AND FINE AND BEAUTIFUL. I AM THERE AS WELL.
I'M IN ALL THOSE PLACES, AND I'M ALSO HERE, TALKING TO YOU.
BUT... I'M NOT YOUR DEATH.
AT LEAST, NOT YET.
WHEN THE FIRST LIVING THING EXISTED, I WAS THERE, WAITING.
WHEN THE LAST LIVING THING DIES, MY JOB WILL BE FINISHED.
I'LL PUT THE CHAIRS ON THE TABLES, TURN OUT THE LIGHTS AND LOCK THE UNIVERSE BEHIND ME WHEN I LEAVE.
I--I DON'T THINK I UNDERSTOOD ALL THAT.
BUT--ARE YOU SAYING YOU WON'T HELP ME? IS THAT WHAT YOU'RE SAYING? THAT I'VE GOT ANOTHER TWO THOUSAND YEARS OF BEING A FREAK?
TWO THOUSAND YEARS OF HELL?

ex-lover from hell, or Michael Zulli's older, wiser monarch, visiting his one friend for a day out of every century, you know Morpheus the moment you see him. He's the guy with the world on his shoulders, arrogant and aloof and immensely powerful, yet as oddly vulnerable as the child kings of old, who were never given a choice of whether or not to be a god.

NEIL'S ADVICE TO READERS WHO WOULD LIKE TO BECOME WRITERS (AND DON'T FEEL PARTICULARLY COMFORTABLE TAKING THE ROUTE OF "CALLIOPE" ANTAGONIST RICHARD MADOC):

"THEY SHOULD WRITE. THEY SHOULD FINISH THINGS. THEY SHOULD READ WITHIN WHATEVER FIELD THEY WANT TO WRITE SO THEY KNOW WHAT'S BEEN DONE BEFORE AND HOW IT'S BEEN DONE AND THEN THEY SHOULD READ LOTS OF OTHER THINGS. IF YOU WANT TO BE A WRITER, READ EVERYTHING. READ GOOD BOOKS. READ BAD BOOKS. BAD BOOKS ARE SO INSPIRING."

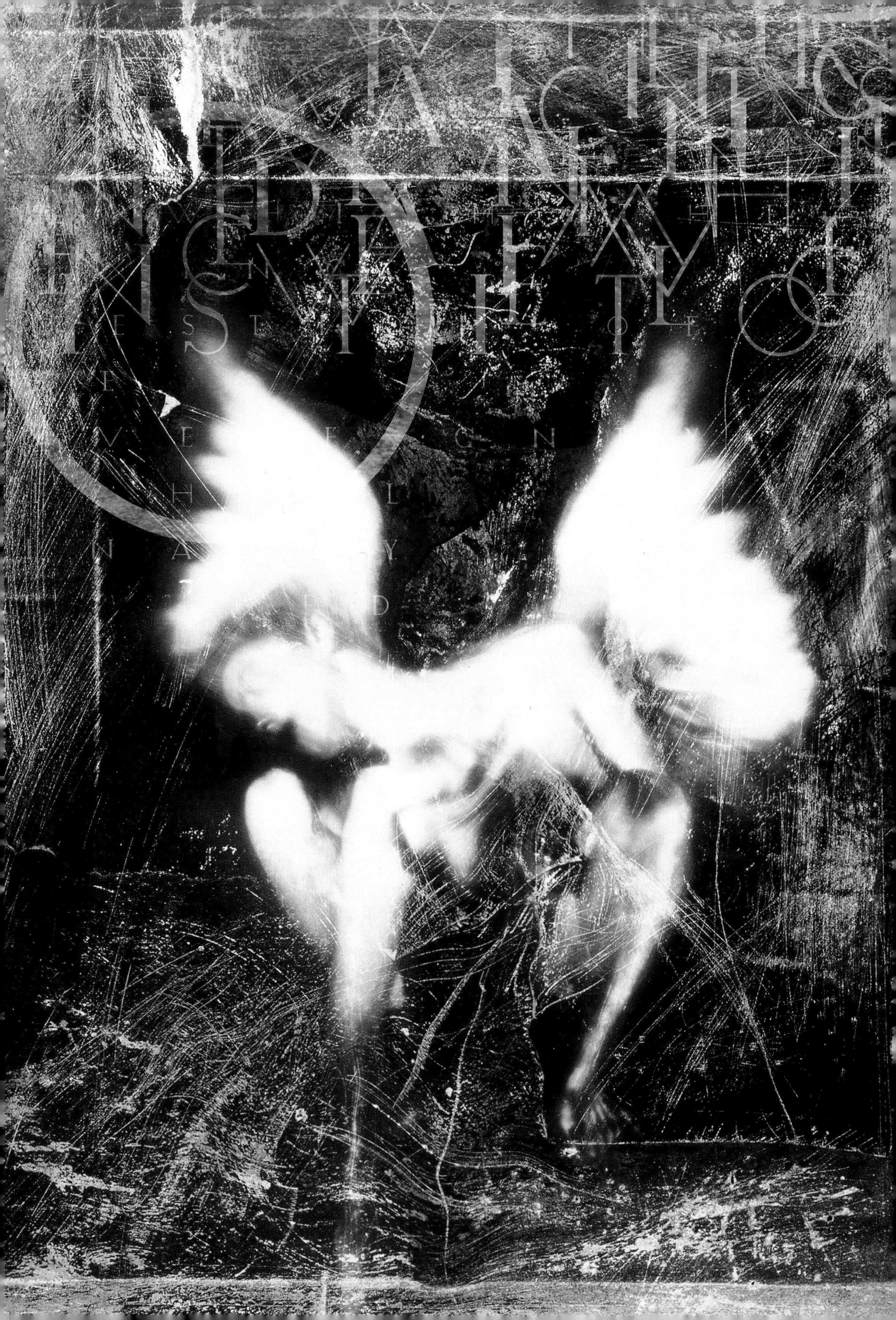

CHAPTER 5

SEASON OF MISTS

IN WHICH WE ARE FORMALLY INTRODUCED TO THE
ENDLESS, AND THE SANDMAN STRUGGLES WITH THE
KEY TO HELL.

At the beginning of the next long storyline, *Season of Mists*, we are formally introduced to the members of the Endless family. (It is actually the first encounter of any kind with Delirium. And a seventh Endless sibling, Destruction – who has abdicated his post – doesn't appear until later, but I'm including him here because, well, he's the Burt Lancaster of the family, and I'm partial to him.)

Each of the Endless has a gallery in which portraits of all his or her (or in Desire's case, his/her) siblings hang. These portraits are used as their means of communicating with one another and of transporting to and from one another's realms. (After all, anthropomorphic beings have better things to do than pick up a phone and be put on hold while their sisters get off the other line.)

PAGE 64 Cover, *The Sandman* no. 27. Artwork by Dave McKean. ABOVE Neil Gaiman's sketches for Despair and Desire taken from his thumbnail comics for the *Season of Mists* prologue.

BELOW Desire. This image is a reproduction of the full painting that, after being rejected as a trading card, was cropped to show only Desire's head. Artwork by Jon J Muth.

At the start of *Season of Mists*, Destiny stands in his gallery and approaches each of his sibling's portraits (with the exception of the prodigal Destruction), beckoning them to his realm. They heed his call and each arrives at Destiny's castle.

"Let us," in the words written by Neil Gaiman, "pause for a moment, as they descend the grey steps toward Destiny's banquet hall, to consider the Endless:"

"IT IS SAID THAT NO PORTRAIT MAY DO DESIRE JUSTICE, FOR TO SEE HER (OR HIM) IS TO LOVE HIM (OR HER) — PASSIONATELY, PAINFULLY, AND TO THE EXCLUSION OF ALL ELSE. DESIRE SMELLS ALMOST SUBLIMINALLY OF SUMMER PEACHES, AND CASTS TWO SHADOWS: ONE BLACK AND SHARP-EDGED, THE OTHER TRANSLUCENT AND FOREVER WAVERING, LIKE HEAT HAZE. DESIRE IS EVERYTHING YOU HAVE EVER WANTED. WHOEVER YOU ARE. WHATEVER YOU ARE. EVERYTHING."

BELOW Despair. Artwork by George Pratt.

"DESIRE'S TWIN IS QUEEN OF HER OWN
BLEAK BOURNE, POCKED WITH A MULTI-
TUDE OF TINY WINDOWS THAT ARE, IN
OUR WORLD, MIRRORS. AT TIMES YOU MAY
LOOK INTO A MIRROR AND FEEL HER EYES
UPON YOU; THEY ARE THE COLOR OF SKY
ON GREY, WET DAYS THAT LEACH THE
WORLD OF COLOR AND MEANING. DESPAIR
SAYS LITTLE, AND IS PATIENT."

BELOW Destiny. Artwork by Kent Williams.

"DESTINY IS THE OLDEST OF THE ENDLESS. THERE ARE SOME WHO BELIEVE HIM TO BE BLIND; WHILE OTHERS, WITH MORE REASON, CLAIM THAT HE HAS TRAVELED FAR BEYOND BLINDNESS, THAT HE CAN DO NOTHING BUT SEE THE INTRICATE PATTERNS LIVING THINGS MAKE ON THEIR JOURNEY THROUGH TIME. DESTINY SMELLS OF DUST AND THE LIBRARIES OF THE NIGHT. HE LEAVES NO FOOTPRINTS. HE CASTS NO SHADOW."

BELOW Delirium. Artwork by Jill Thompson.

"DELIRIUM IS THE YOUNGEST OF THE
ENDLESS; ONCE, SHE WAS DELIGHT, BUT
THAT WAS LONG AGO. SHE SMELLS OF
SWEAT, SOUR WINES, LATE NIGHTS, OLD
LEATHER. HER APPEARANCE IS THE MOST
VARIABLE OF ALL THE ENDLESS, WHO, AT
BEST, ARE IDEAS CLOAKED IN THE SEM-
BLANCE OF FLESH. THE POET COLERIDGE
CLAIMED TO HAVE KNOWN HER INTIMATELY,
BUT THE MAN WAS AN INVETERATE LIAR.
WHO CAN KNOW WHAT DELIRIUM SEES
THROUGH HER MISMATCHED EYES?"

BELOW Destruction. Artwork by Glenn Fabry.

"NO ONE EVER KISSED DESPAIR, EXCEPT HER BROTHER DESTRUCTION; CENTURIES AGO; HIS BEARD WAS ROUGH AGAINST HER CHEEK. SHE MISSES HIM NOW, AS DO THE OTHERS, SINCE HE FLED HIS REALM. THINGS ARE STILL CREATED; STILL EXIST; ARE STILL DESTROYED, BUT IT'S NO LONGER HIS RESPONSIBILITY . . . NO LONGER HIS FAULT."

BELOW Dream. Artwork by Dave McKean.

"DREAM OF THE ENDLESS; AH, THERE'S A CONUNDRUM. IN THIS ASPECT (AND WE PERCEIVE BUT ASPECTS OF THE ENDLESS, AS WE SEE THE LIGHT GLINTING FROM ONE TINY FACET OF SOME HUGE AND FLAWLESSLY CUT PRECIOUS STONE) HE IS RAKE-THIN, WITH SKIN THE COLOR OF FALLING SNOW. DREAM ACCUMULATES NAMES TO HIMSELF LIKE OTHERS MAKE FRIENDS; BUT HE PERMITS HIMSELF FEW FRIENDS. IF HE IS CLOSEST TO ANYONE, IT IS TO HIS ELDER SISTER, WHOM HE SEES BUT RARELY. OF ALL THE ENDLESS, SAVE PERHAPS DESTINY, HE IS MOST CONSCIOUS OF HIS RESPONSIBILITIES, THE MOST METICULOUS IN THEIR EXECUTION."

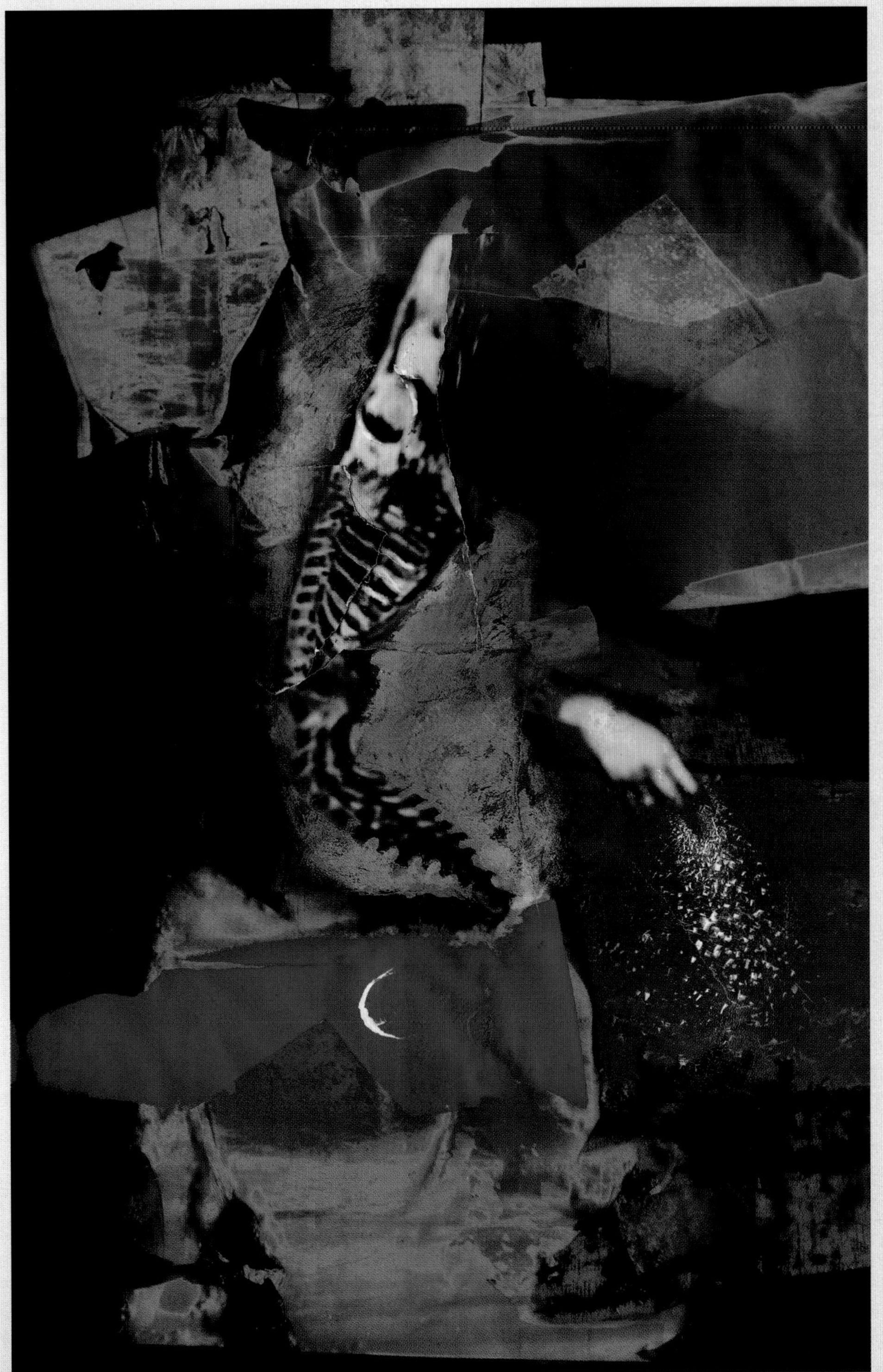

BELOW Death. Artwork by Bill Sienkiewicz. PAGE 73 An Endless family portrait. Artwork by Mike Allred, from *The Endless Gallery*.

NOTE **All quoted text on pages 66 through 72 was taken from the Sandman trading cards, after being abridged from Neil Gaiman's original text, which appeared in *Season of Mists*, "Episode 0."**

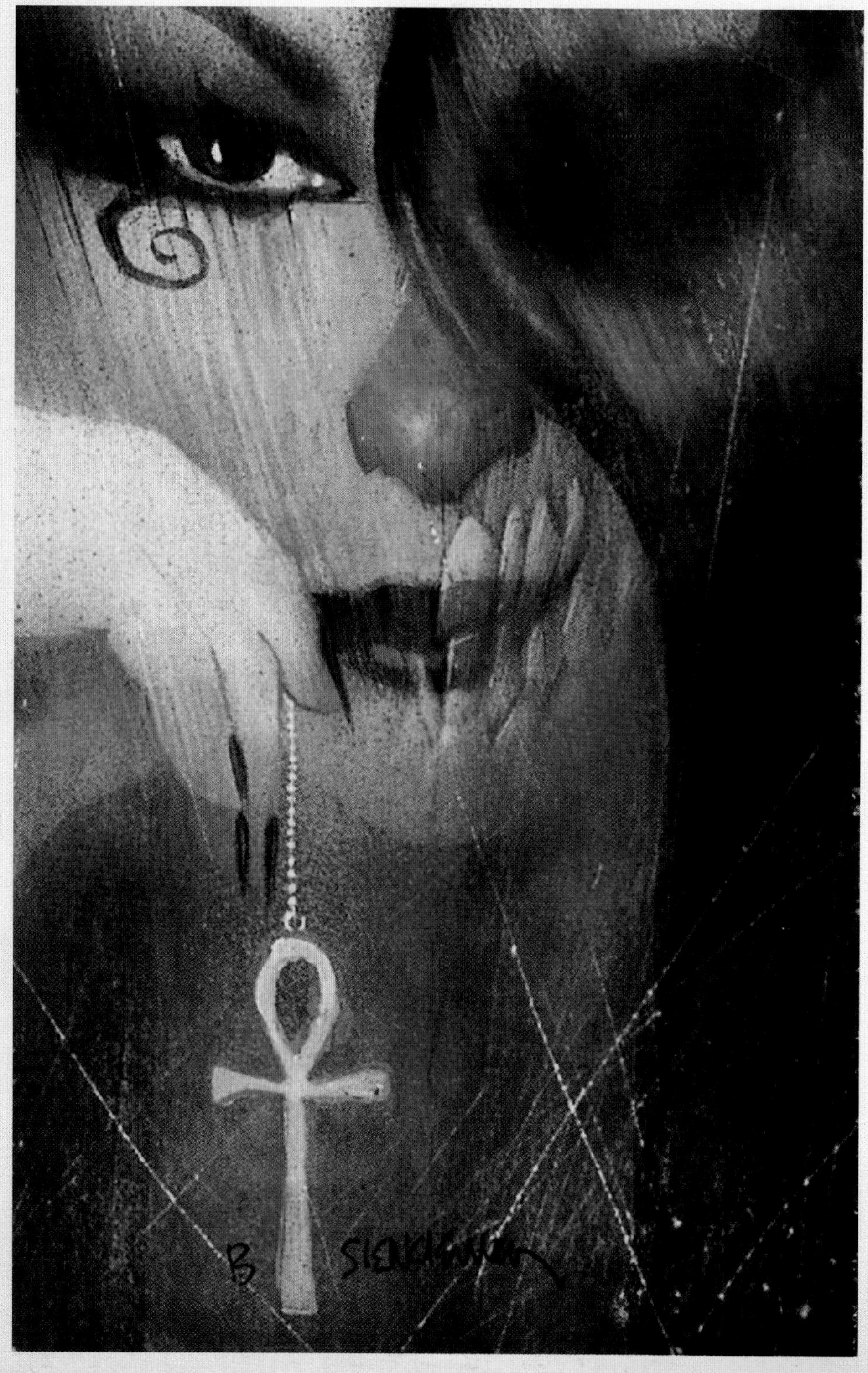
B SIENKIEWICZ

"AND THERE IS DEATH."

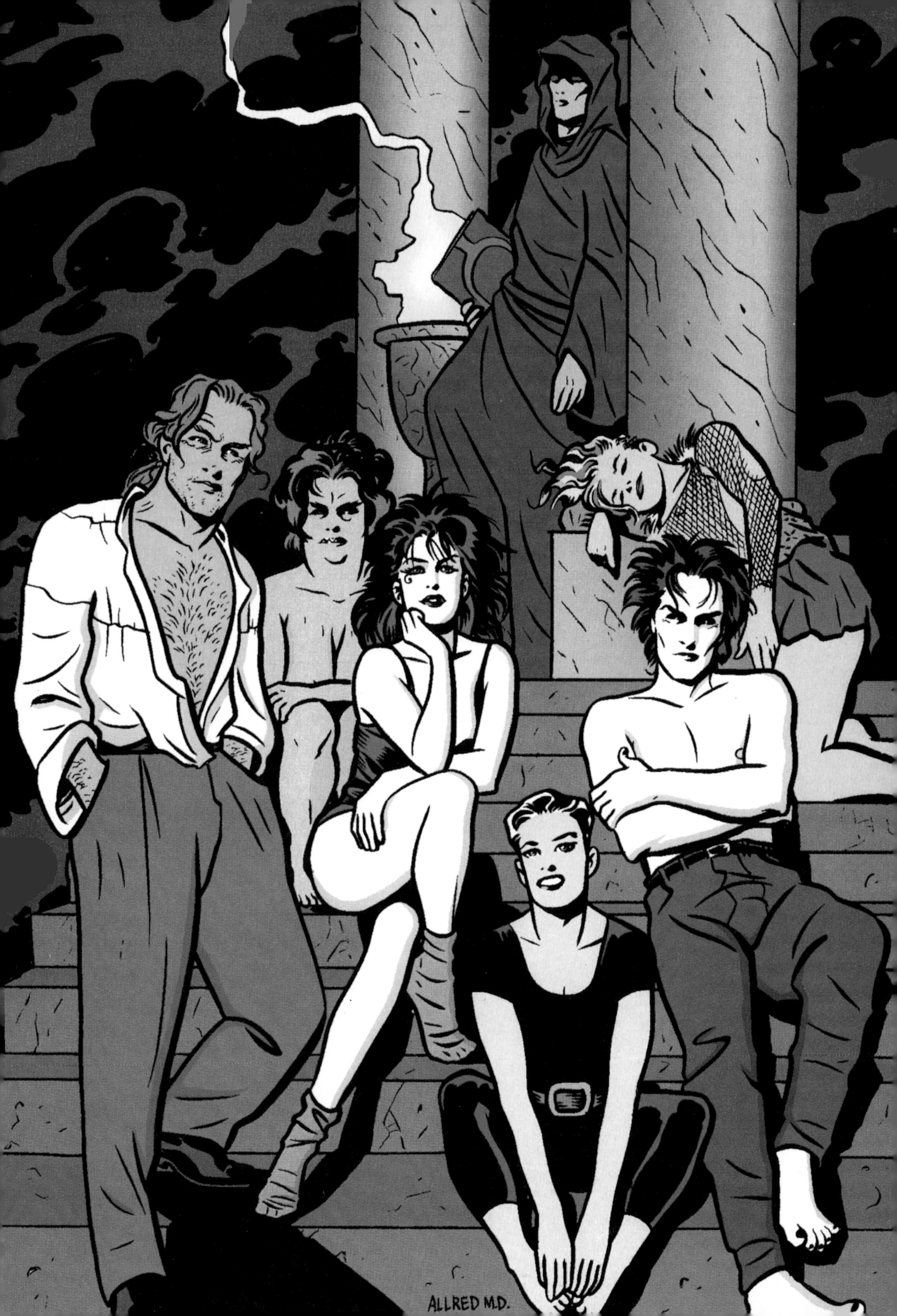
ALLRED M.D.

The Dreaming.
OUR LORD BIDS YOU **ENTER**. YOU ARE ONE OF **MANY** TO ARRIVE THIS DAY, CLURACAN. THE LORD OF DREAMS IS HOLDING A FEAST FOR HIS VISITORS.
IF YOU AND YOUR COMPANION ADVANCE, YOU WILL FIND YOURSELVES IN THE BANQUETING HALL.
GREETINGS TO YOU, GOOD GATEKEEPER.
I PRAY YOU: TELL YOUR MASTER THAT CLURACAN OF FAERIE IS HERE, AS A MESSENGER, AND WOULD HAVE WORDS WITH HIM.

With the introduction of the Endless, the theme of the Sandman's consciousness of his duties and obligations is reiterated. Knowing that Destruction relinquished his role gives a context both to the Sandman's refusal to absolve himself of responsibility and to his actions toward the end of the saga.

Because of this storyline's popularity, the Sandman as he is represented in *Season of Mists* is the version of the character that first broke into the wider consciousness of the public. The story works as a star vehicle for Morpheus. It's so easy to imagine *Season of*

PAGES 74–76 Mythical beings descend on the Dreaming for a banquet. Artwork by Kelley Jones and George Pratt. Daniel Vozzo, colorist.

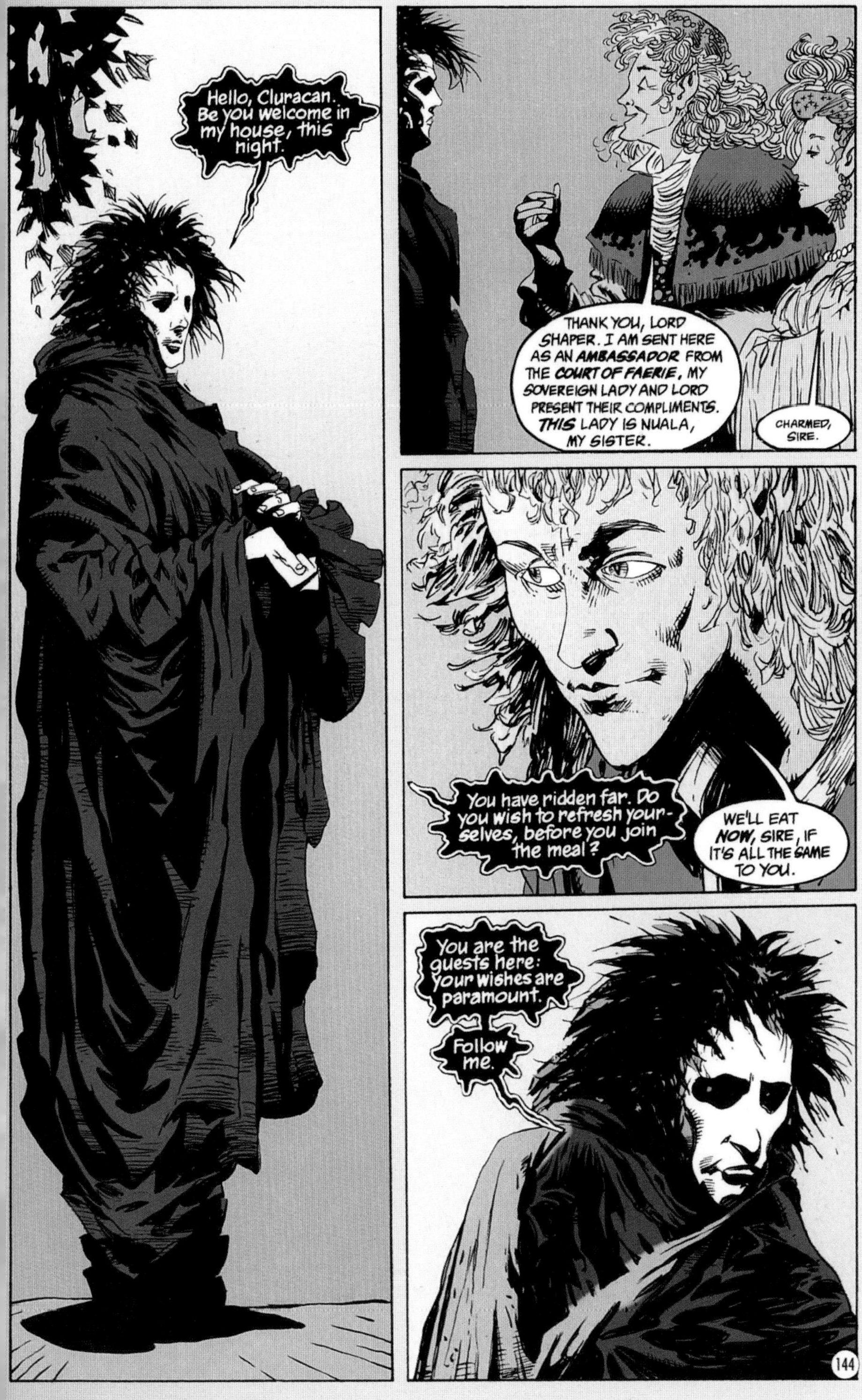
Hello, Cluracan. Be you welcome in my house, this night.
THANK YOU, LORD SHAPER. I AM SENT HERE AS AN AMBASSADOR FROM THE COURT OF FAERIE, MY SOVEREIGN LADY AND LORD PRESENT THEIR COMPLIMENTS. THIS LADY IS NUALA, MY SISTER.
CHARMED, SIRE.
You have ridden far. Do you wish to refresh yourselves, before you join the meal?
WE'LL EAT NOW, SIRE, IF IT'S ALL THE SAME TO YOU.
You are the guests here: your wishes are paramount.
Follow me.
144

Mists as an old-style Hollywood historical saga: A cast of thousands! The splendor of the Dreaming! The grand horror that is Hell! More demons than you can shake a stick at, and not one, not two, but three scantily clad beauties! (Nada, the Sandman's long-suffering and usually naked ex; the voluptuously glamoured faerie, Nuala; and the buxom cat goddess, Bast.) Artist Kelley Jones, who could be counted on to go for broke on the wide-angle shots of hell and all the myriad demons, also gave a wonderful, over-the-top feel to the banquet scenes.

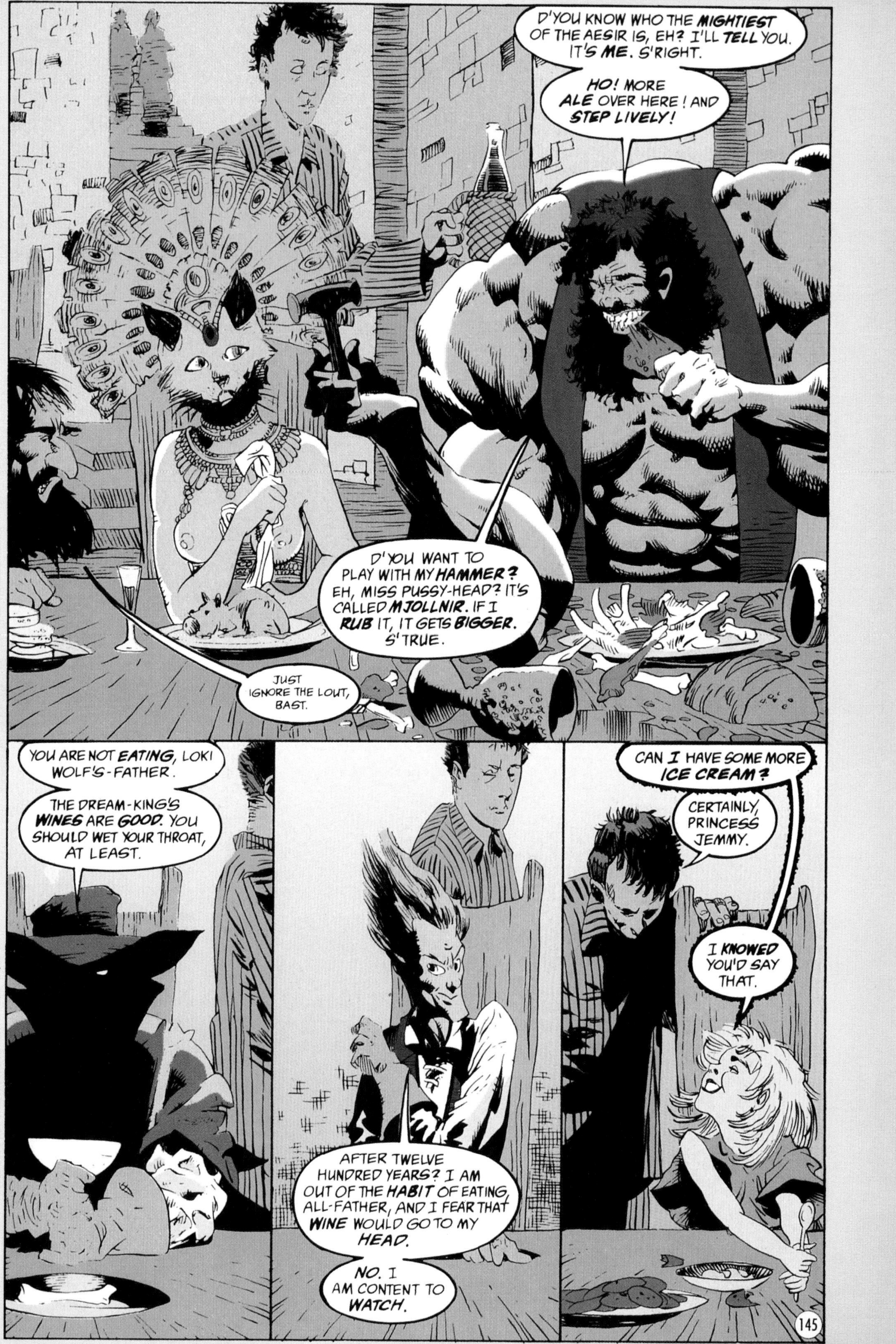
D'YOU KNOW WHO THE MIGHTIEST OF THE AESIR IS, EH? I'LL TELL YOU. IT'S ME. S'RIGHT.
HO! MORE ALE OVER HERE! AND STEP LIVELY!
D'YOU WANT TO PLAY WITH MY HAMMER? EH, MISS PUSSY-HEAD? IT'S CALLED MJOLLNIR. IF I RUB IT, IT GETS BIGGER. S'TRUE.
JUST IGNORE THE LOUT, BAST.
YOU ARE NOT EATING, LOKI WOLF'S-FATHER.
THE DREAM-KING'S WINES ARE GOOD. YOU SHOULD WET YOUR THROAT, AT LEAST.
AFTER TWELVE HUNDRED YEARS? I AM OUT OF THE HABIT OF EATING, ALL-FATHER, AND I FEAR THAT WINE WOULD GO TO MY HEAD.
NO. I AM CONTENT TO WATCH.
CAN I HAVE SOME MORE ICE CREAM?
CERTAINLY, PRINCESS JEMMY.
I KNOWED YOU'D SAY THAT.

BELOW When *Season of Mists* was first collected, it was published as a hardcover with the look of an old family bible. Says Neil, "It was the first hardcover *Sandman* collection, and the first printing has become very rare, and consequently very valuable. Dave McKean's Key to Hell design (embossed in copper on the cover) became very popular both as a tattoo and as an item of jewelry." DC Comics eventually released a sculpted version of the popular key.

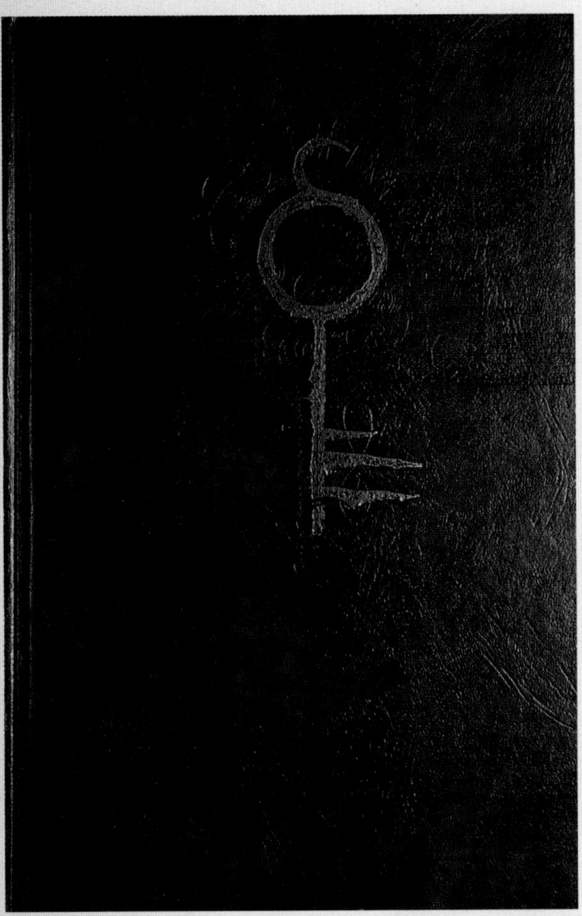

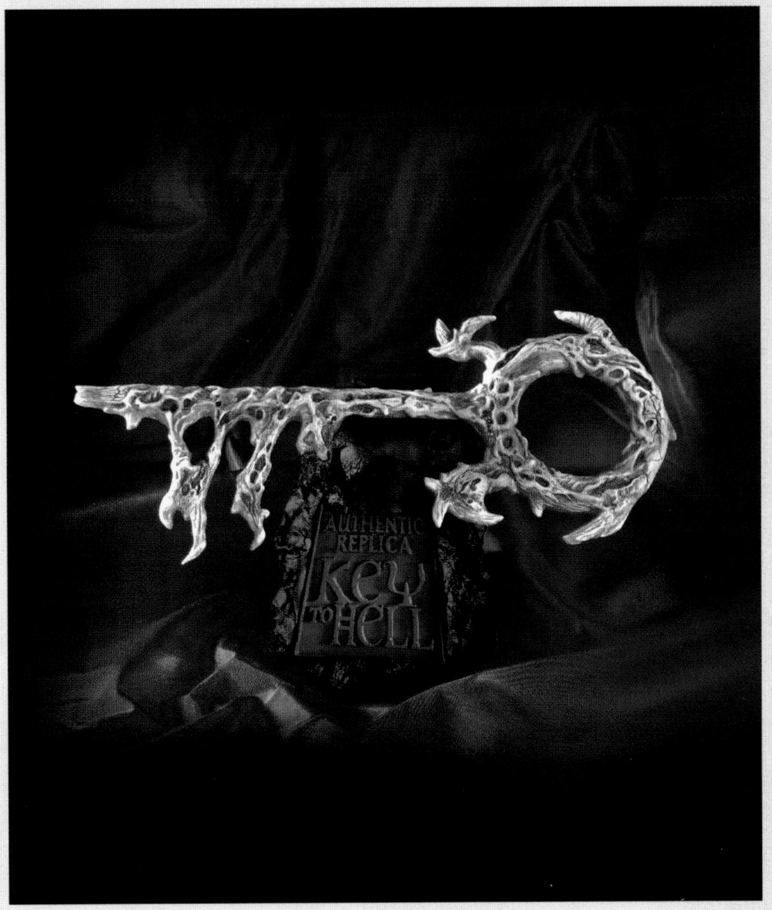
AUTHENTIC
REPLICA
KEY
TO HELL

The plotline is fittingly baroque: Brought to the realization that he has acted in error, the Sandman feels duty-bound to risk reentering Hell so that he may release an old lover he has caused to be imprisoned there. But Hell holds a danger Morpheus isn't expecting: Lucifer is abdicating, leaving the Sandman in charge of the key to the kingdom. No sooner do the floodgates of Hell open than the emissaries from a smorgasbord of world mythologies pour into the Dreaming castle to make their case for receiving the key, offering bribes, threats, and an utterly entertaining assortment of in-fights, subplots, and sub-subplots.

BELOW Nuala, with and without glamour. Artwork by Joe Phillips.   PAGES 79–81 The Sandman and Lucifer have a nice long chat. Artwork by Kelley Jones and Malcolm Jones III. Daniel Vozzo, colorist.

Perhaps the most important plot nugget of *Season of Mists* is the revelation that a de-glamoured Nuala must remain in the Dreaming or risk the censure of the faerie queen. Of little consequence now, Nuala will prove in time to be a far more dangerous gift than the key ever was.

There are so many, er, key moments in this storyline that it is hard to single out only a few. But the scenes in which Morpheus, king of a realm of dreamers, walks with Lucifer, king of a realm of sinners, deserve special notice. These two make such a wonderful pair of contrasts: Morpheus, introspective and rightfully cautious of one of the few beings more powerful than himself, and Lucifer, mocking and sly, yet implicitly respectful of one of the few beings able to comprehend his plight. They share the flaw of pride, although their meeting clearly marks a turning point for both, as Morpheus is beginning to question his pride, and Lucifer seems to be moving beyond his.

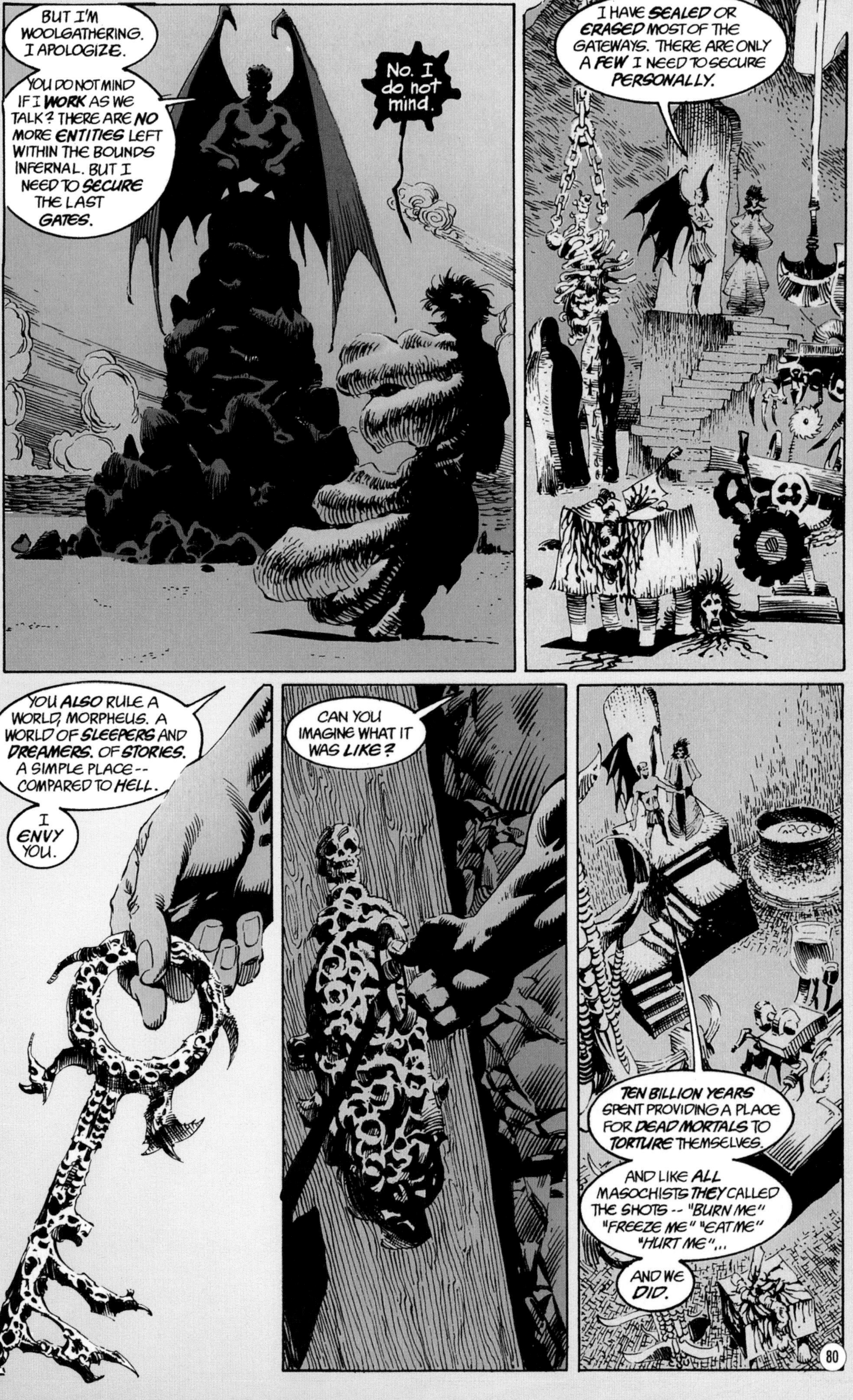

BUT I'M WOOLGATHERING. I APOLOGIZE.
YOU DO NOT MIND IF I WORK AS WE TALK? THERE ARE NO MORE ENTITIES LEFT WITHIN THE BOUNDS INFERNAL. BUT I NEED TO SECURE THE LAST GATES.
No. I do not mind.
I HAVE SEALED OR ERASED MOST OF THE GATEWAYS. THERE ARE ONLY A FEW I NEED TO SECURE PERSONALLY.
YOU ALSO RULE A WORLD, MORPHEUS. A WORLD OF SLEEPERS AND DREAMERS. OF STORIES. A SIMPLE PLACE-- COMPARED TO HELL.
I ENVY YOU.
CAN YOU IMAGINE WHAT IT WAS LIKE?
TEN BILLION YEARS SPENT PROVIDING A PLACE FOR DEAD MORTALS TO TORTURE THEMSELVES.
AND LIKE ALL MASOCHISTS THEY CALLED THE SHOTS -- "BURN ME" "FREEZE ME" "EAT ME" "HURT ME"...
AND WE DID.

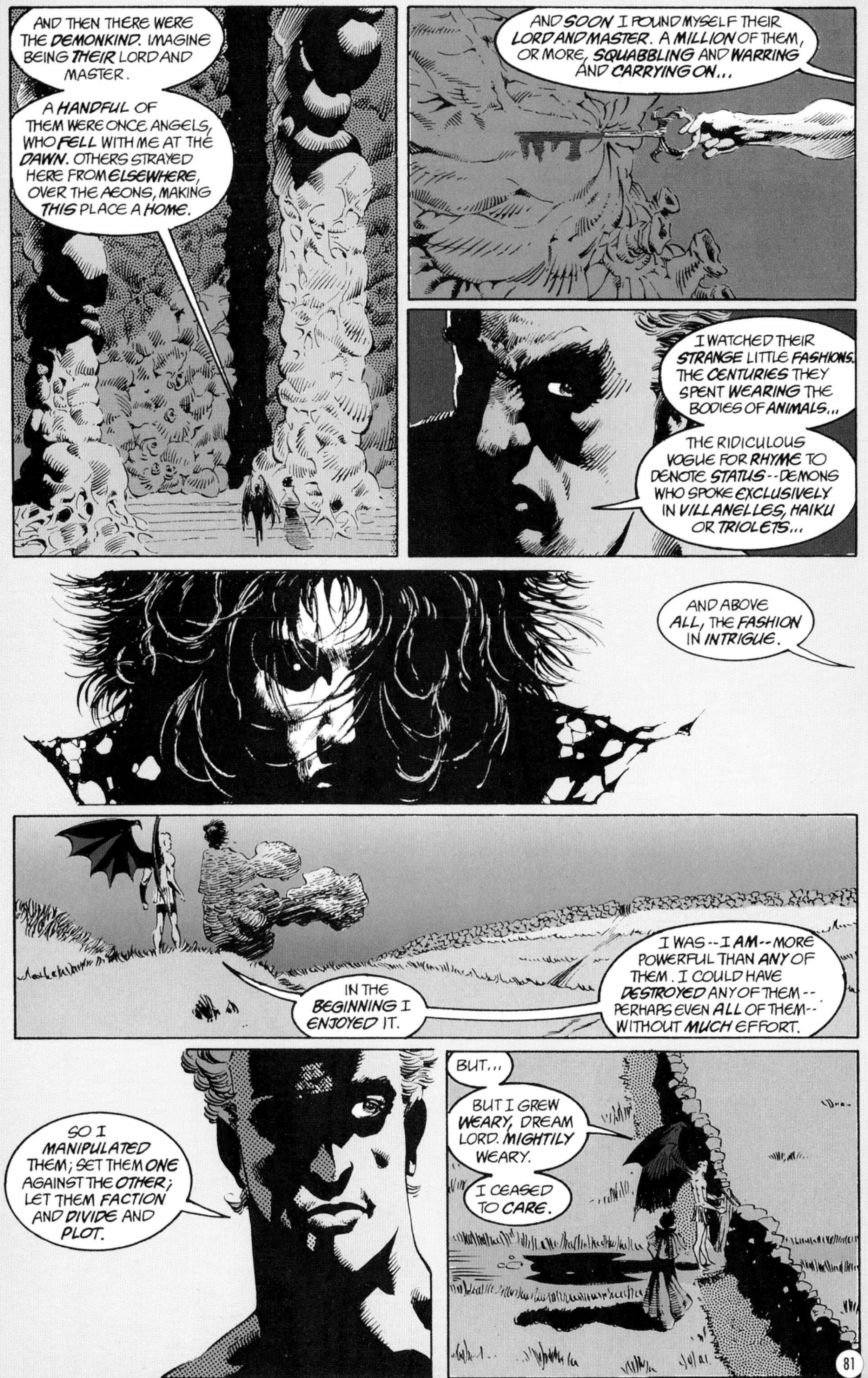
AND THEN THERE WERE THE DEMONKIND. IMAGINE BEING THEIR LORD AND MASTER.
A HANDFUL OF THEM WERE ONCE ANGELS, WHO FELL WITH ME AT THE DAWN. OTHERS STRAYED HERE FROM ELSEWHERE, OVER THE AEONS, MAKING THIS PLACE A HOME.
AND SOON I FOUND MYSELF THEIR LORD AND MASTER. A MILLION OF THEM, OR MORE, SQUABBLING AND WARRING AND CARRYING ON...
I WATCHED THEIR STRANGE LITTLE FASHIONS. THE CENTURIES THEY SPENT WEARING THE BODIES OF ANIMALS...
THE RIDICULOUS VOGUE FOR RHYME TO DENOTE STATUS--DEMONS WHO SPOKE EXCLUSIVELY IN VILLANELLES, HAIKU OR TRIOLETS...
AND ABOVE ALL, THE FASHION IN INTRIGUE.
IN THE BEGINNING I ENJOYED IT.
I WAS--I AM--MORE POWERFUL THAN ANY OF THEM. I COULD HAVE DESTROYED ANY OF THEM--PERHAPS EVEN ALL OF THEM--WITHOUT MUCH EFFORT.
SO I MANIPULATED THEM; SET THEM ONE AGAINST THE OTHER; LET THEM FACTION AND DIVIDE AND PLOT.
BUT...
BUT I GREW WEARY, DREAM LORD. MIGHTILY WEARY.
I CEASED TO CARE.
81

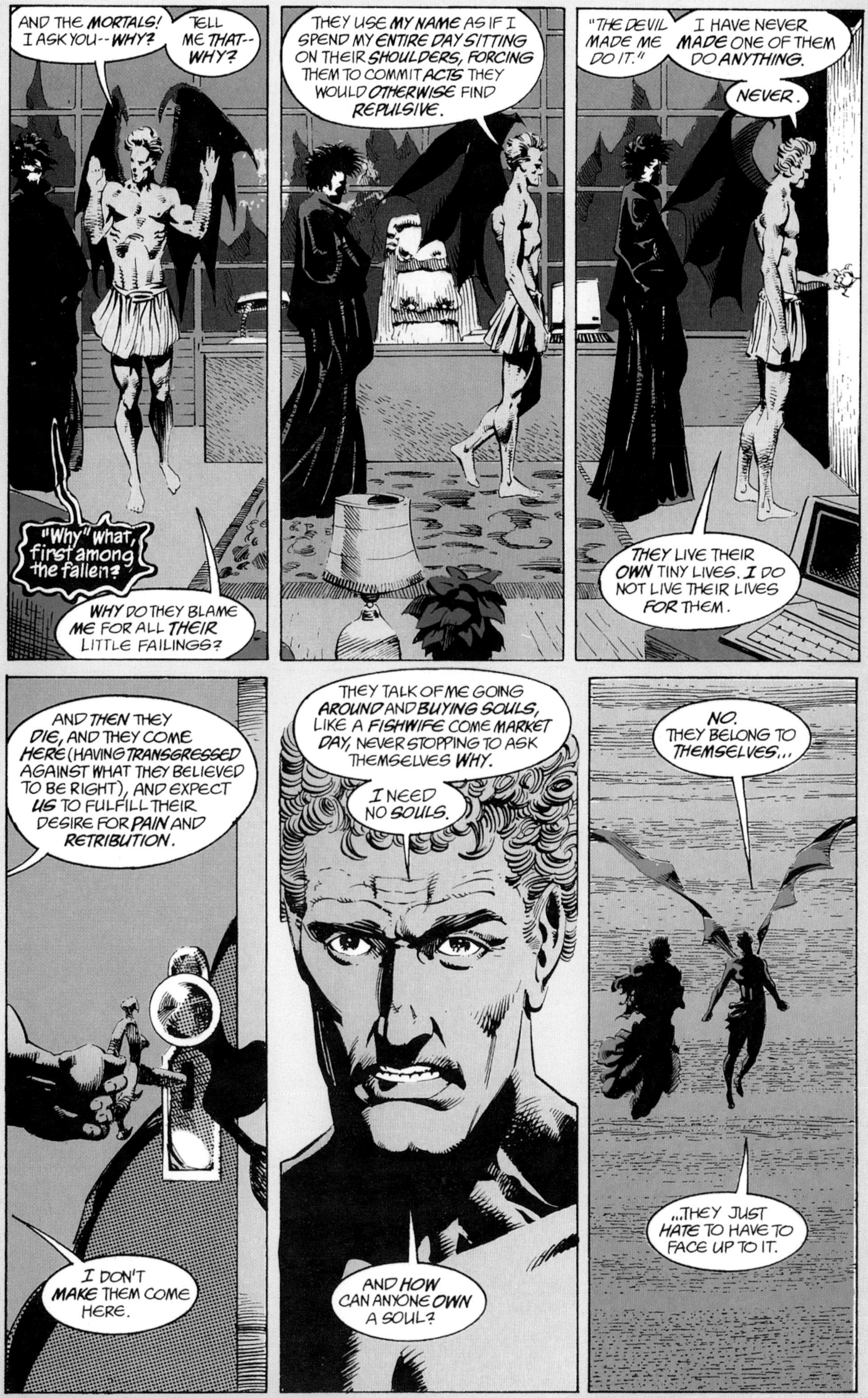
AND THE MORTALS! I ASK YOU--WHY?
TELL ME THAT--WHY?
"Why" what, first among the fallen?
WHY DO THEY BLAME ME FOR ALL THEIR LITTLE FAILINGS?
THEY USE MY NAME AS IF I SPEND MY ENTIRE DAY SITTING ON THEIR SHOULDERS, FORCING THEM TO COMMIT ACTS THEY WOULD OTHERWISE FIND REPULSIVE.
"THE DEVIL MADE ME DO IT."
I HAVE NEVER MADE ONE OF THEM DO ANYTHING.
NEVER.
THEY LIVE THEIR OWN TINY LIVES. I DO NOT LIVE THEIR LIVES FOR THEM.
AND THEN THEY DIE, AND THEY COME HERE (HAVING TRANSGRESSED AGAINST WHAT THEY BELIEVED TO BE RIGHT), AND EXPECT US TO FULFILL THEIR DESIRE FOR PAIN AND RETRIBUTION.
I DON'T MAKE THEM COME HERE.
THEY TALK OF ME GOING AROUND AND BUYING SOULS, LIKE A FISHWIFE COME MARKET DAY, NEVER STOPPING TO ASK THEMSELVES WHY.
I NEED NO SOULS.
AND HOW CAN ANYONE OWN A SOUL?
NO. THEY BELONG TO THEMSELVES...
...THEY JUST HATE TO HAVE TO FACE UP TO IT.

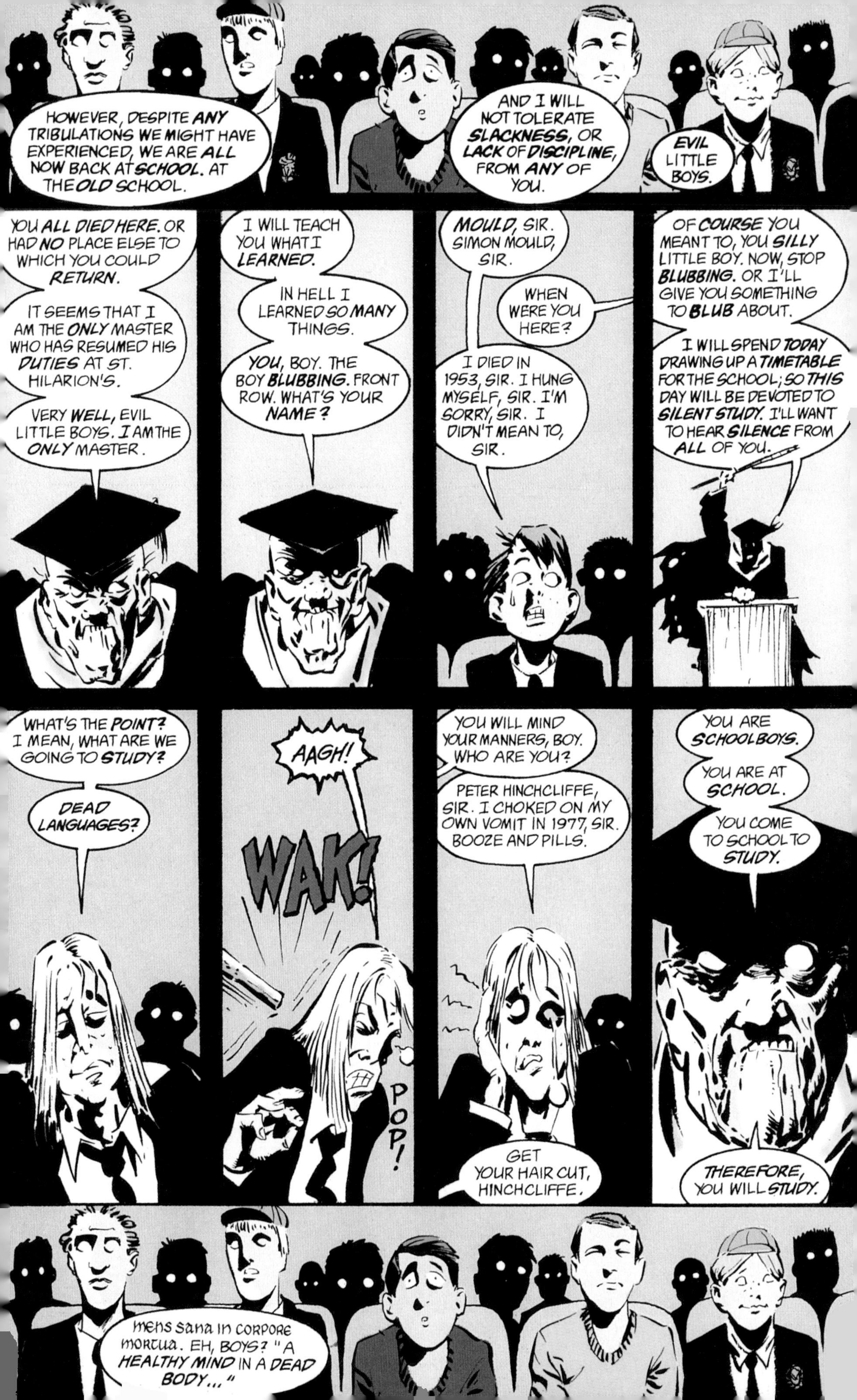
HOWEVER, DESPITE ANY TRIBULATIONS WE MIGHT HAVE EXPERIENCED, WE ARE ALL NOW BACK AT SCHOOL. AT THE OLD SCHOOL.
AND I WILL NOT TOLERATE SLACKNESS, OR LACK OF DISCIPLINE, FROM ANY OF YOU.
EVIL LITTLE BOYS.
YOU ALL DIED HERE. OR HAD NO PLACE ELSE TO WHICH YOU COULD RETURN.
IT SEEMS THAT I AM THE ONLY MASTER WHO HAS RESUMED HIS DUTIES AT ST. HILARION'S.
VERY WELL, EVIL LITTLE BOYS. I AM THE ONLY MASTER.
I WILL TEACH YOU WHAT I LEARNED.
IN HELL I LEARNED SO MANY THINGS.
YOU, BOY. THE BOY BLUBBING. FRONT ROW. WHAT'S YOUR NAME?
MOULD, SIR. SIMON MOULD, SIR.
WHEN WERE YOU HERE?
I DIED IN 1953, SIR. I HUNG MYSELF, SIR. I'M SORRY, SIR. I DIDN'T MEAN TO, SIR.
OF COURSE YOU MEANT TO, YOU SILLY LITTLE BOY. NOW, STOP BLUBBING. OR I'LL GIVE YOU SOMETHING TO BLUB ABOUT.
I WILL SPEND TODAY DRAWING UP A TIMETABLE FOR THE SCHOOL; SO THIS DAY WILL BE DEVOTED TO SILENT STUDY. I'LL WANT TO HEAR SILENCE FROM ALL OF YOU.
WHAT'S THE POINT? I MEAN, WHAT ARE WE GOING TO STUDY?
DEAD LANGUAGES?
AAGH!
WAK!
POP!
YOU WILL MIND YOUR MANNERS, BOY. WHO ARE YOU?
PETER HINCHCLIFFE, SIR. I CHOKED ON MY OWN VOMIT IN 1977, SIR. BOOZE AND PILLS.
GET YOUR HAIR CUT, HINCHCLIFFE.
YOU ARE SCHOOLBOYS.
YOU ARE AT SCHOOL.
YOU COME TO SCHOOL TO STUDY.
THEREFORE, YOU WILL STUDY.
mens sana in corpore mortua. EH, BOYS? "A HEALTHY MIND IN A DEAD BODY..."

PAGE 82 For many, far scarier than Hell is the thought of an English boarding school. Artwork by Matt Wagner and Malcolm Jones III. Daniel Vozzo, colorist.

If *The Sandman* does finally get made into a film (and there has been much talk in that direction, for a very long time), the easiest storyline to adapt would be *Season of Mists*. But filmmakers would surely leave out the one strange gem of a story not set in Hell or any mythic realm: episode 4 of *Season of Mists*, subtitled "In which the dead return; and Charles Rowland concludes his education."

This episode differs in setting and mood from the rest of *Season of Mists*, although it is a story that occurs as a direct consequence of Lucifer's decision to quit his leadership position. As the gates of Hell are flung open and the dead escape, a harried Death tries to keep up with the sudden increase in her workload, and Charles Rowland, the one boy left in an English boarding school over holidays, discovers that all the bullies who ever got sent to Hell are now his classmates.

With its nightmarish evocation of childhood cruelties and its youthfully defiant and optimistic ending, this little outpost of the Dreaming, above all the others, garners my vote for the most overlooked attraction *The Sandman* has to offer.

Charles Rowland, together with his detective partner Edwin Paine, reappears in *The Children's Crusade*, a 1993 comic book crossover event (meaning different writers would write elements of the story into their monthly scripts).

Neil was tapped to write the bookends — the comics that would begin and end the saga. But, well, to make a long storyline short, the whole thing got a bit complicated, as the other writers were busy with their own plots and Neil was busy with *The Sandman*'s writing commitments . . . And since desperate times call for desperate measures, I was called in to write (as Gaimanishly as I could) some sections of *The Children's Crusade*.

I suggested having some fun, and in a big double-page spread where all the children are cavorting, I asked the book's artist, Peter Snejbjerg, to draw a very youthful Neil, oblivious to the frenetic play around him, calmly reading a comic book.

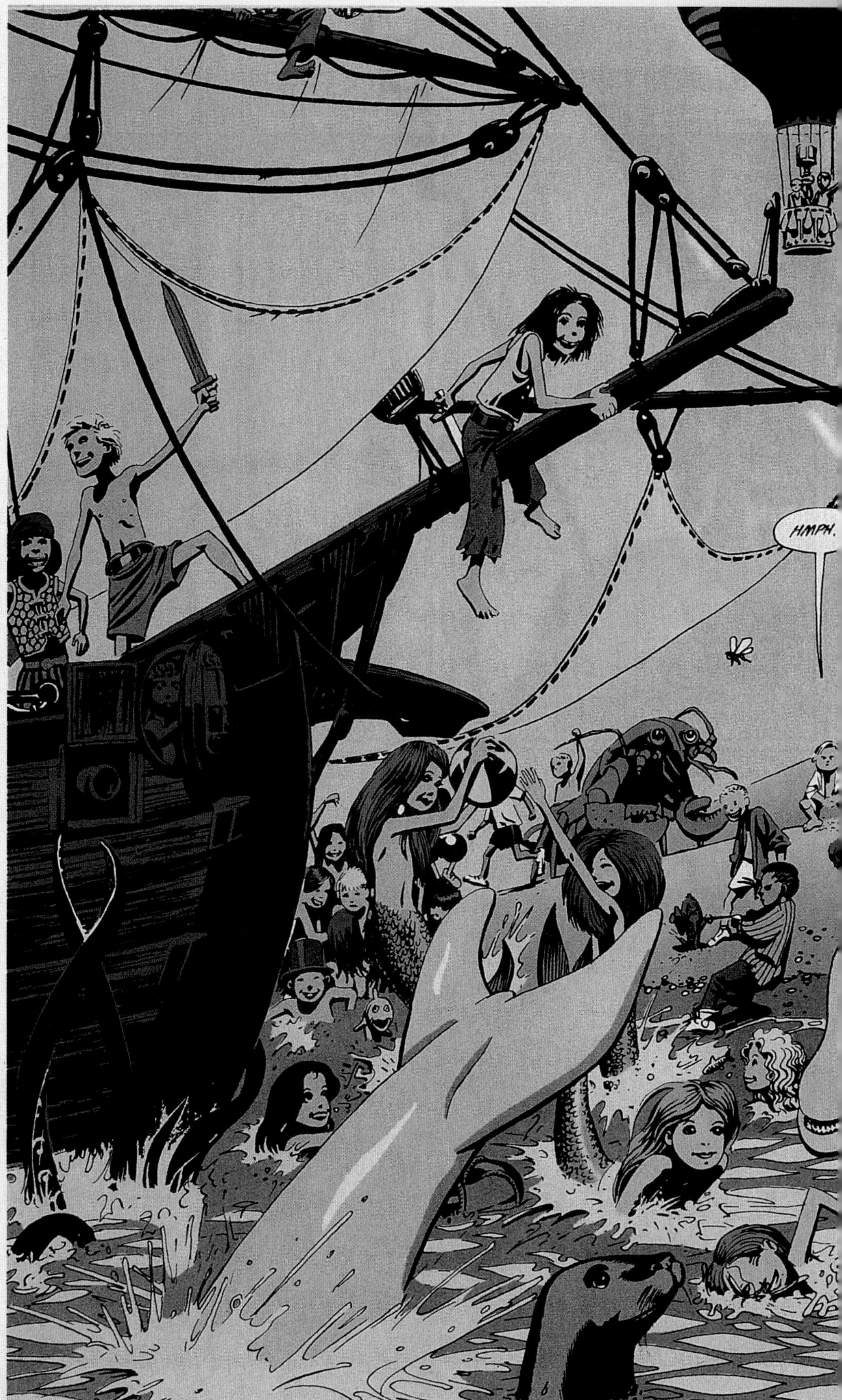
HMPH.

PAGES 84–85 Where's Neil? From the Alisa Kwitney–scripted second volume of *The Children's Crusade*. Artwork by Peter Snejbjerg. Daniel Vozzo, colorist.

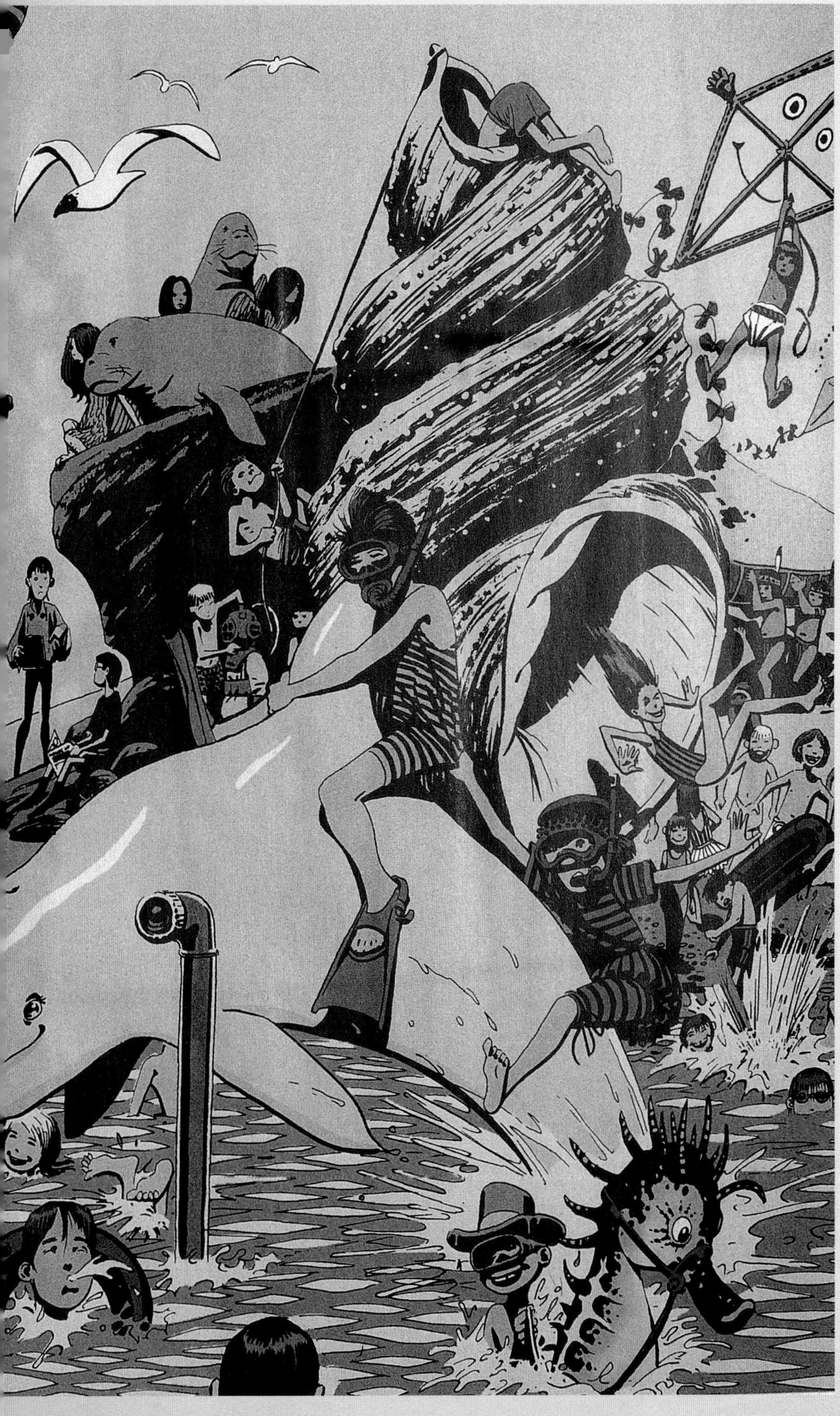

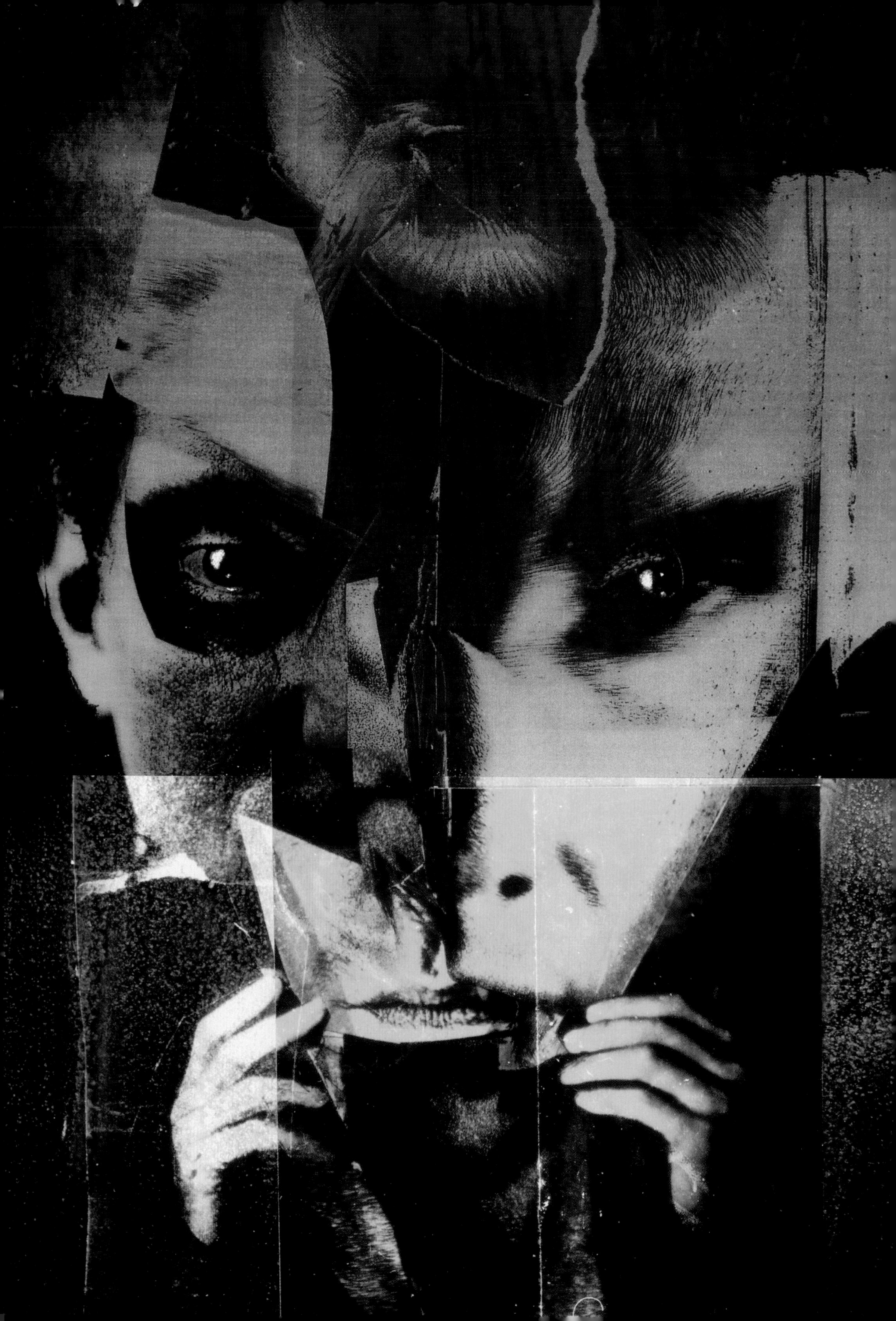

CHAPTER 6

A GAME OF YOU

IN WHICH THE WOMEN STEAL THE SHOW, AND AN ANCIENT WITCH NAMED THESSALY PERFORMS A NEAT TRICK WITH THE SKIN OF A MAN'S FACE.

"YOU KNOW, PEOPLE COME UP TO ME TO THIS DAY AND TELL ME I WRITE GOOD WOMEN AND ASK HOW DO I DO IT. AND I TELL THEM MY SECRET, WHICH IS YOU WRITE HUMAN BEINGS, YOU WRITE PEOPLE." —NEIL GAIMAN

It's easy to demystify a hero; just keep him on stage too long. As we begin the next installment of the Sandman saga, it's interesting to note how the Dream King becomes conspicuous by his absence. *A Game of You* is a book where we explore the nature of dreams, and of the Dreaming; in the end, we will learn that the king and his kingdom are, like conjoined twins, not easily separated.

Intellectually among the most provocative of the collections, *A Game of You* is a storyline about fantasy and gender, and it takes a journey into one of the distant skerries of Dream. This is about as far from the center of the Dreaming as you can get – if the Sandman's castle were in Moscow, this story would be set in far-off Uzbekistan – and Morpheus does not figure largely in the plot until the very end. This may be why the storyline did not, when first published, have the broad commercial appeal of *Season of Mists*.

Yet even those who pine for more Morpheus will find plenty to recommend this tale of tripping the dark fantastic.

PAGE 86 Cover, *The Sandman* no. 37. Artwork by Dave McKean.

BELOW Dream. Artwork by Barron Storey.

BELOW Dream. Artwork by Barron Storey.

BELOW Matthew and Dream contemplate what feels like a seismic disturbance in the Dreaming. Artwork by Shawn McManus. Daniel Vozzo, colorist.

The story begins with the revelation that this far-off island of the Dreaming, populated largely by the creatures of a young woman's childhood imagining, is in crisis. The disturbances begin to make themselves felt in the waking world, and in one New York City apartment building because the young woman in question – Barbie – lives there. (We've met Barbie before, in *The Doll's House:* She's the blandly pretty blonde with the remarkably vivid dream life.)

Her dream life has become so vivid lately that it is spilling over into the lives of her neighbors: Wanda, a preoperative transsexual; Hazel and Foxglove, a lesbian couple; George, a mild-mannered evil emissary of the villainous Cuckoo; and Thessaly, a primly bespectacled witch-woman of the lowlands.

Thessaly takes Hazel and Foxglove on a journey into Barbie's dream, not by asking Morpheus for help, but by taking the alternate route – the moon's road. Along the way, the women – and Wanda, who straddles the borderlands of gender – discover much about the nature of dreams, and of the Dreaming.

And, the catty exchanges between Morpheus and Thessaly at the end of *A Game of You* are twice as much fun when reread with the knowledge that there's more going on between them than meets the eye.

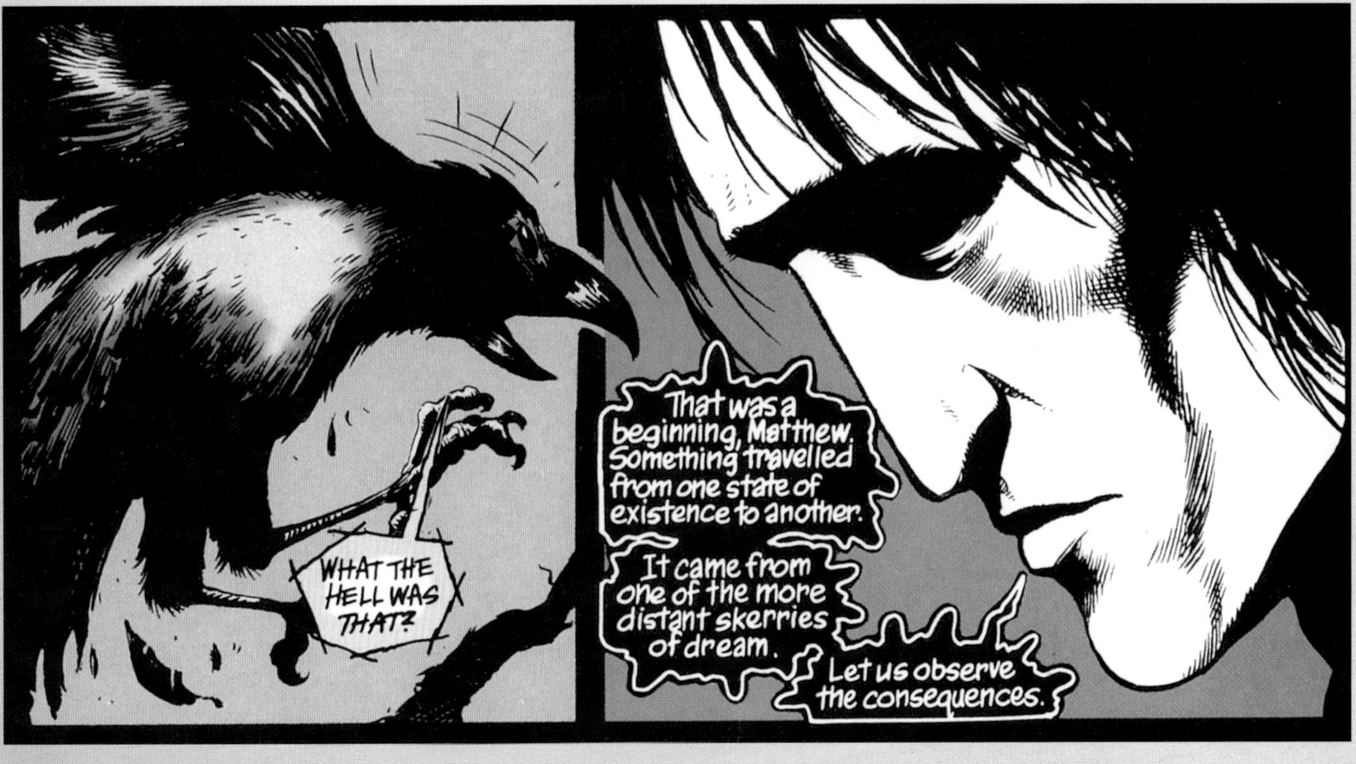
WHAT THE HELL WAS THAT?
That was a beginning, Matthew. Something travelled from one state of existence to another.
It came from one of the more distant skerries of dream.
Let us observe the consequences.

BELOW The Cuckoo explains the real difference between boys and girls. Artwork by Bryan Talbot and Stan Woch. Daniel Vozzo, colorist.

BOYS AND GIRLS ARE DIFFERENT, YOU KNOW THAT?
LITTLE BOYS HAVE FANTASIES IN WHICH THEY'RE FASTER, OR SMARTER, OR ABLE TO FLY.
WHERE THEY HIDE THEIR FACES IN SECRET IDENTITIES, AND LISTEN TO THE PEOPLE WHO DESPISE THEM ADMIRING THEIR REMARKABLE DEEDS.
PATHETIC, BESPECTACLED, REJECTED PERRY PORTER IS SECRETLY THE AMAZING SPIDER. GAWKY, BESPECTACLED, UNLOVED CLINT CLARKE IS REALLY HYPERMAN. YES?
WHAT HAS THIS GOT TO DO WITH--?
SHUSH.
125
NOW, LITTLE GIRLS, ON THE OTHER HAND, HAVE DIFFERENT FANTASIES. MUCH LESS CONVOLUTED. THEIR PARENTS ARE NOT THEIR PARENTS. THEIR LIVES ARE NOT THEIR LIVES.
THEY ARE PRINCESSES.
LOST PRINCESSES FROM DISTANT LANDS.
AND ONE DAY THE KING AND QUEEN, THEIR REAL PARENTS, WILL TAKE THEM BACK TO THEIR LAND, AND THEN THEY'LL BE HAPPY FOR EVER AND EVER.
LITTLE CUCKOOS.
DID I DREAM THAT? I DON'T REMEMBER...
SURE YOU DID. YOU MADE UP A MAGIC LAND, AND YOU POPULATED IT WITH YOUR TOYS.
Barbara's ROOM
...TOYS?
YEAH. THEY'RE ALL IN HERE. IN THE SHRINE. COME ON IN.
THIS IS MY BEDROOM.
THAT'S RIGHT.

BELOW The Sandman's unhappy love affair (does he have any other kind?) with Thessaly takes place offstage. Artwork by Colleen Doran.

WHO WAS THE GREAT ROMANTIC LOVE OF MORPHEUS'S LIFE? NADA? ALIANORA? THESSALY? OR SOMEONE WE DON'T KNOW ABOUT? NEIL SAYS, "PROBABLY SOMEONE WE DON'T KNOW ABOUT. EVEN ALLOWING FOR ONE RELATIONSHIP EVERY COUPLE OF THOUSAND YEARS, YOU STILL HAVE A NUMBER OF RELATIONSHIPS THAT COULD EACH GO WRONG IN ITS OWN DIFFERENT WAY."

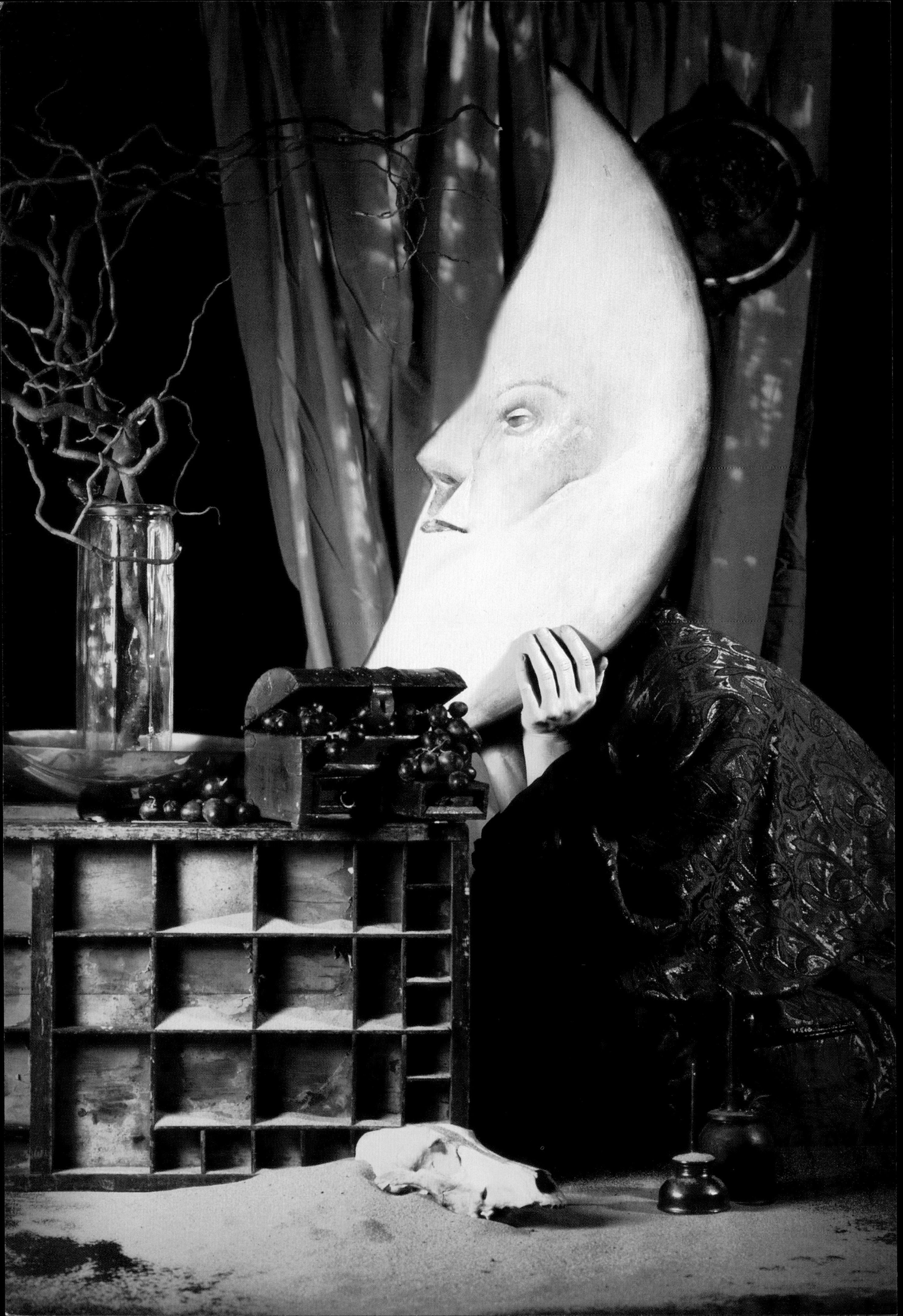

CHAPTER 7

FABLES & REFLECTIONS

IN WHICH MORPHEUS VISITS HAROUN AL RASCHID, JOHANNA CONSTANTINE, AND JOSHUA NORTON.

The next collection, *Fables & Reflections*, is as deeply rooted in history as *A Game of You* is rooted in fantasy. These are short stories, all based on a premise of historical fact. "Three Septembers and a January" concerns the life of Joshua Norton, the self-appointed Emperor of America, and features the first time Delirium gets a real walking, talking role in the plot.

The next story, "Thermidor," introduces the redoubtable Johanna Constantine, ancestress of John Constantine of *Hellblazer* fame. (Neil holds me personally responsible for "Thermidor," as I called him insisting on a blurb for the "next issue" box that ran at the end of each monthly issue of *The Sandman*. Neil claims he was totally unprepared and simply blurted out "Lady Johanna Constantine and the French Revolution" without any prior planning.)

WHO WOULD WIN IN A FIGHT: LADY JOHANNA CONSTANTINE OR HER DESCENDANT, JOHN CONSTANTINE? ACCORDING TO NEIL GAIMAN, THERE WOULD BE NO CONTEST: "LADY JOHANNA. 'CAUSE SHE'S MORE RUTHLESS, AND BECAUSE JOHN WOULD HESITATE, JUST FOR A MOMENT, DURING WHICH TIME SHE WILL HAVE KICKED HIM IN THE NUTS AND PUSHED HIM OFF A CLIFF. THAT'S JUST MY OPINION, OF COURSE."

PAGE 92 Cover, *The Sandman* no. 39. Artwork by Dave McKean

PAGES 94–95 From "Three Septembers and a January." Artist Shawn McManus did a memorable Delirium. If she looks vaguely Asian here, it is probably because she's spent the afternoon with suicidal young Chinese prostitutes. Daniel Vozzo, colorist.

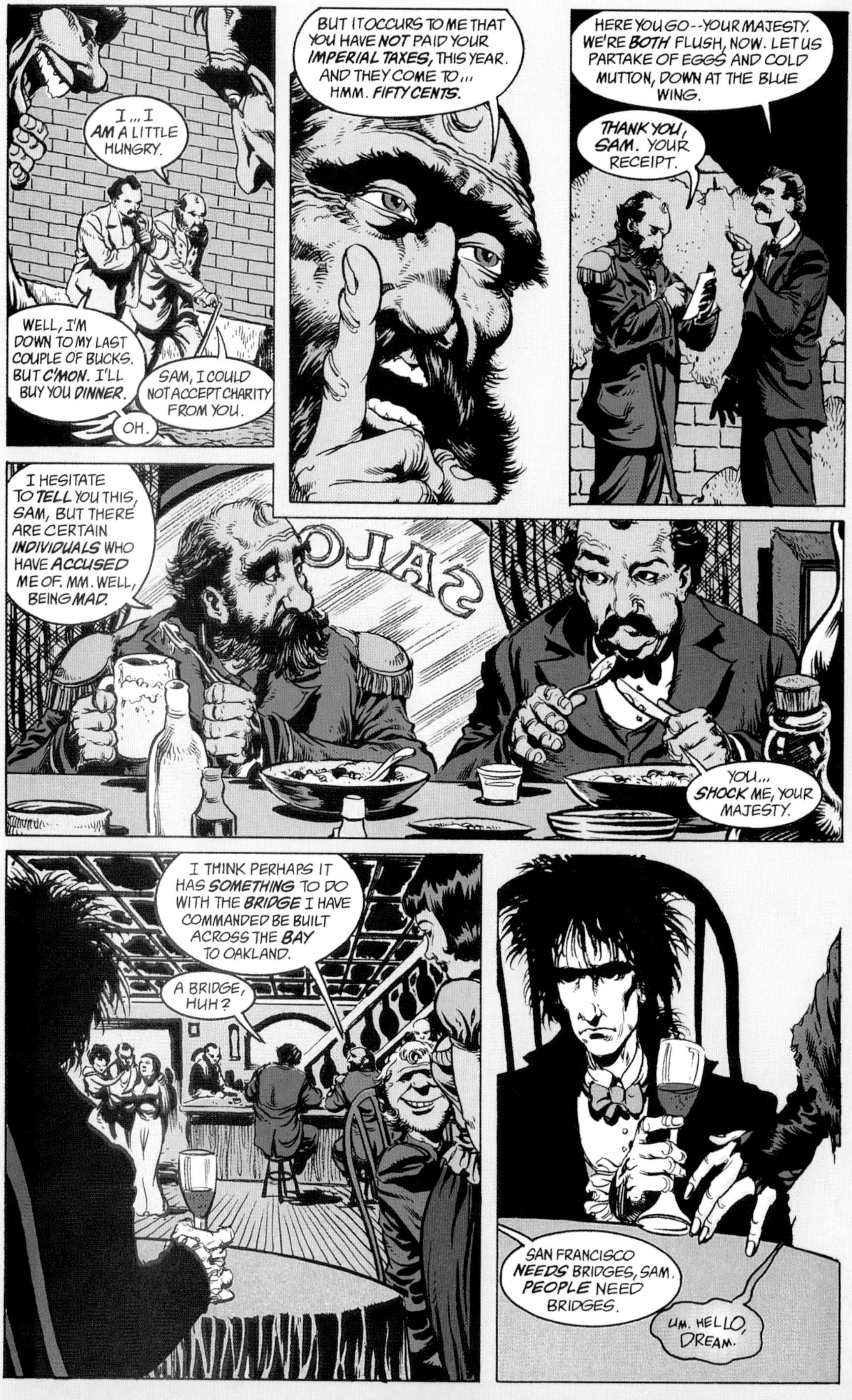
I ... I AM A LITTLE HUNGRY.
WELL, I'M DOWN TO MY LAST COUPLE OF BUCKS. BUT C'MON. I'LL BUY YOU DINNER.
SAM, I COULD NOT ACCEPT CHARITY FROM YOU.
OH.
BUT IT OCCURS TO ME THAT YOU HAVE NOT PAID YOUR IMPERIAL TAXES, THIS YEAR. AND THEY COME TO ... HMM. FIFTY CENTS.
HERE YOU GO--YOUR MAJESTY. WE'RE BOTH FLUSH, NOW. LET US PARTAKE OF EGGS AND COLD MUTTON, DOWN AT THE BLUE WING.
THANK YOU, SAM. YOUR RECEIPT.
I HESITATE TO TELL YOU THIS, SAM, BUT THERE ARE CERTAIN INDIVIDUALS WHO HAVE ACCUSED ME OF. MM. WELL, BEING MAD.
SALO
YOU... SHOCK ME, YOUR MAJESTY.
I THINK PERHAPS IT HAS SOMETHING TO DO WITH THE BRIDGE I HAVE COMMANDED BE BUILT ACROSS THE BAY TO OAKLAND.
A BRIDGE, HUH?
SAN FRANCISCO NEEDS BRIDGES, SAM. PEOPLE NEED BRIDGES.
UM. HELLO, DREAM.

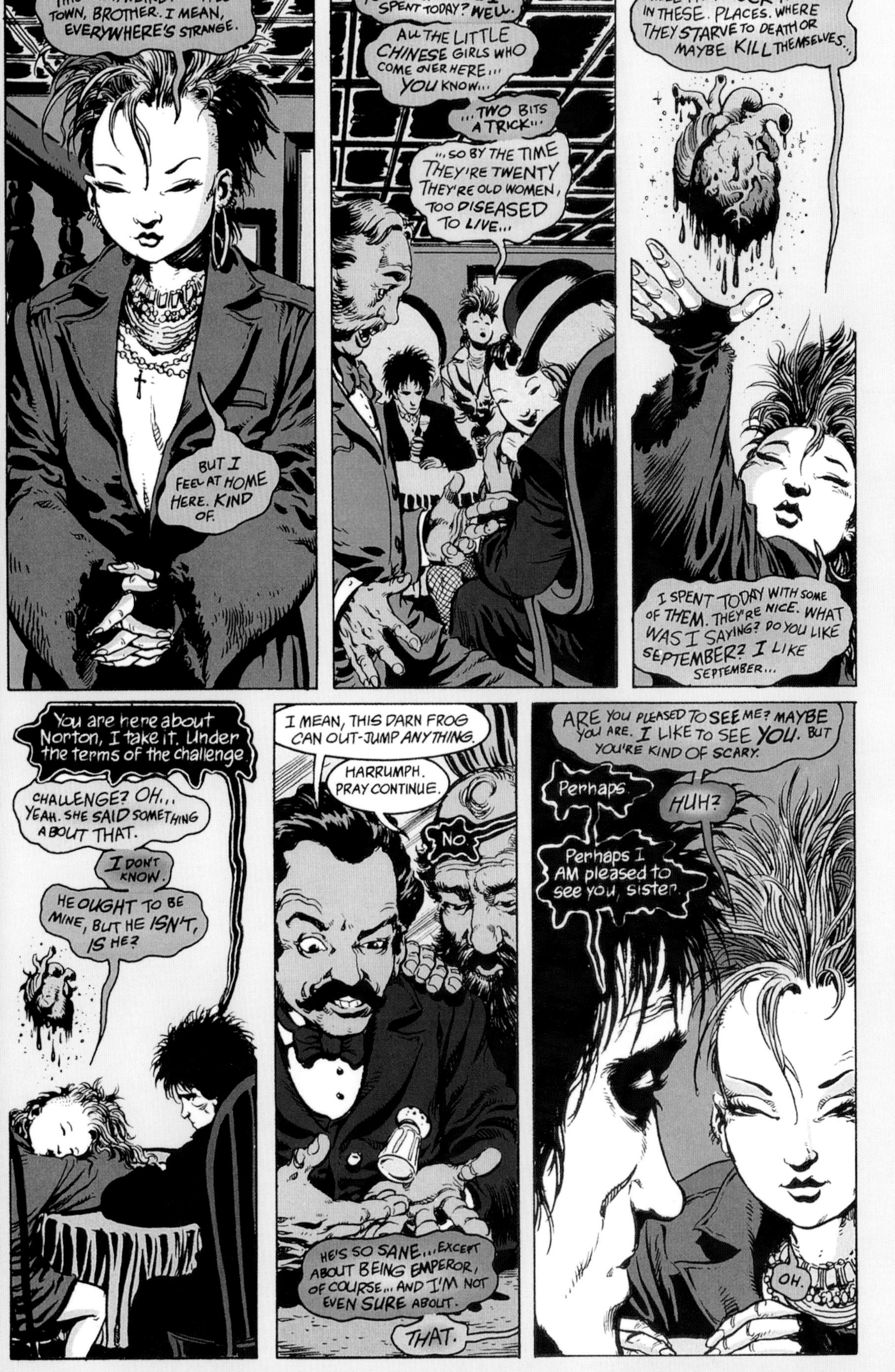
THIS IS A... WEIRD... LITTLE TOWN, BROTHER. I MEAN, EVERYWHERE'S STRANGE.
BUT I FEEL AT HOME HERE. KIND OF.
YOU KNOW WHERE I SPENT TODAY? WELL.
ALL THE LITTLE CHINESE GIRLS WHO COME OVER HERE... YOU KNOW...
...TWO BITS A TRICK...
...SO BY THE TIME THEY'RE TWENTY THEY'RE OLD WOMEN, TOO DISEASED TO LIVE...
WELL THEY LOCK THEM AWAY IN THESE. PLACES. WHERE THEY STARVE TO DEATH OR MAYBE KILL THEMSELVES...
I SPENT TODAY WITH SOME OF THEM. THEY'RE NICE. WHAT WAS I SAYING? DO YOU LIKE SEPTEMBER? I LIKE SEPTEMBER...
You are here about Norton, I take it. Under the terms of the challenge.
CHALLENGE? OH... YEAH. SHE SAID SOMETHING ABOUT THAT.
I DON'T KNOW.
HE OUGHT TO BE MINE, BUT HE ISN'T, IS HE?
I MEAN, THIS DARN FROG CAN OUT-JUMP ANYTHING.
HARRUMPH. PRAY CONTINUE.
NO.
HE'S SO SANE... EXCEPT ABOUT BEING EMPEROR, OF COURSE... AND I'M NOT EVEN SURE ABOUT.
THAT.
ARE YOU PLEASED TO SEE ME? MAYBE YOU ARE. I LIKE TO SEE YOU. BUT YOU'RE KIND OF SCARY.
Perhaps.
HUH?
Perhaps I AM pleased to see you, sister.
OH.

BELOW A woman with two heads. From "Thermidor." The artist for this piece, Stan Woch, had previously penciled issues of Alan Moore's run on *Swamp Thing*. Inked by Dick Giordano. Daniel Vozzo, colorist.

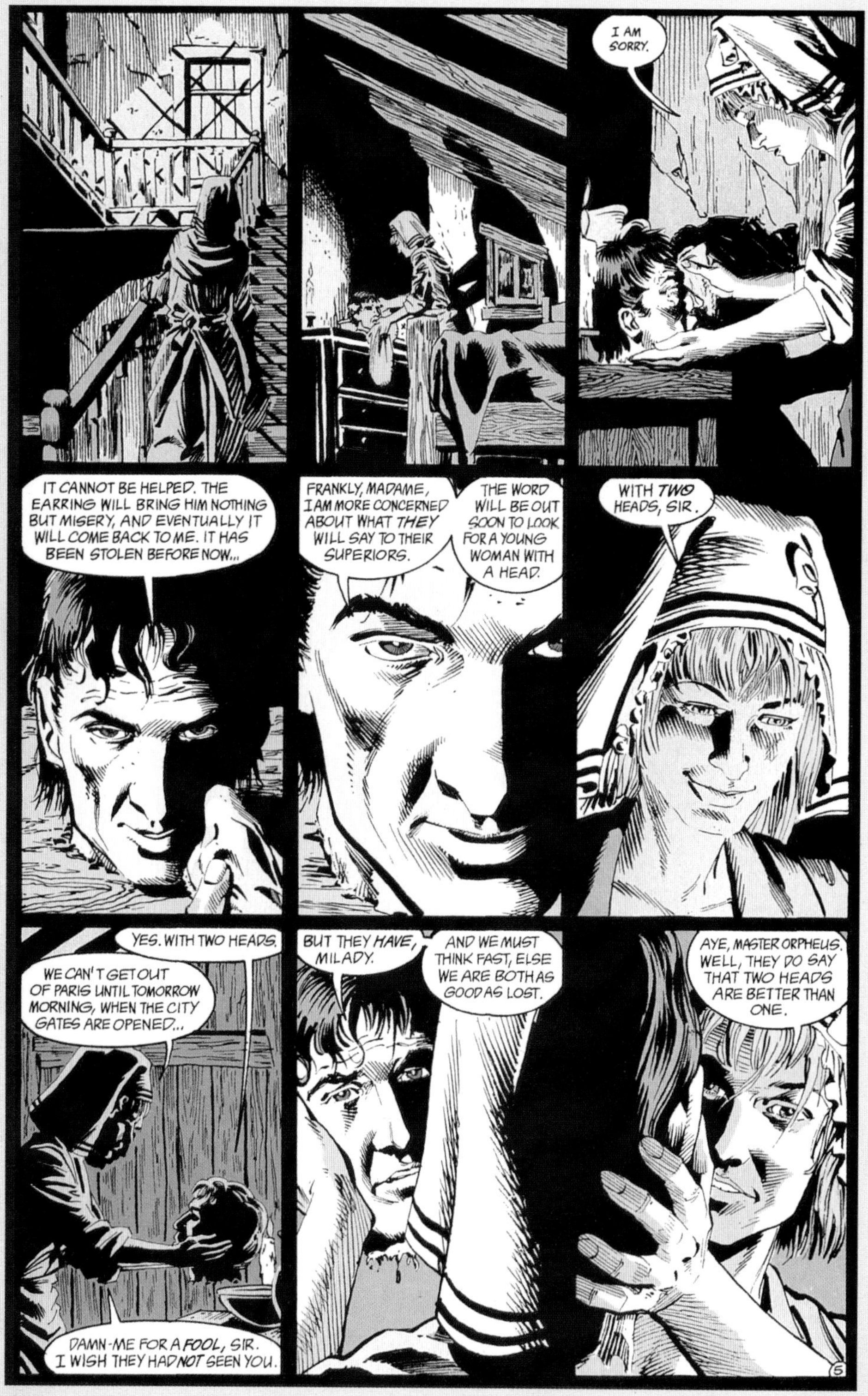
I AM SORRY.
IT CANNOT BE HELPED. THE EARRING WILL BRING HIM NOTHING BUT MISERY, AND EVENTUALLY IT WILL COME BACK TO ME. IT HAS BEEN STOLEN BEFORE NOW...
FRANKLY, MADAME, I AM MORE CONCERNED ABOUT WHAT THEY WILL SAY TO THEIR SUPERIORS.
THE WORD WILL BE OUT SOON TO LOOK FOR A YOUNG WOMAN WITH A HEAD.
WITH TWO HEADS, SIR.
YES. WITH TWO HEADS.
WE CAN'T GET OUT OF PARIS UNTIL TOMORROW MORNING, WHEN THE CITY GATES ARE OPENED...
DAMN-ME FOR A FOOL, SIR. I WISH THEY HAD NOT SEEN YOU.
BUT THEY HAVE, MILADY.
AND WE MUST THINK FAST, ELSE WE ARE BOTH AS GOOD AS LOST.
AYE, MASTER ORPHEUS. WELL, THEY DO SAY THAT TWO HEADS ARE BETTER THAN ONE.
5

With consummate skill, in this story Neil introduces us to the Sandman's son—or rather his son's living head: Orpheus "who bested Death, and who now cannot die." It is revealed to us that Orpheus lost his body to the Bacchante, the women of the frenzy.

PAGES 97–99 From "Orpheus." Artwork by Bryan Talbot and Mark Buckingham. Daniel Vozzo, colorist.

We also learn, at the end of this tale, that Orpheus is poignantly hoping for reconciliation with his father, a tidbit that whets the appetite for the whole story told from the beginning – which we get later in the collection in "Orpheus," originally from *The Sandman Special.*

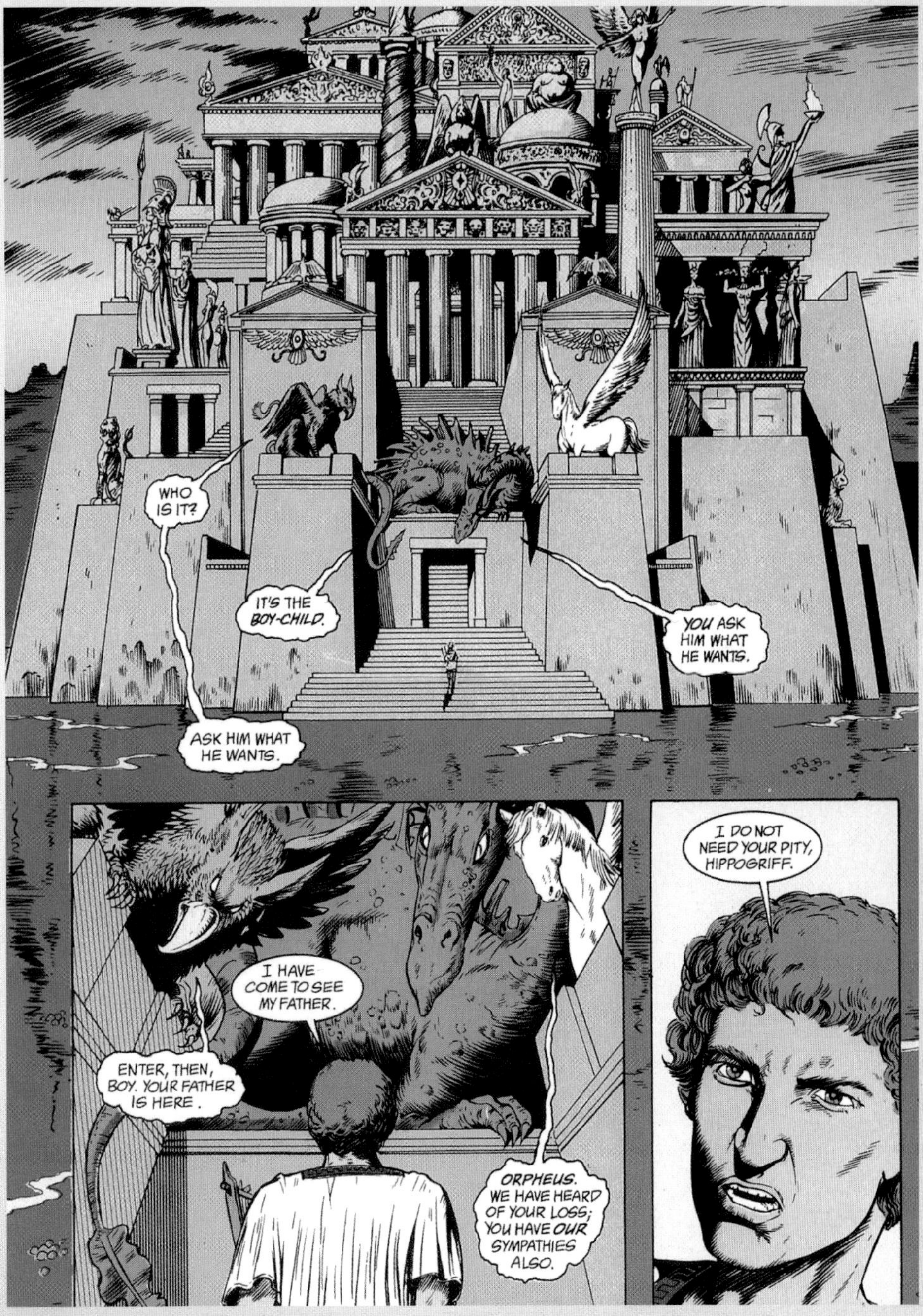
WHO IS IT?
IT'S THE BOY-CHILD.
YOU ASK HIM WHAT HE WANTS.
ASK HIM WHAT HE WANTS.
I HAVE COME TO SEE MY FATHER.
ENTER, THEN, BOY. YOUR FATHER IS HERE.
ORPHEUS. WE HAVE HEARD OF YOUR LOSS; YOU HAVE OUR SYMPATHIES ALSO.
I DO NOT NEED YOUR PITY, HIPPOGRIFF.

IT WAS FREELY GIVEN, BOY. YOU SHOULD NOT SCORN IT.
DON'T PITY ME.
You should have gone to her funeral.
WHY?
To say goodbye.
I HAVE NOT YET SAID GOOD-BYE TO EURYDICE.
You should. You are mortal: it is the mortal way. You attend the funeral, you bid the dead farewell. You grieve. Then you continue with your life.
And at times the fact of her absence will hit you like a blow to the chest, and you will weep. But this will happen less and less as time goes on.
She is dead. You are alive.
So live.
15

WHEN "ORPHEUS" WAS ORIGINALLY RELEASED AS *THE SANDMAN SPECIAL*, ITS COVER WAS EMBOSSED WITH A GLOW-IN-THE-DARK INK. A SUBTLE GLOWING INK, THAT IS. SO SUBTLE, IN FACT, THAT MANY PEOPLE DON'T KNOW IT IS MEANT TO BECOME ILLUMINATED UNTIL THEY SEE A LITTLE GREEN SPIRIT RISING UP FROM THEIR COMIC COLLECTION. ACCORDING TO NEIL, "TO THIS DAY PEOPLE COME UP TO ME AND SAY, 'YOU KNOW, I HAD NO IDEA THAT COVER WAS SUPPOSED TO GLOW, UNTIL ONE NIGHT I CAME HOME PISSED DRUNK AND TURNED AROUND TO LOOK AT IT ONLY TO HAVE THE CRAP SCARED OUT OF ME!'"

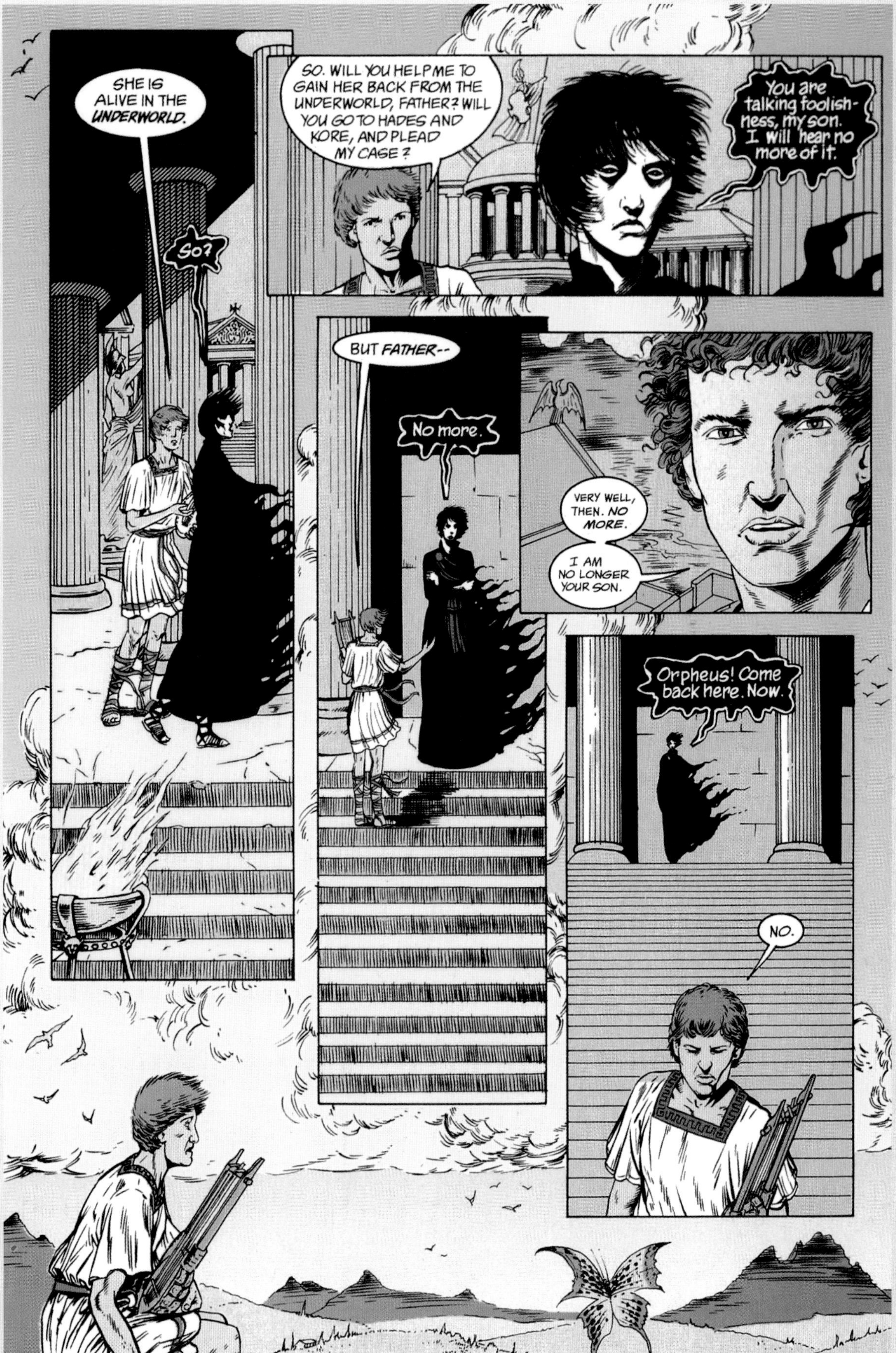
SHE IS ALIVE IN THE UNDERWORLD.
So?
SO. WILL YOU HELP ME TO GAIN HER BACK FROM THE UNDERWORLD, FATHER? WILL YOU GO TO HADES AND KORE, AND PLEAD MY CASE?
You are talking foolishness, my son. I will hear no more of it.
BUT FATHER--
No more.
VERY WELL, THEN. NO MORE.
I AM NO LONGER YOUR SON.
Orpheus! Come back here. Now.
NO.
16

PAGES 100–102 Orpheus and his mother discuss his predicament. From "Orpheus." Artwork by Bryan Talbot and Mark Buckingham. Daniel Vozzo, colorist.

ORPHEUS?
YOU SCARED THEM. YOU SCARED MY FRIENDS.
ORPHEUS? IT'S ME.
I KNOW IT'S YOU, MOTHER. YOU SCARED MY FRIENDS.
I--I'M SORRY.

Denied his father's help, Orpheus turns to his aunt, Death, to request safe passage into the underworld where he can try to reclaim Eurydice, his dead bride. Granted his aunt's reluctant promise never to take him, Orpheus travels to the underworld, and as the legend goes, he convinces Hades to allow Eurydice to follow him out of there – so long as he does not look back. But Orpheus does look back, and utterly destroyed by the second and irreversible

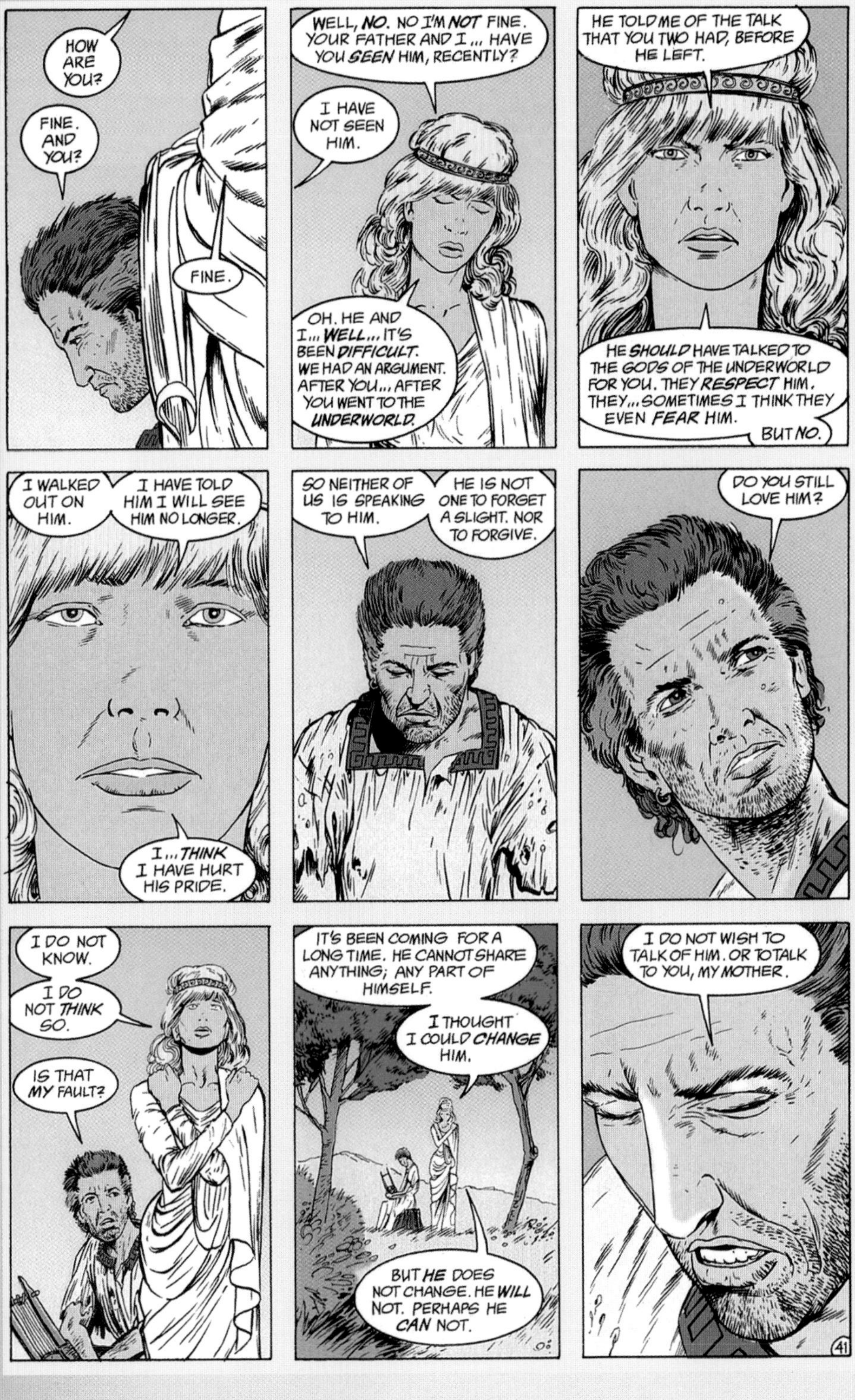
HOW ARE YOU?
FINE. AND YOU?
FINE.
WELL, NO. NO I'M NOT FINE. YOUR FATHER AND I ... HAVE YOU SEEN HIM, RECENTLY?
I HAVE NOT SEEN HIM.
OH. HE AND I... WELL... IT'S BEEN DIFFICULT. WE HAD AN ARGUMENT. AFTER YOU... AFTER YOU WENT TO THE UNDERWORLD.
HE TOLD ME OF THE TALK THAT YOU TWO HAD, BEFORE HE LEFT.
HE SHOULD HAVE TALKED TO THE GODS OF THE UNDERWORLD FOR YOU. THEY RESPECT HIM. THEY... SOMETIMES I THINK THEY EVEN FEAR HIM.
BUT NO.
I WALKED OUT ON HIM.
I HAVE TOLD HIM I WILL SEE HIM NO LONGER.
I... THINK I HAVE HURT HIS PRIDE.
SO NEITHER OF US IS SPEAKING TO HIM.
HE IS NOT ONE TO FORGET A SLIGHT. NOR TO FORGIVE.
DO YOU STILL LOVE HIM?
I DO NOT KNOW.
I DO NOT THINK SO.
IS THAT MY FAULT?
IT'S BEEN COMING FOR A LONG TIME. HE CANNOT SHARE ANYTHING; ANY PART OF HIMSELF.
I THOUGHT I COULD CHANGE HIM.
BUT HE DOES NOT CHANGE. HE WILL NOT. PERHAPS HE CAN NOT.
I DO NOT WISH TO TALK OF HIM. OR TO TALK TO YOU, MY MOTHER.
41

loss of his love, he allows himself to fall into the path of the drunken, lawless followers of Bacchus.

Torn to pieces yet unable to die, Orpheus beseeches his father to kill him. Morpheus, in this chronologically early story, younger and less compromising, refuses. But he does not forget his son. In time, he will reconsider Orpheus's plea, knowing full well that there will be a terrible price to pay for his actions.

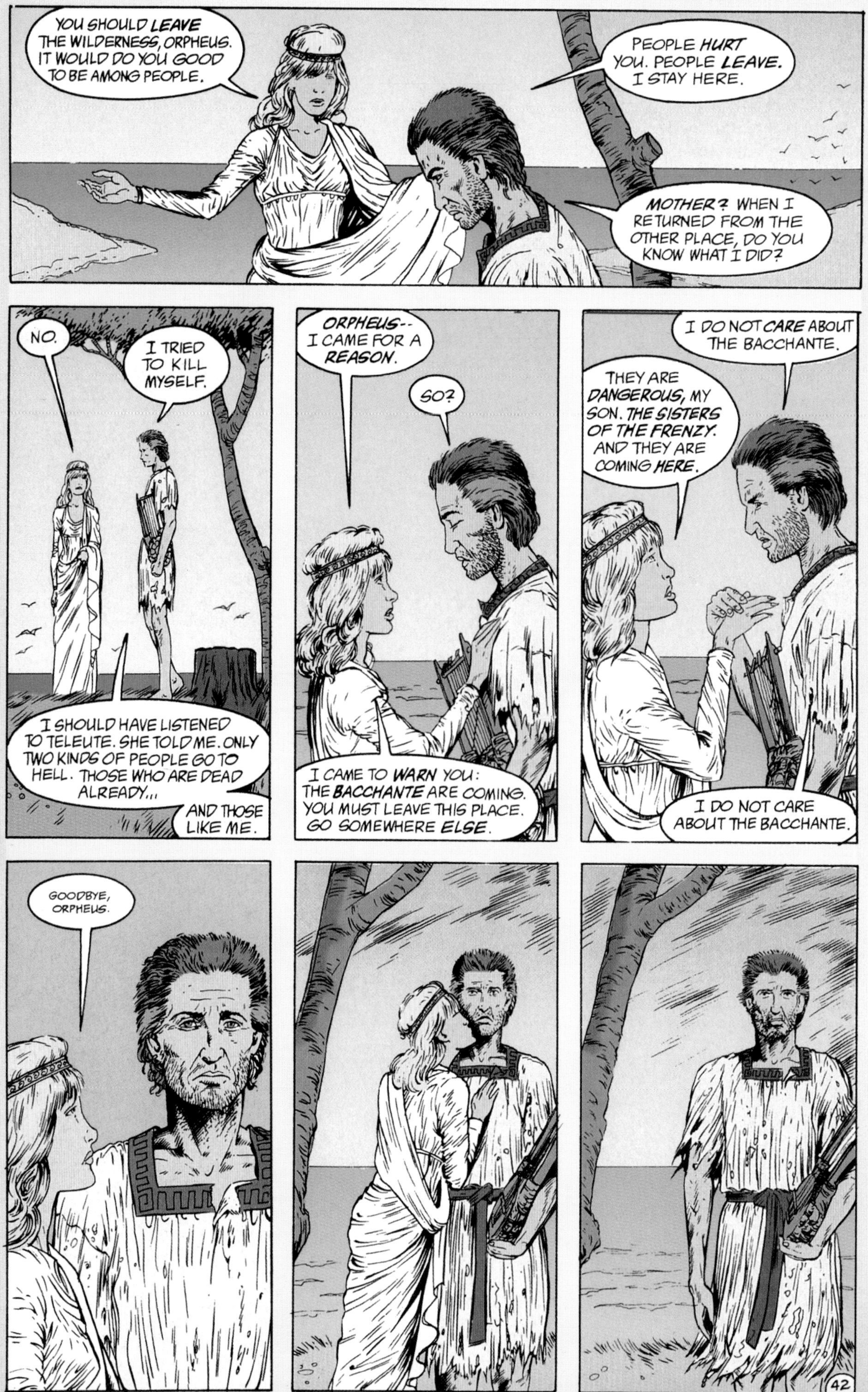
YOU SHOULD LEAVE THE WILDERNESS, ORPHEUS. IT WOULD DO YOU GOOD TO BE AMONG PEOPLE.
PEOPLE HURT YOU. PEOPLE LEAVE. I STAY HERE.
MOTHER? WHEN I RETURNED FROM THE OTHER PLACE, DO YOU KNOW WHAT I DID?
NO.
I TRIED TO KILL MYSELF.
I SHOULD HAVE LISTENED TO TELEUTE. SHE TOLD ME. ONLY TWO KINDS OF PEOPLE GO TO HELL. THOSE WHO ARE DEAD ALREADY...
AND THOSE LIKE ME.
ORPHEUS-- I CAME FOR A REASON.
SO?
I CAME TO WARN YOU: THE BACCHANTE ARE COMING. YOU MUST LEAVE THIS PLACE. GO SOMEWHERE ELSE.
I DO NOT CARE ABOUT THE BACCHANTE.
THEY ARE DANGEROUS, MY SON. THE SISTERS OF THE FRENZY. AND THEY ARE COMING HERE.
I DO NOT CARE ABOUT THE BACCHANTE.
GOODBYE, ORPHEUS.
42

BELOW Orpheus meets the women who will tear his body to shreds. Artwork by Bryan Talbot and Mark Buckingham. Daniel Vozzo, colorist.

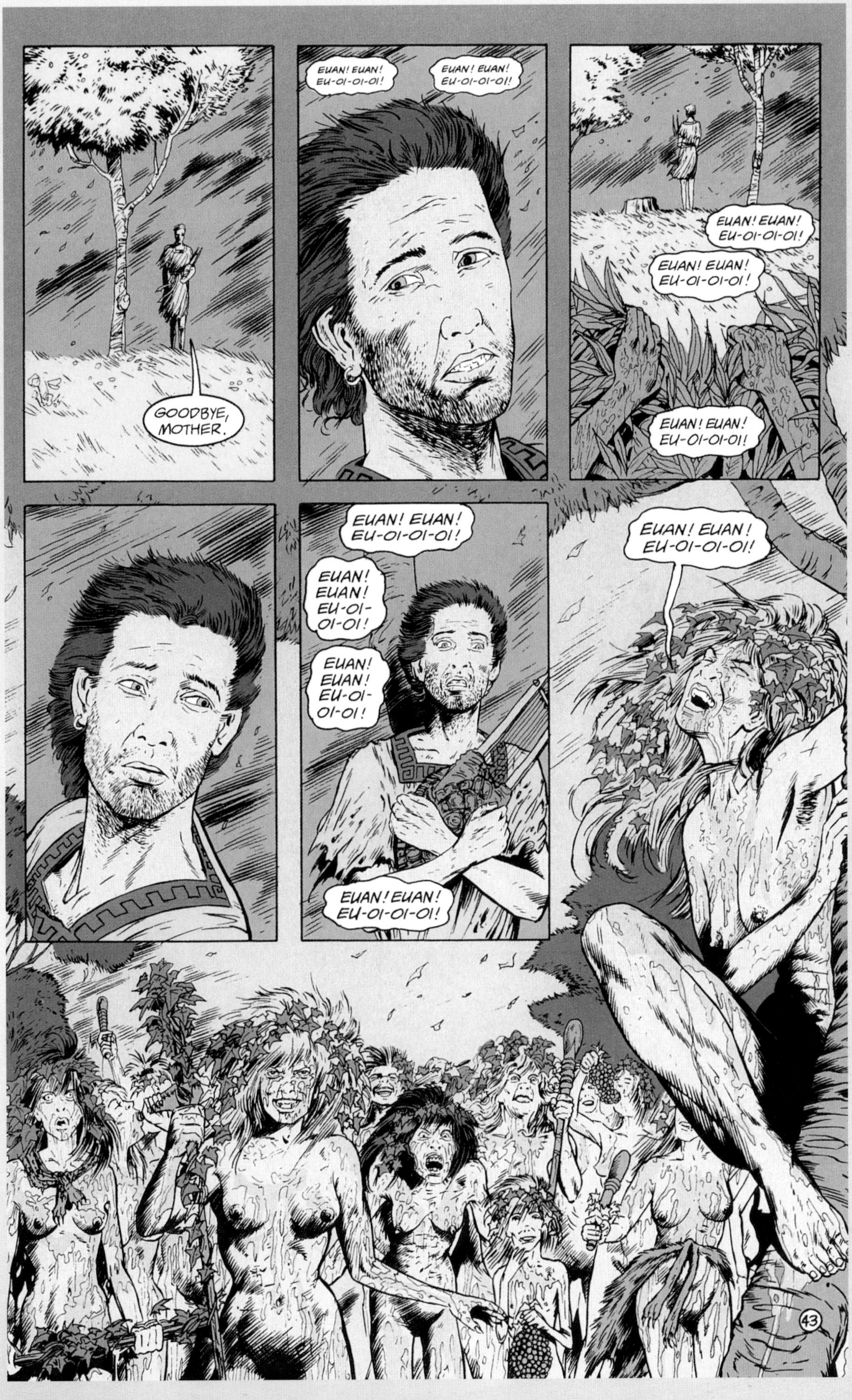
GOODBYE, MOTHER.
EUAN! EUAN! EU-OI-OI-OI!
EUAN! EUAN! EU-OI-OI-OI!
EUAN! EUAN! EU-OI-OI-OI!
EUAN! EUAN! EU-OI-OI-OI!
EUAN! EUAN! EU-OI-OI-OI!
EUAN! EUAN! EU-OI-OI-OI!
EUAN! EUAN! EU-OI-OI-OI!
EUAN! EUAN! EU-OI-OI-OI!
EUAN! EUAN! EU-OI-OI-OI!
EUAN! EUAN! EU-OI-OI-OI!
43

PAGES 105–109 "Ramadan." Artwork by P. Craig Russell. Colored by Lovern Kindzierski / Digital Chameleon.

The final story in this collection, "Ramadan," is so preternaturally beautiful that the reader runs the risk of overlooking the brilliance of the story. Highlighting the disconnect between dream and reality, it takes as its metaphor the Baghdad of the Arabian Nights, a composite dream of the enlightened, magical glory of a vanish'ed Middle East.

Of all *The Sandman* stories, this one is the most jewel-like, as perfect in concept as it is in execution. Neil deviated from his usual script-writing method, writing this issue first as a prose story, and then allowing artist P. Craig Russell to adapt it. With plenty of time — this story was written an entire year ahead of its publication — Russell researched several centuries of Islamic art. Throughout "Ramadan," Russell makes extensive use of traditional patterns, balancing a genie's hoard of ornate detail with simplified, even cartoony lines. As for the other elements, one can almost imagine a mind link between the artist, colorist Lovern Kindzierski, and letterer Todd Klein, as each contribution — panel composition, the shape of the words and word balloons, and the lavish palette — works in harmony with the others to enhance the whole.

As "Ramadan" eloquently makes clear, now more than ever we need to be reminded that the cities of imagination that fill our dreams and inspire us to greatness or to violence are as important as the ones that exist on maps in the real world. We may fight inside the cities of the real world, but we fight *for* the cities that we have imagined in a thousand and one nights.

In the
name of Allah,
the compassionate,
the all-merciful,
I tell my tale.
For there is no
God but Allah,
and Mohammed
is his Prophet.

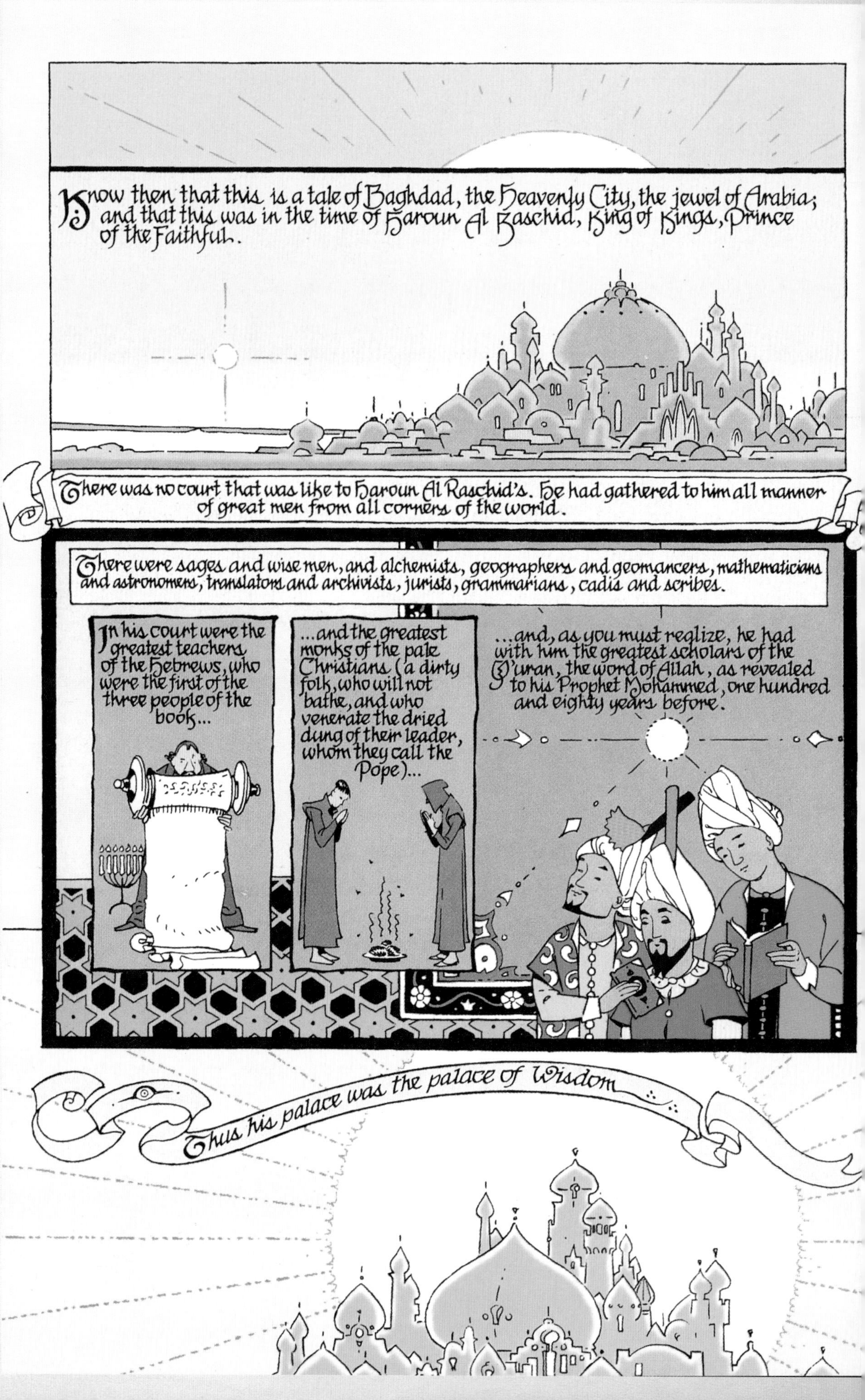
Know then that this is a tale of Baghdad, the Heavenly City, the jewel of Arabia; and that this was in the time of Haroun Al Raschid, King of Kings, Prince of the Faithful.
There was no court that was like to Haroun Al Raschid's. He had gathered to him all manner of great men from all corners of the world.
There were sages and wise men, and alchemists, geographers and geomancers, mathematicians and astronomers, translators and archivists, jurists, grammarians, cadis and scribes.
In his court were the greatest teachers of the Hebrews, who were the first of the three people of the book...
...and the greatest monks of the pale Christians (a dirty folk, who will not bathe, and who venerate the dried dung of their leader, whom they call the Pope)...
...and, as you must realize, he had with him the greatest scholars of the Q'uran, the word of Allah, as revealed to his Prophet Mohammed, one hundred and eighty years before.
Thus his palace was the palace of Wisdom

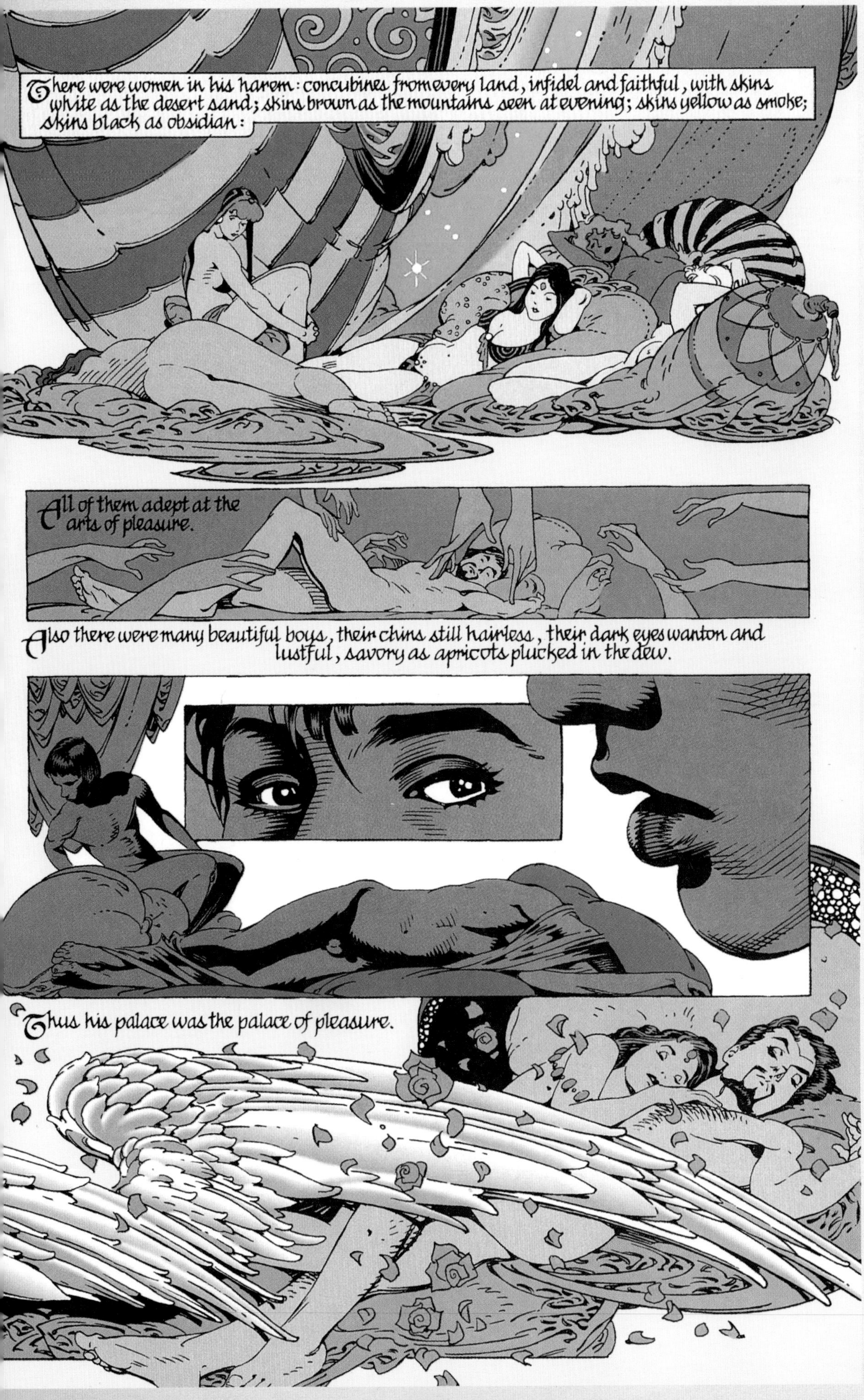
There were women in his harem: concubines from every land, infidel and faithful, with skins white as the desert sand; skins brown as the mountains seen at evening; skins yellow as smoke; skins black as obsidian:
All of them adept at the arts of pleasure.
Also there were many beautiful boys, their chins still hairless, their dark eyes wanton and lustful, savory as apricots plucked in the dew.
Thus his palace was the palace of pleasure.

There were magicians in his palace: astrologers, who could interpret the will of Allah from the high dances of the distant stars;

Enchanters from China and the Mongol lands, with high fur hats and long sleeves full of secrets;

Ascetic Bedouin sorcerers, who knew the secrets of angels and of djinn and of men.

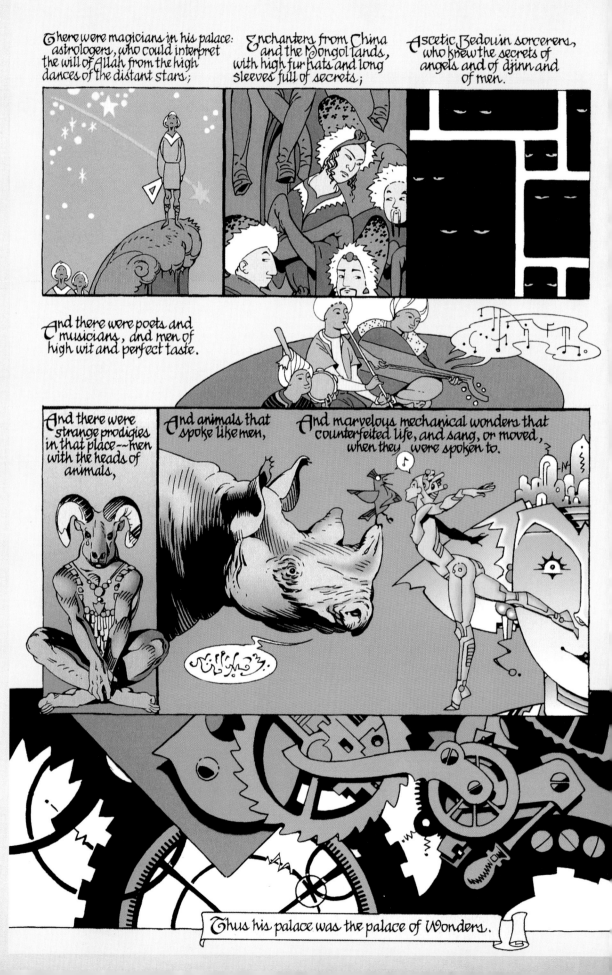

And there were poets and musicians, and men of high wit and perfect taste.

And there were strange prodigies in that place—men with the heads of animals,

And animals that spoke like men,

And marvelous mechanical wonders that counterfeited life, and sang, or moved, when they were spoken to.

Thus his palace was the palace of Wonders.

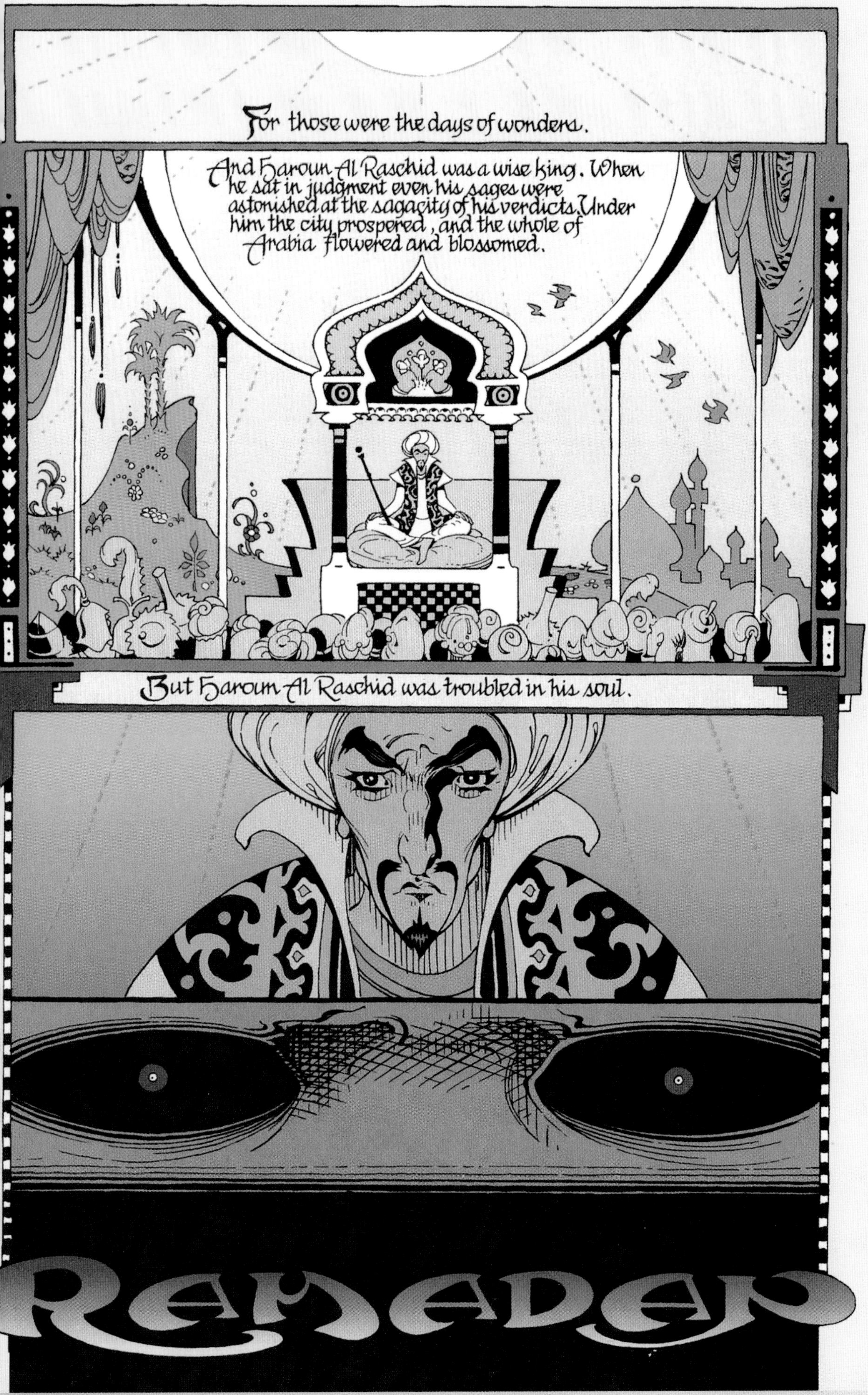
For those were the days of wonders.
And Haroun Al Raschid was a wise king. When he sat in judgment even his sages were astonished at the sagacity of his verdicts. Under him the city prospered, and the whole of Arabia flowered and blossomed.
But Haroun Al Raschid was troubled in his soul.
RAMADAN

PAGES 110–111 Haroun Al Raschid makes a bargain with the Dream King in some of the final pages of "Ramadan." Artwork by P. Craig Russell. Colored by Lovern Kindzierski / Digital Chameleon.

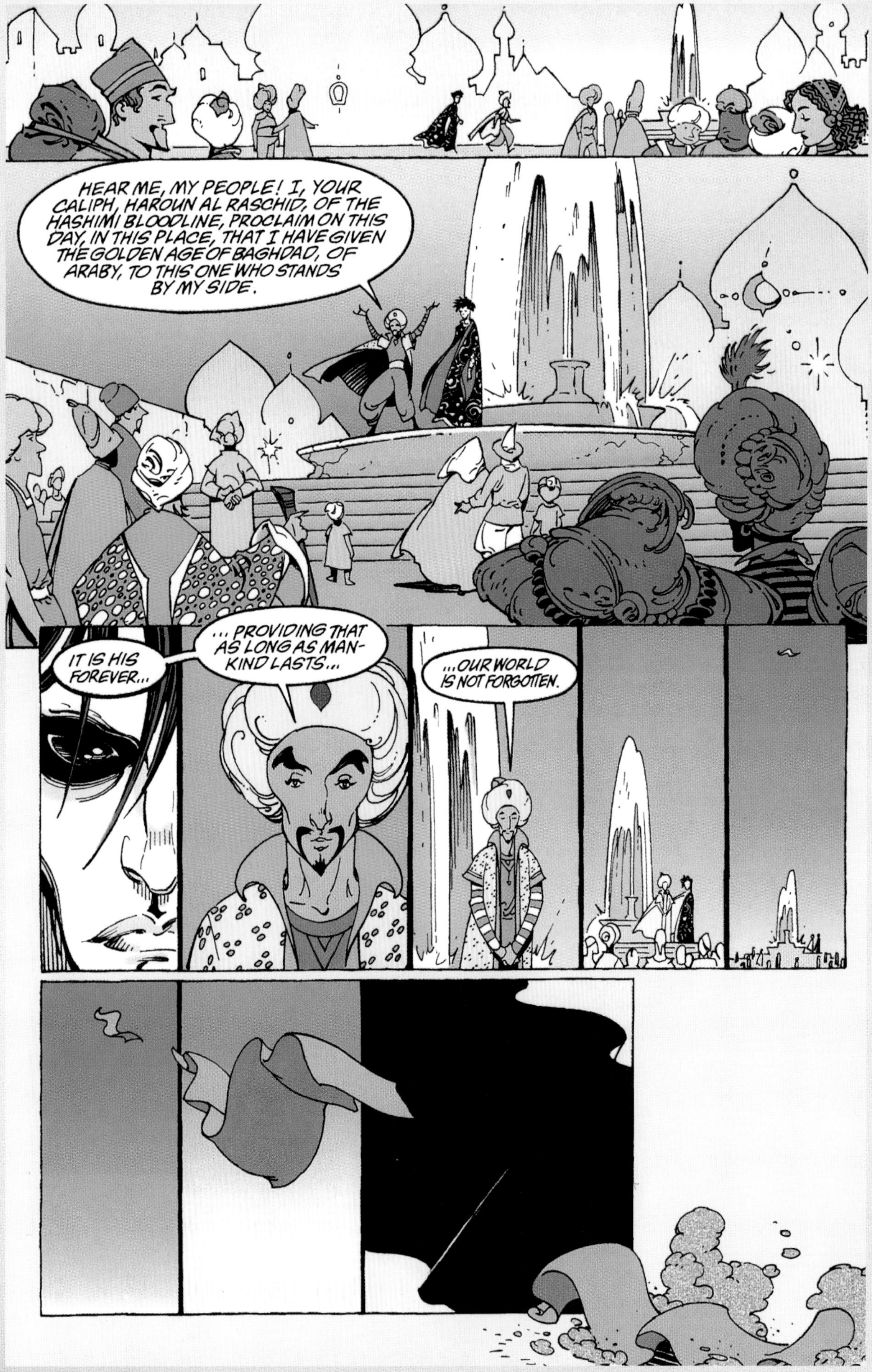
HEAR ME, MY PEOPLE! I, YOUR CALIPH, HAROUN AL RASCHID, OF THE HASHIMI BLOODLINE, PROCLAIM ON THIS DAY, IN THIS PLACE, THAT I HAVE GIVEN THE GOLDEN AGE OF BAGHDAD, OF ARABY, TO THIS ONE WHO STANDS BY MY SIDE.
IT IS HIS FOREVER...
...PROVIDING THAT AS LONG AS MAN-KIND LASTS...
...OUR WORLD IS NOT FORGOTTEN.

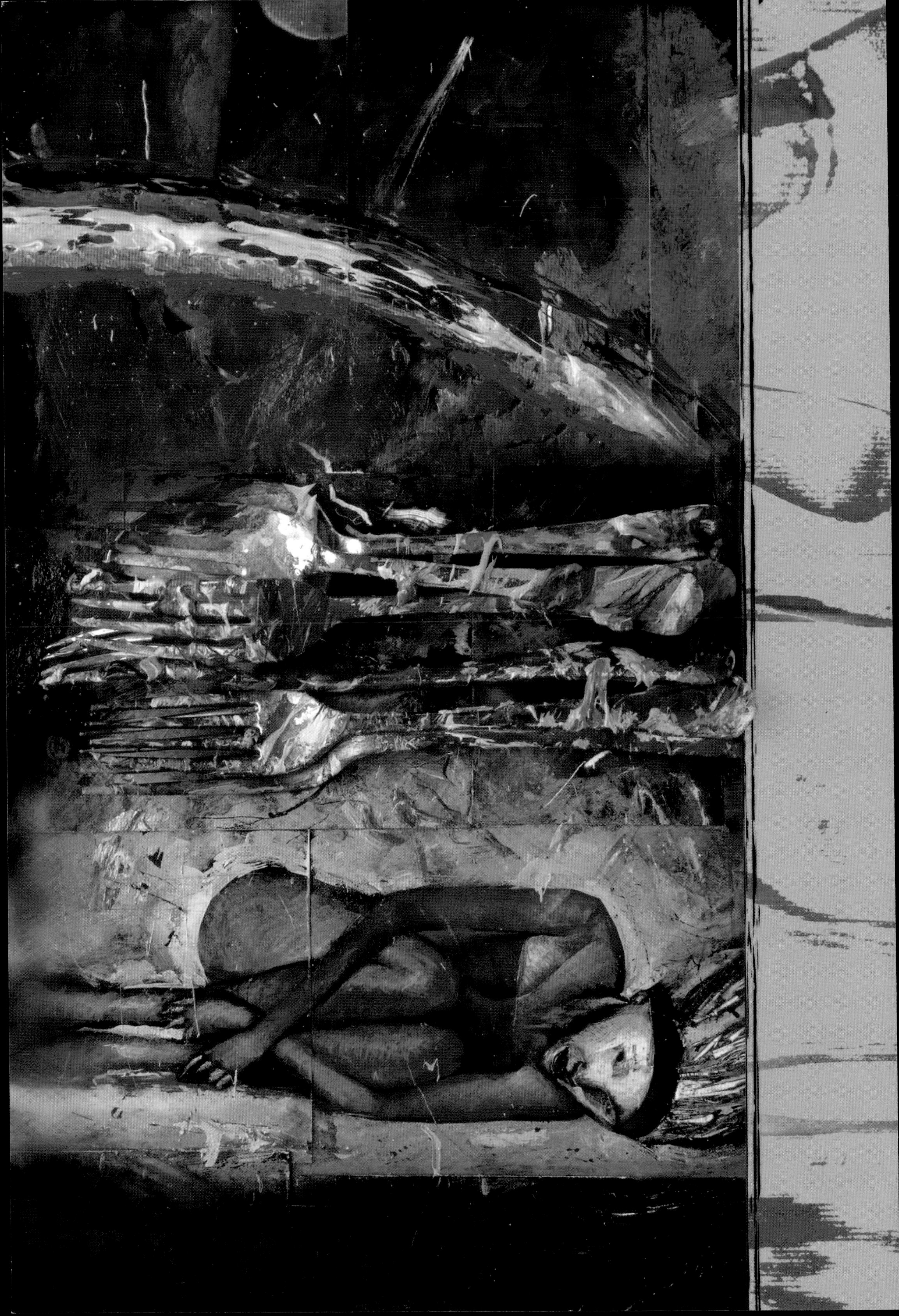

CHAPTER *8*

BRIEF LIVES

IN WHICH DREAM TAKES A ROAD TRIP WITH HIS SISTER
DELIRIUM IN SEARCH OF THEIR BROTHER DESTRUCTION
(WHO HAPPENS TO HAVE A PET DOG NAMED BARNABUS).

Brief Lives is the very beginning of the end of the Sandman's journey, and beneath its picaresque surface, there is a sense of gathering darkness. Artist Jill Thompson's relaxed, expressive art style, as well as the delicious contrast between the dour Sandman and his free-spirited sister Delirium, give this storyline its sense of fun adventure; colorist Danny Vozzo reflects this in his light, at times psychedelic, palette. And yet, despite the fact that the Sandman serves as an impeccable straight man for his dizzy sister, much happens here that is somber.

Brief Lives is another quest – Delirium's quest for her brother Destruction, the one Endless who abdicated his role. Brooding and depressed in the aftermath of a failed love affair, Dream begins this storyline aloof and detached, accompanying his sister as a distraction, or perhaps hoping to meet the ex-lover who's had him raining all over his realm. As the search for Destruction proves more complicated and dangerous than he expected, Morpheus grows in compassion, acting more like a father than an older brother to the unstable Delirium, and then, finally, crucially, acting as a father to his own son – by killing him.

PAGE 112 Cover, *The Sandman* no. 48. Artwork by Dave McKean.

BELOW Dream. Artwork by Mark Chiarello.

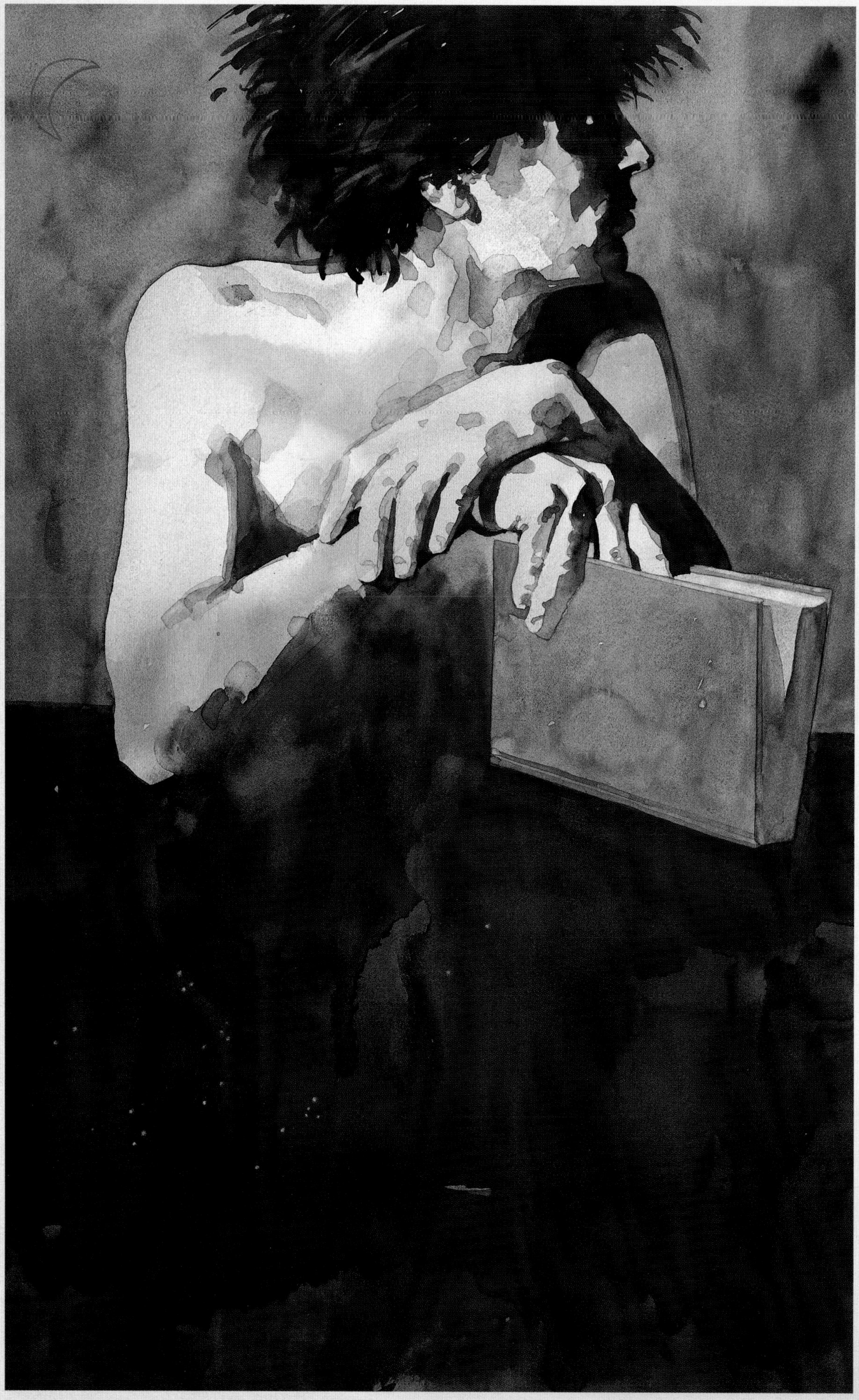

BELOW Delirium, with her fish. Artwork by Richard Case.

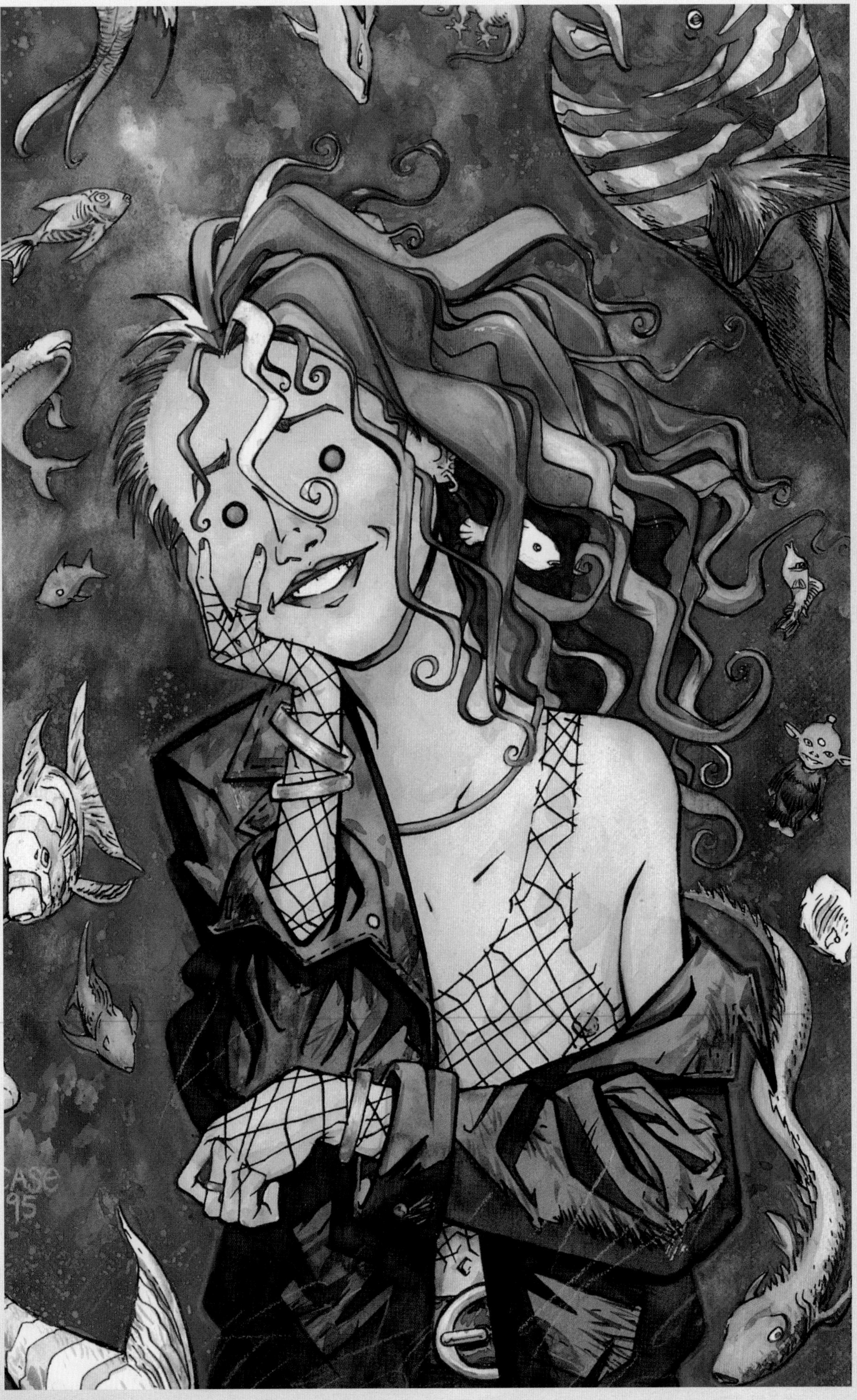
CASE
95

BELOW A little Dream, from Brief Lives artist Jill Thompson's *The Little Endless Storybook.*

BY THE END OF THE SERIES' FIRST YEAR, NEIL KNEW THAT DESTRUCTION WAS THE PRODIGAL SIBLING OF THE ENDLESS. HE EVEN USED TO TELL THAT TO FANS AT SIGNINGS. "BUT THAT WAS BEFORE THE INTERNET," HE ADDS. "I'M MUCH CAGIER NOW."

In *Brief Lives* — chapter 7 to be exact — Orpheus is again mentioned. Dream approaches Destiny for an answer as to where Destruction can be found. Destiny tells him that there is an oracle who can not only tell *of* the Endless, but is related to them. Orpheus is the oracle in question thand his life, of course, has been anything but brief. In granting his son the death he so greatly desires, the Sandman must spill family blood, just as Desire has been plotting for him to do since the events that transpired in *The Doll's House.*

PAGES 117–119 Dream and Delirium exhaust all possibilities in their search for Destruction. Artwork by Jill Thompson and Vince Locke. Daniel Vozzo, colorist.

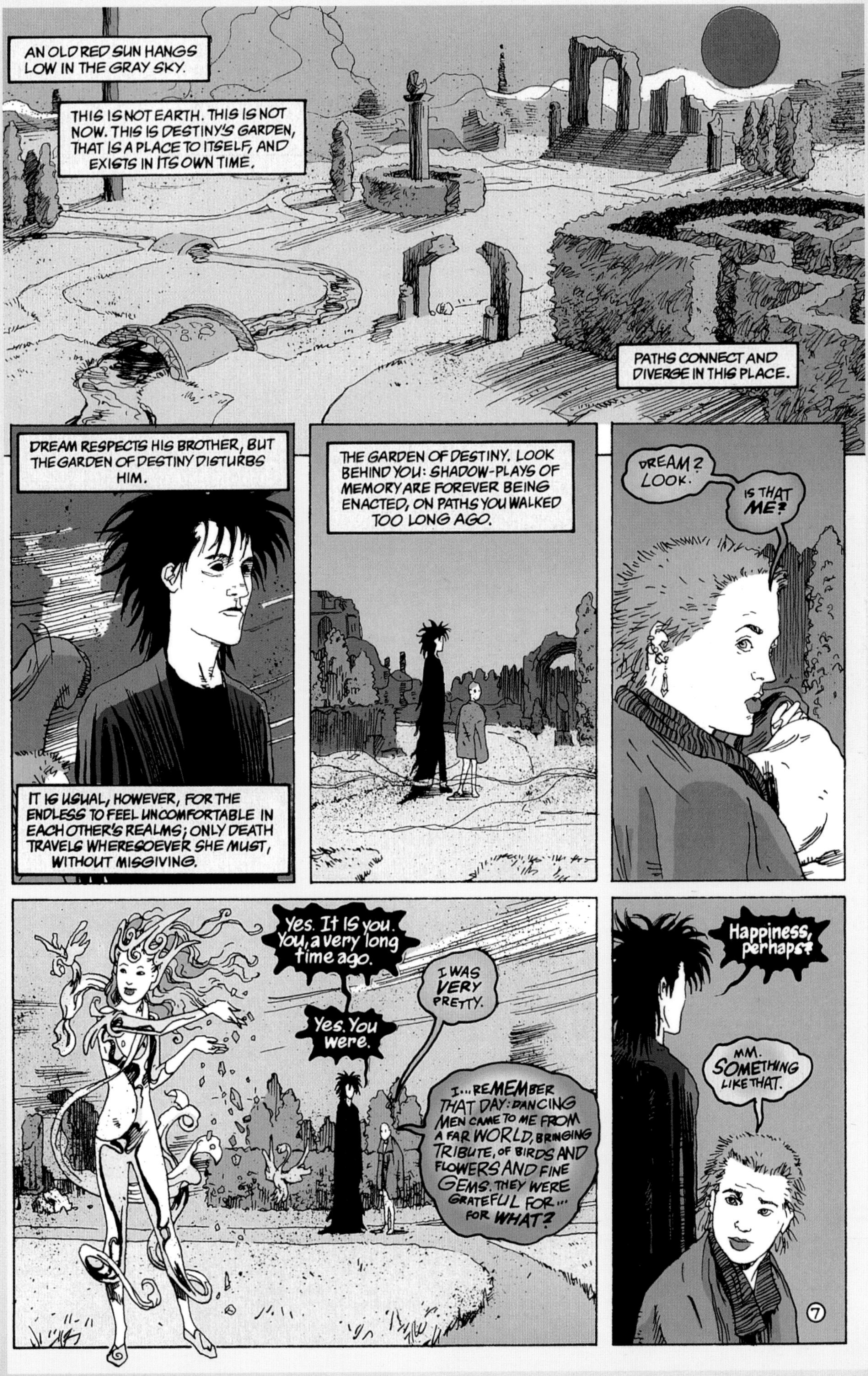
AN OLD RED SUN HANGS LOW IN THE GRAY SKY.
THIS IS NOT EARTH. THIS IS NOT NOW. THIS IS DESTINY'S GARDEN, THAT IS A PLACE TO ITSELF, AND EXISTS IN ITS OWN TIME.
PATHS CONNECT AND DIVERGE IN THIS PLACE.
DREAM RESPECTS HIS BROTHER, BUT THE GARDEN OF DESTINY DISTURBS HIM.
IT IS USUAL, HOWEVER, FOR THE ENDLESS TO FEEL UNCOMFORTABLE IN EACH OTHER'S REALMS; ONLY DEATH TRAVELS WHERESOEVER SHE MUST, WITHOUT MISGIVING.
THE GARDEN OF DESTINY. LOOK BEHIND YOU: SHADOW-PLAYS OF MEMORY ARE FOREVER BEING ENACTED, ON PATHS YOU WALKED TOO LONG AGO.
DREAM? LOOK.
IS THAT ME?
Yes. It IS you. You, a very long time ago.
I WAS VERY PRETTY.
Yes. You were.
I... REMEMBER THAT DAY: DANCING MEN CAME TO ME FROM A FAR WORLD, BRINGING TRIBUTE, OF BIRDS AND FLOWERS AND FINE GEMS. THEY WERE GRATEFUL FOR... FOR WHAT?
Happiness, perhaps?
MM. SOMETHING LIKE THAT.
7

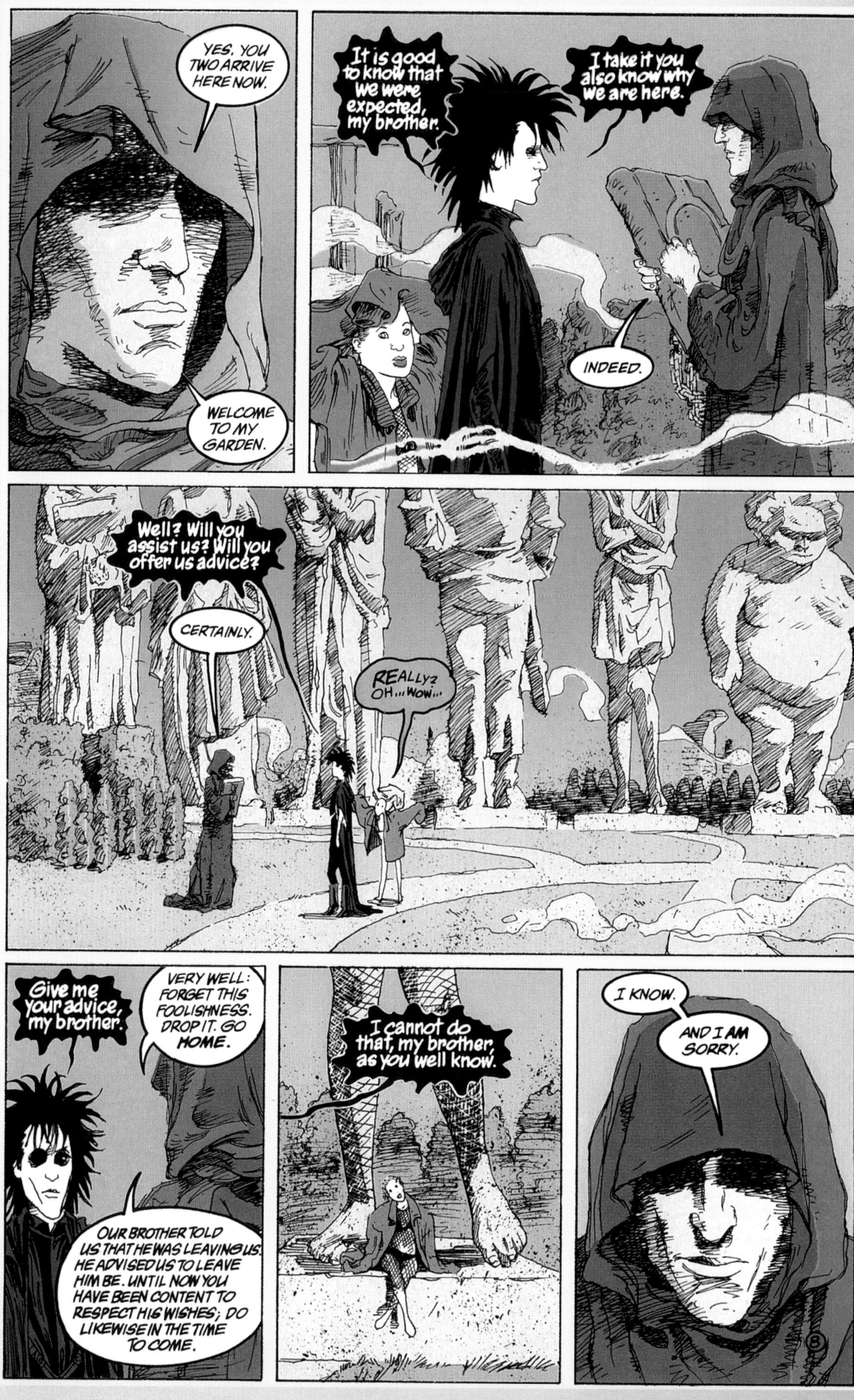
YES. YOU TWO ARRIVE HERE NOW.
WELCOME TO MY GARDEN.
It is good to know that we were expected, my brother.
I take it you also know why we are here.
INDEED.
Well? Will you assist us? Will you offer us advice?
CERTAINLY.
REALLY? OH... WOW...
Give me your advice, my brother.
VERY WELL: FORGET THIS FOOLISHNESS. DROP IT. GO HOME.
OUR BROTHER TOLD US THAT HE WAS LEAVING US. HE ADVISED US TO LEAVE HIM BE. UNTIL NOW YOU HAVE BEEN CONTENT TO RESPECT HIS WISHES; DO LIKEWISE IN THE TIME TO COME.
I cannot do that, my brother, as you well know.
I KNOW.
AND I AM SORRY.
8

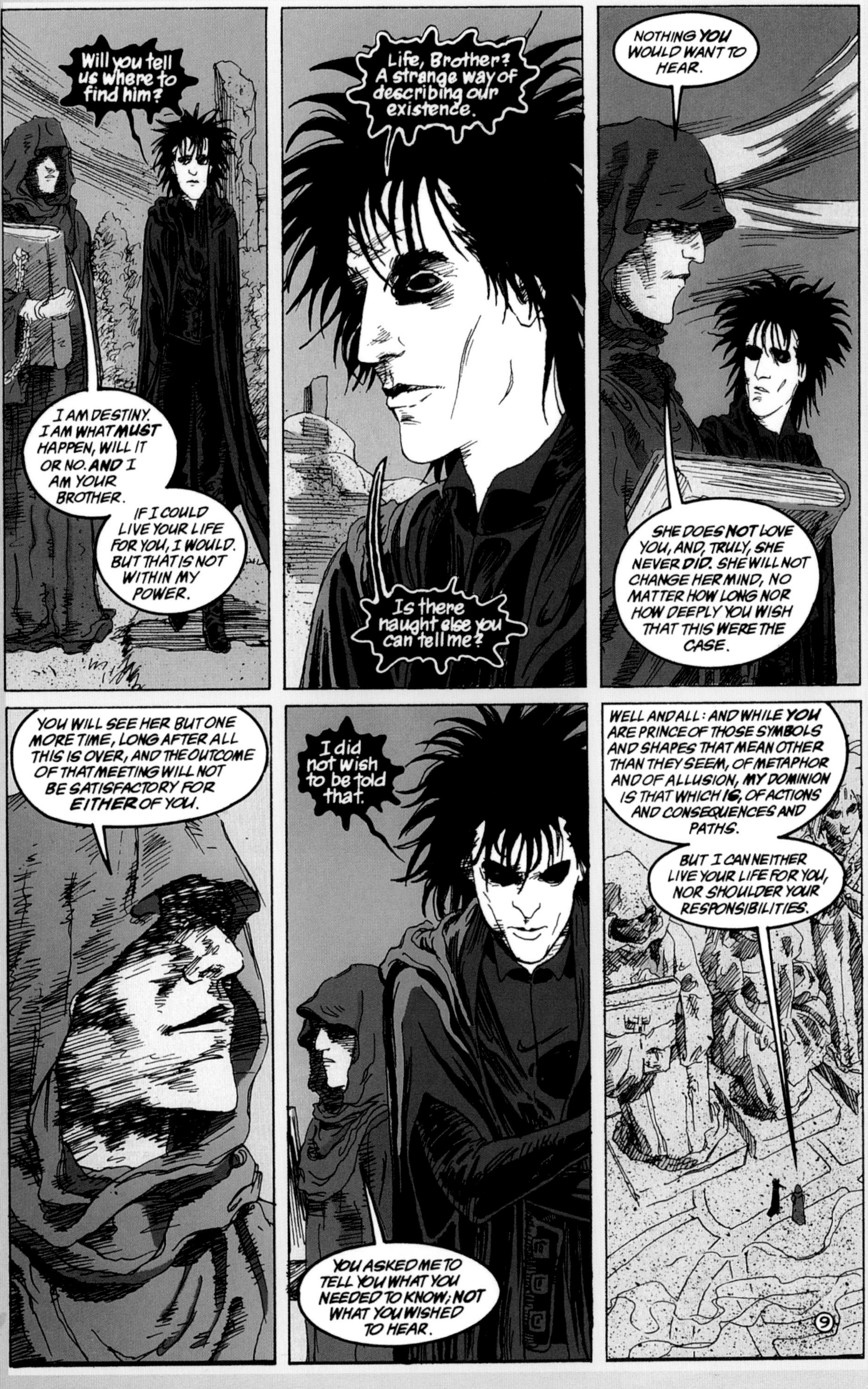
Will you tell us where to find him?
I AM DESTINY. I AM WHAT MUST HAPPEN, WILL IT OR NO. AND I AM YOUR BROTHER.
IF I COULD LIVE YOUR LIFE FOR YOU, I WOULD. BUT THAT IS NOT WITHIN MY POWER.
Life, Brother? A strange way of describing our existence.
Is there naught else you can tell me?
NOTHING YOU WOULD WANT TO HEAR.
SHE DOES NOT LOVE YOU, AND, TRULY, SHE NEVER DID. SHE WILL NOT CHANGE HER MIND, NO MATTER HOW LONG NOR HOW DEEPLY YOU WISH THAT THIS WERE THE CASE.
YOU WILL SEE HER BUT ONE MORE TIME, LONG AFTER ALL THIS IS OVER, AND THE OUTCOME OF THAT MEETING WILL NOT BE SATISFACTORY FOR EITHER OF YOU.
I did not wish to be told that.
YOU ASKED ME TO TELL YOU WHAT YOU NEEDED TO KNOW; NOT WHAT YOU WISHED TO HEAR.
WELL AND ALL: AND WHILE YOU ARE PRINCE OF THOSE SYMBOLS AND SHAPES THAT MEAN OTHER THAN THEY SEEM, OF METAPHOR AND OF ALLUSION, MY DOMINION IS THAT WHICH IS, OF ACTIONS AND CONSEQUENCES AND PATHS.
BUT I CAN NEITHER LIVE YOUR LIFE FOR YOU, NOR SHOULDER YOUR RESPONSIBILITIES.
9

BELOW Delirium has a moment of coherence. Artwork by Jill Thompson and Vince Locke. Daniel Vozzo, colorist.

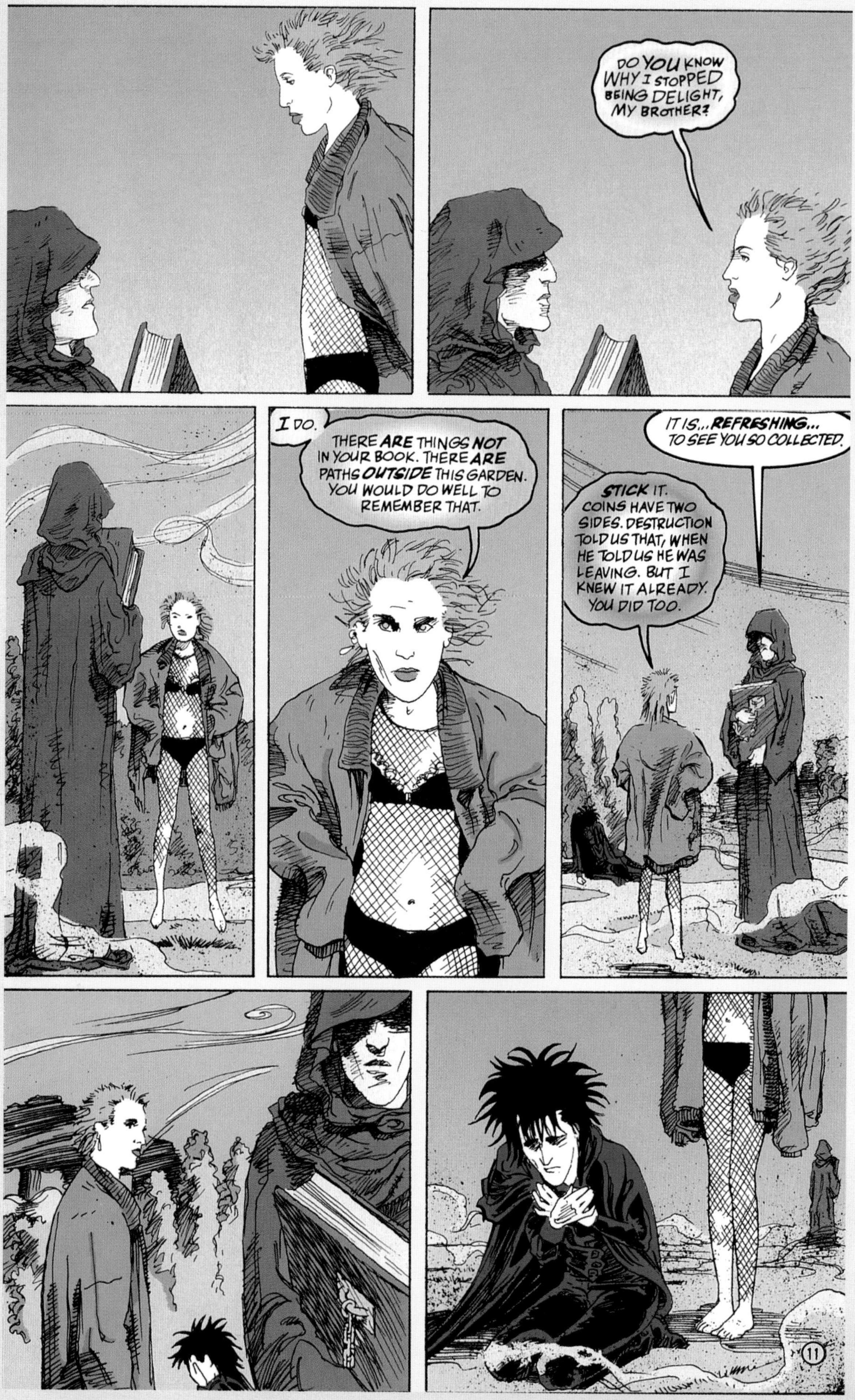
DO YOU KNOW WHY I STOPPED BEING DELIGHT, MY BROTHER?
I DO.
THERE ARE THINGS NOT IN YOUR BOOK. THERE ARE PATHS OUTSIDE THIS GARDEN. YOU WOULD DO WELL TO REMEMBER THAT.
IT IS... REFRESHING... TO SEE YOU SO COLLECTED.
STICK IT. COINS HAVE TWO SIDES. DESTRUCTION TOLD US THAT, WHEN HE TOLD US HE WAS LEAVING. BUT I KNEW IT ALREADY. YOU DID TOO.
11

BELOW Dream returns to his sister after having spoken to Orpheus, who reveals Destruction's location. For the revelation there is a price, however, and Morpheus owes his son a boon. Artwork by Jill Thompson and Vince Locke. Daniel Vozzo, colorist.

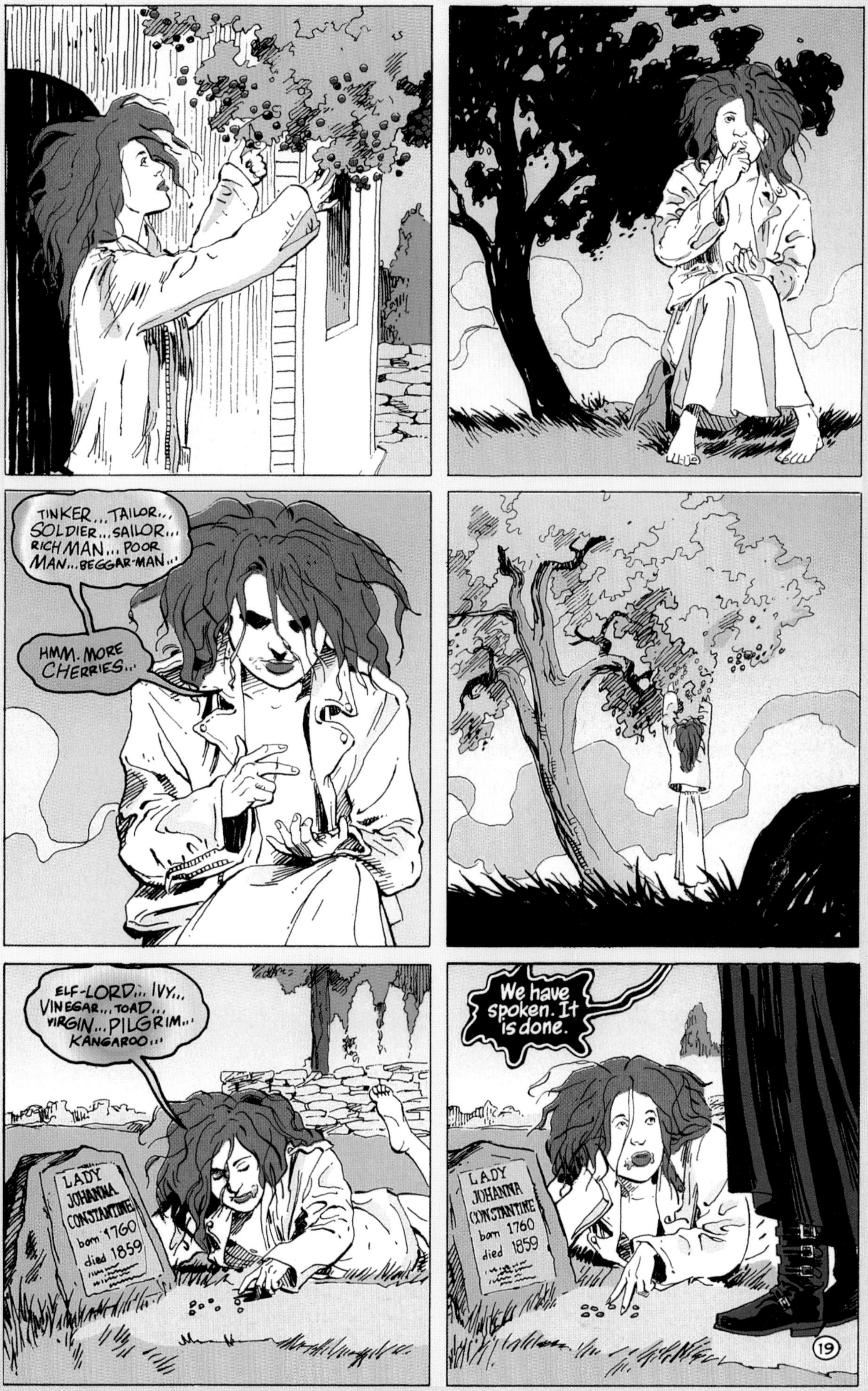
TINKER... TAILOR... SOLDIER... SAILOR... RICH MAN... POOR MAN... BEGGAR-MAN...
HMM. MORE CHERRIES...
ELF-LORD... IVY... VINEGAR... TOAD... VIRGIN... PILGRIM... KANGAROO...
LADY JOHANNA CONSTANTINE born 1760 died 1859
We have spoken. It is done.
LADY JOHANNA CONSTANTINE born 1760 died 1859
19

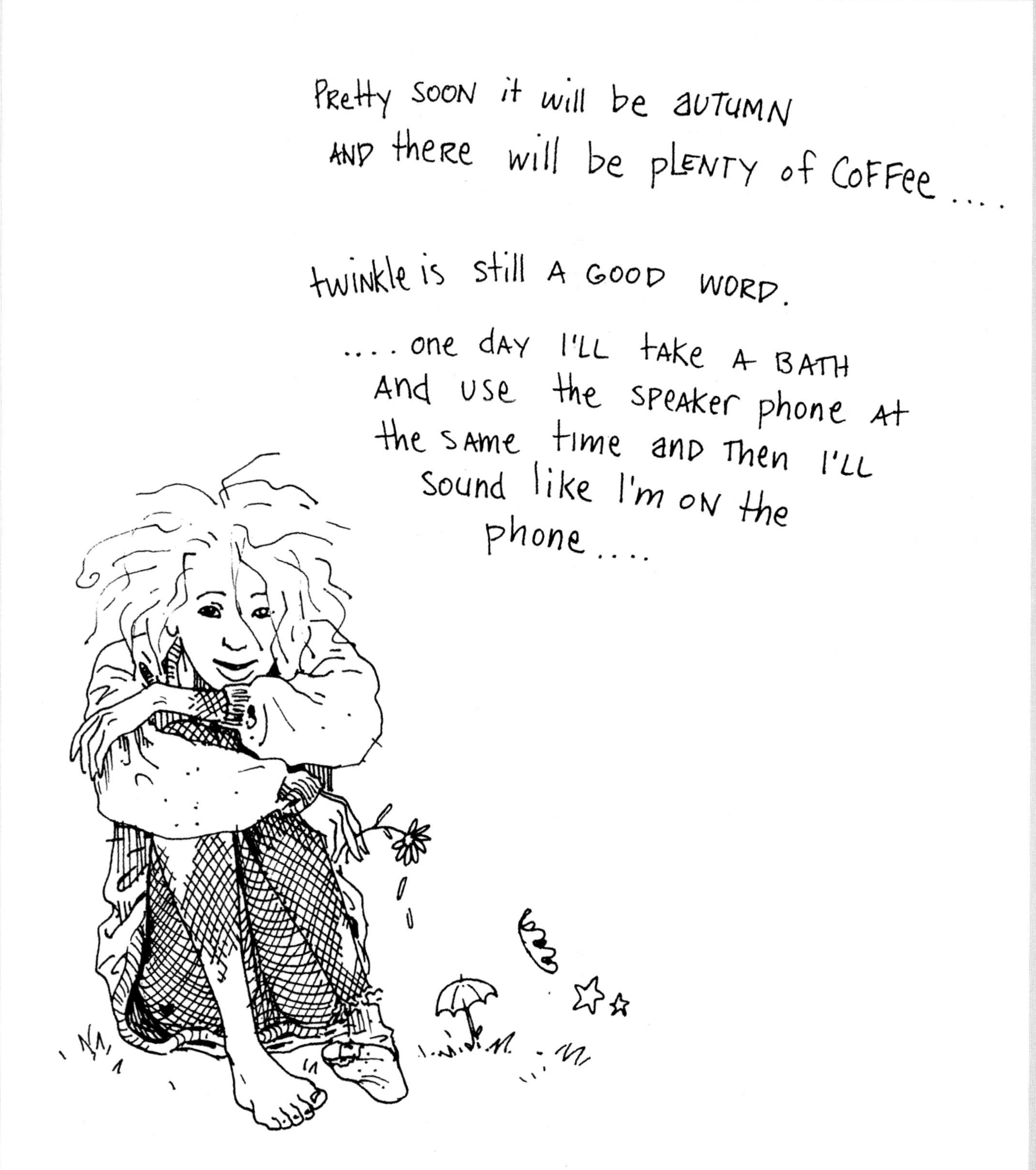
Pretty soon it will be autumn
and there will be plenty of coffee....
twinkle is still a good word.
....one day I'll take a bath
and use the speaker phone at
the same time and then I'll
sound like I'm on the
phone....

Brief Lives, unlike the other long storylines, is more about the journey than about the destination. What the Sandman learns, he learns on the road, not from the brother he finally rediscovers (although Destruction confirms what many readers have intuited all along about the change in Dream, and hints at what we will soon discover about the consequence of that change). Morpheus has learned regret. He has lost some of his arrogant certainty and gained compassion for others. *Brief Lives* is all about mortality and change, and its lesson – if there is one – is to take pleasure in the moment.

PAGE 122 One of Jill Thompson's unique fax cover notes to Neil. Jill explained that she would often talk to Neil on the speaker phone and he'd complain that she sounded like she was in the bathtub. BELOW Delirium plays with her food. Artwork by Jill Thompson and Vince Locke. Daniel Vozzo, colorist

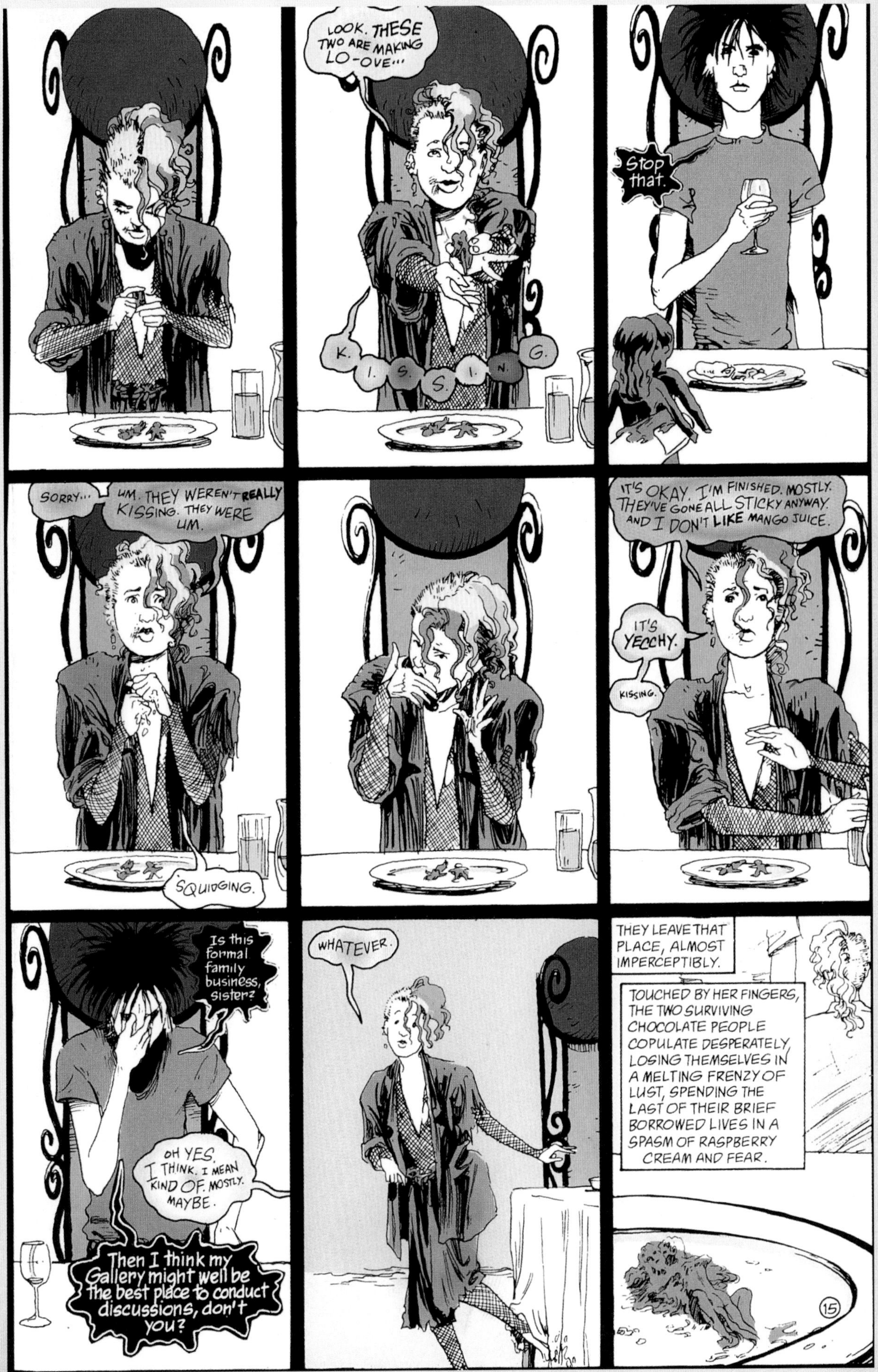
LOOK. THESE TWO ARE MAKING LO-OVE...
K. I. S. S. I. N. G.
Stop that.
SORRY...
UM. THEY WEREN'T REALLY KISSING. THEY WERE UM.
SQUIDGING.
IT'S OKAY. I'M FINISHED. MOSTLY. THEY'VE GONE ALL STICKY ANYWAY. AND I DON'T LIKE MANGO JUICE.
IT'S YECCHY.
KISSING.
Is this formal family business, sister?
OH YES. I THINK. I MEAN KIND OF. MOSTLY. MAYBE.
Then I think my Gallery might well be the best place to conduct discussions, don't you?
WHATEVER.
THEY LEAVE THAT PLACE, ALMOST IMPERCEPTIBLY.
TOUCHED BY HER FINGERS, THE TWO SURVIVING CHOCOLATE PEOPLE COPULATE DESPERATELY, LOSING THEMSELVES IN A MELTING FRENZY OF LUST, SPENDING THE LAST OF THEIR BRIEF BORROWED LIVES IN A SPASM OF RASPBERRY CREAM AND FEAR.
15

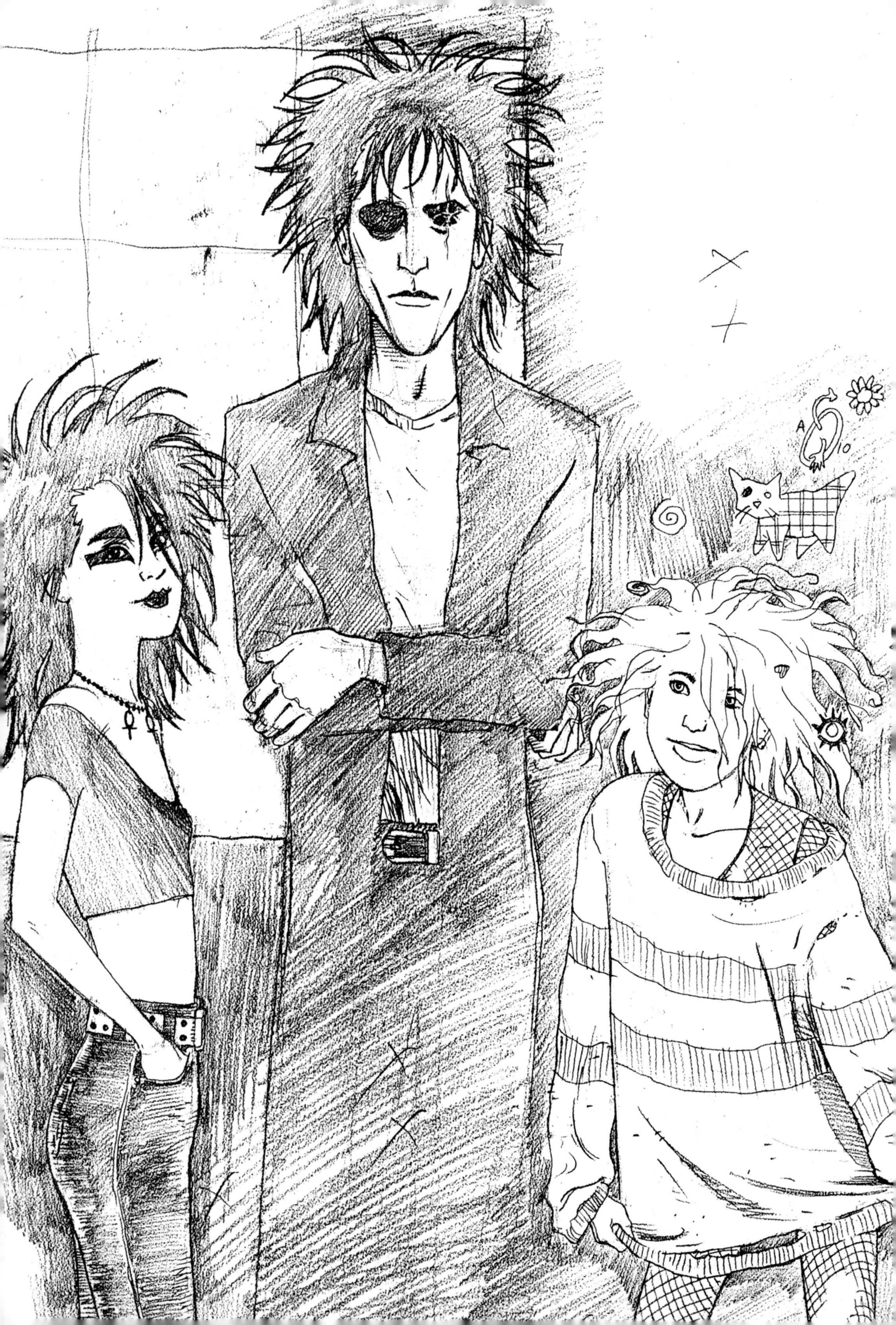

PAGE 124   Jill Thompson's pencils for a Sandman T-shirt.

There are plenty of moments here to savor — moments of quiet insight, moments poignant and absurd, when Delirium's madness reveals the sad wisdom beneath. A particularly strong example of these vignettes takes place in the beginning, when Delirium sits with her brother in the Dreaming and orders milk chocolate people (Dream orders an omelet, a light salad, and a glass of white wine). As Delirium plays with her food, the Sandman snaps, "Stop that." Like a chastised child, Delirium stops, ("Sorry . . . hm. They weren't *really* kissing. They were um. Squidging.") The Sandman, clearly getting a headache, urges his sister away from the table and into his Gallery — a more appropriate place, he suggests, for formal family business.

What happens next is Delirium's special brand of magic, and a metaphor for all of our sticky, fragile little lives. As the text says, touched by Delirium "the two surviving chocolate people copulate desperately, losing themselves in a melting frenzy of lust, spending the last of their brief borrowed lives in a spasm of raspberry cream and fear."

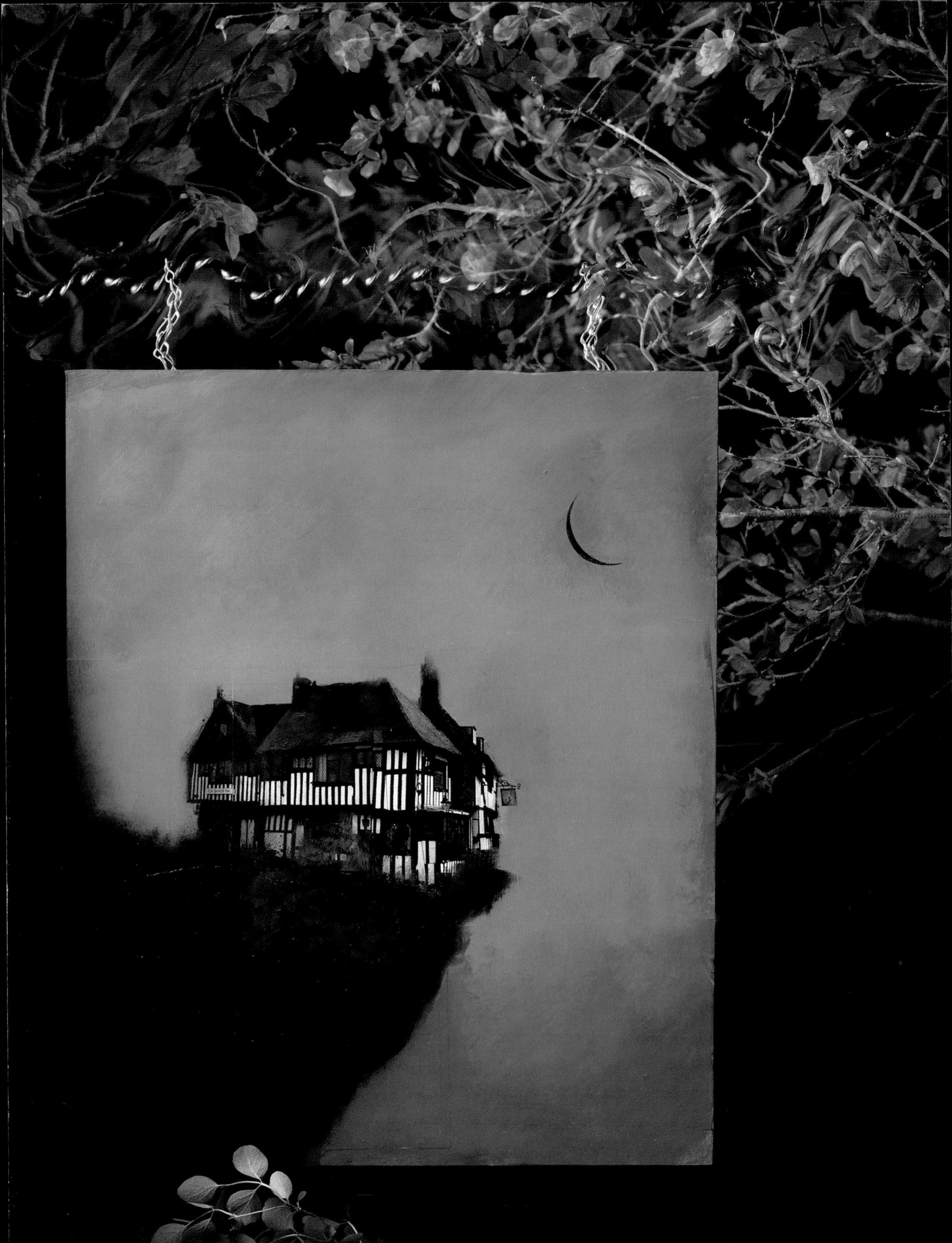

CHAPTER 9

WORLDS' END

IN WHICH WE VISIT A MYSTERIOUS INN AND HEAR THE PATRONS' TALES.

The last of the collections of Sandman short stories, *Worlds' End*, like Chaucer's *Canterbury Tales* and *The Decameron* by Boccaccio, is framed by a bunch of travelers telling stories, in this case, as they take refuge from a storm. But this is a reality storm, and bits of the future keep getting blown around. The inn where the story takes place is one of several free houses that stand on the borderlands of different worlds.

In the first story, "A Tale of Two Cities," Brant and his unconscious companion, Charlene, stumble from a road in our world into the Inn, where they listen to the stories of other travelers. In the stories of *Worlds' End* there are meditations on the nature of place and leadership that resonate with the events to come, but the most pertinent tale is "Cerements," which is a story of death and burial in the Necropolis Litharge.

The clue to Morpheus's fate revealed in this story – that the Endless can, in effect, die and be replaced in their function – adds to the chilling nature of the following scene, where the travelers look out of the Inn's windows and see a funeral procession walking across the sky.

Altogether, the short tales in *Worlds' End* offer a quick breather before the big finish. The following arc is a long journey to the end.

 Cover, *The Sandman* no. 51. Artwork by Dave McKean.

BELOW LEFT Mike Allred's pencils for "The Golden Boy." BELOW RIGHT The finished art from "The Golden Boy." Artwork by Michael Allred. Daniel Vozzo, colorist.

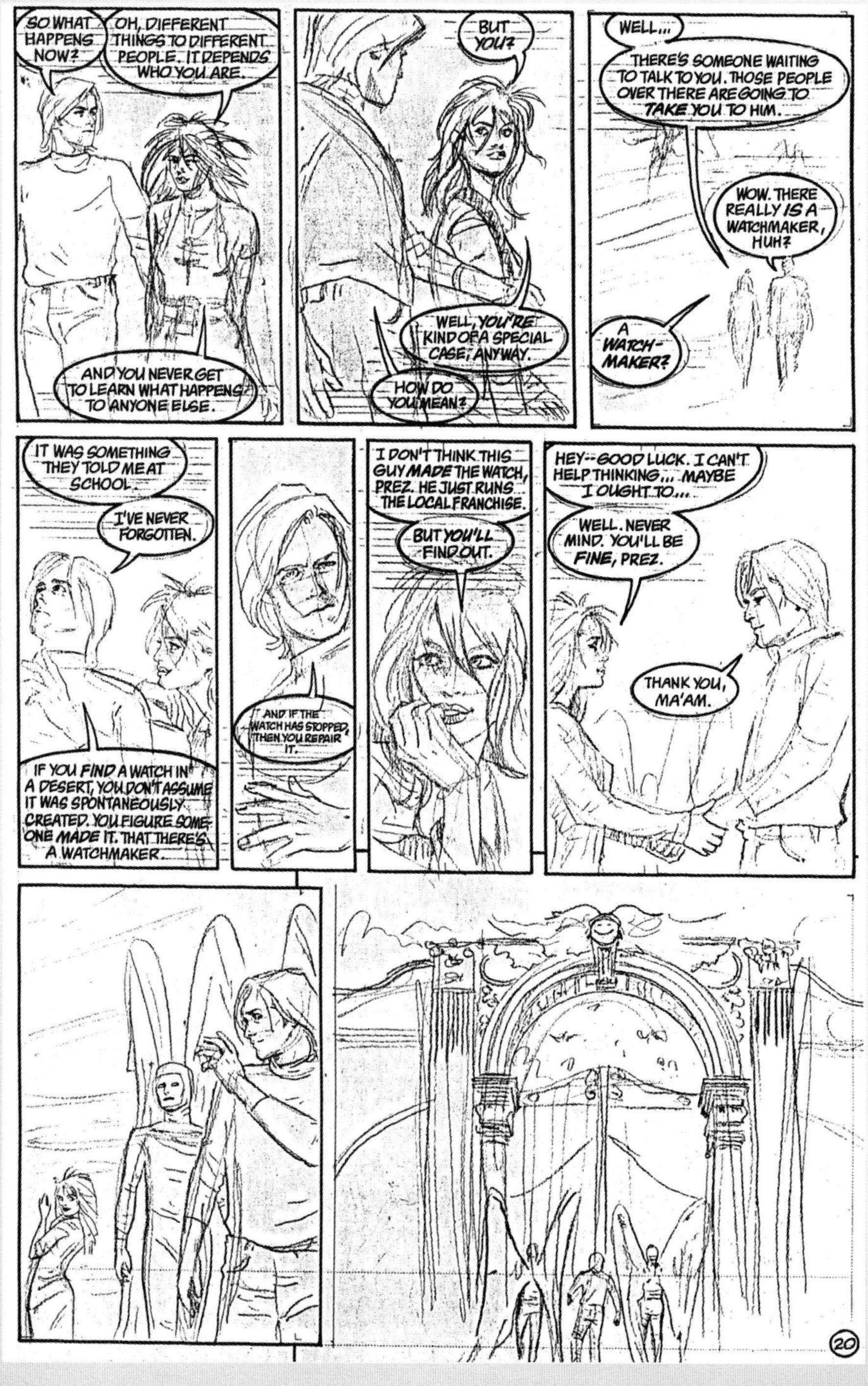
SO WHAT HAPPENS NOW?
OH, DIFFERENT THINGS TO DIFFERENT PEOPLE. IT DEPENDS WHO YOU ARE.
AND YOU NEVER GET TO LEARN WHAT HAPPENS TO ANYONE ELSE.
BUT YOU?
WELL, YOU'RE KIND OF A SPECIAL CASE, ANYWAY.
HOW DO YOU MEAN?
WELL...
THERE'S SOMEONE WAITING TO TALK TO YOU. THOSE PEOPLE OVER THERE ARE GOING TO TAKE YOU TO HIM.
WOW. THERE REALLY IS A WATCHMAKER, HUH?
A WATCH-MAKER?
IT WAS SOMETHING THEY TOLD ME AT SCHOOL.
I'VE NEVER FORGOTTEN.
IF YOU FIND A WATCH IN A DESERT, YOU DON'T ASSUME IT WAS SPONTANEOUSLY CREATED. YOU FIGURE SOME-ONE MADE IT. THAT THERE'S A WATCHMAKER.
AND IF THE WATCH HAS STOPPED, THEN YOU REPAIR IT.
I DON'T THINK THIS GUY MADE THE WATCH, PREZ. HE JUST RUNS THE LOCAL FRANCHISE.
BUT YOU'LL FIND OUT.
HEY--GOOD LUCK. I CAN'T HELP THINKING... MAYBE I OUGHT TO...
WELL. NEVER MIND. YOU'LL BE FINE, PREZ.
THANK YOU, MA'AM.
20

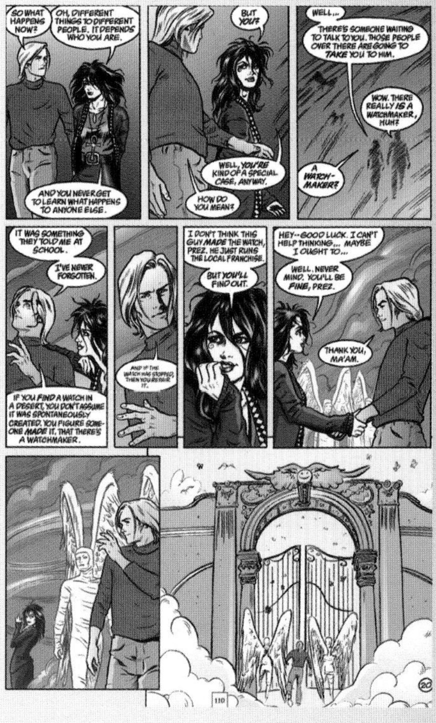
SO WHAT HAPPENS NOW?
OH, DIFFERENT THINGS TO DIFFERENT PEOPLE. IT DEPENDS WHO YOU ARE.
AND YOU NEVER GET TO LEARN WHAT HAPPENS TO ANYONE ELSE.
BUT YOU?
WELL, YOU'RE KIND OF A SPECIAL CASE, ANYWAY.
HOW DO YOU MEAN?
WELL...
THERE'S SOMEONE WAITING TO TALK TO YOU. THOSE PEOPLE OVER THERE ARE GOING TO TAKE YOU TO HIM.
WOW. THERE REALLY IS A WATCHMAKER, HUH?
A WATCH-MAKER?
IT WAS SOMETHING THEY TOLD ME AT SCHOOL.
I'VE NEVER FORGOTTEN.
IF YOU FIND A WATCH IN A DESERT, YOU DON'T ASSUME IT WAS SPONTANEOUSLY CREATED. YOU FIGURE SOME-ONE MADE IT. THAT THERE'S A WATCHMAKER.
AND IF THE WATCH HAS STOPPED, THEN YOU REPAIR IT.
I DON'T THINK THIS GUY MADE THE WATCH, PREZ. HE JUST RUNS THE LOCAL FRANCHISE.
BUT YOU'LL FIND OUT.
HEY--GOOD LUCK. I CAN'T HELP THINKING... MAYBE I OUGHT TO...
WELL. NEVER MIND. YOU'LL BE FINE, PREZ.
THANK YOU, MA'AM.
110
20

PAGES 129–130 The guests arrive at the inn. The guests' story provides a framing sequence around the tales presented in *Worlds' End*. Artwork by Bryan Talbot and Mark Buckingham. Daniel Vozzo, colorist.

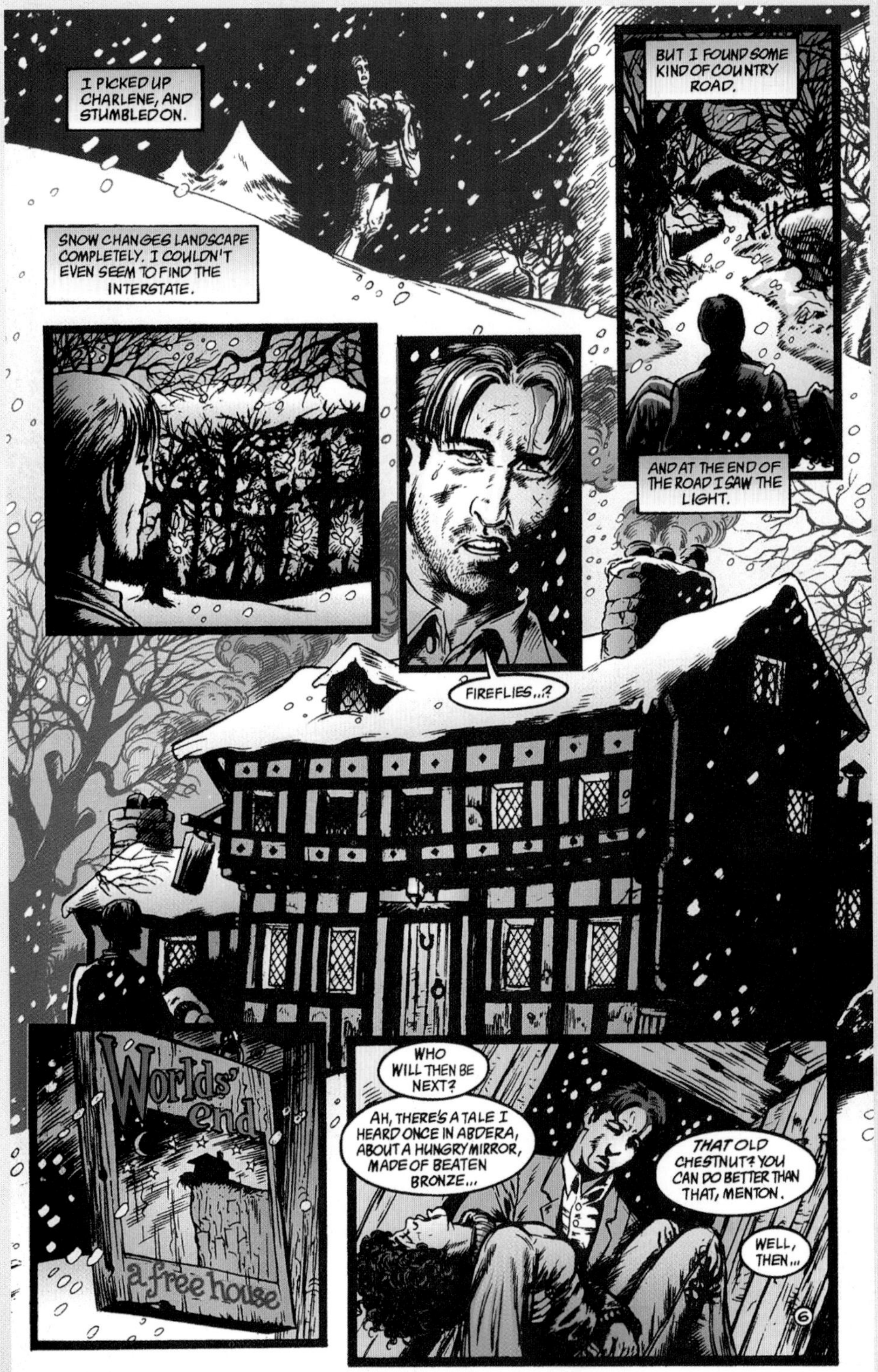
I PICKED UP CHARLENE, AND STUMBLED ON.
SNOW CHANGES LANDSCAPE COMPLETELY. I COULDN'T EVEN SEEM TO FIND THE INTERSTATE.
BUT I FOUND SOME KIND OF COUNTRY ROAD.
AND AT THE END OF THE ROAD I SAW THE LIGHT.
FIREFLIES...?
Worlds' end
a free house
WHO WILL THEN BE NEXT?
AH, THERE'S A TALE I HEARD ONCE IN ABDERA, ABOUT A HUNGRY MIRROR, MADE OF BEATEN BRONZE...
THAT OLD CHESTNUT? YOU CAN DO BETTER THAN THAT, MENTON.
WELL, THEN...
6

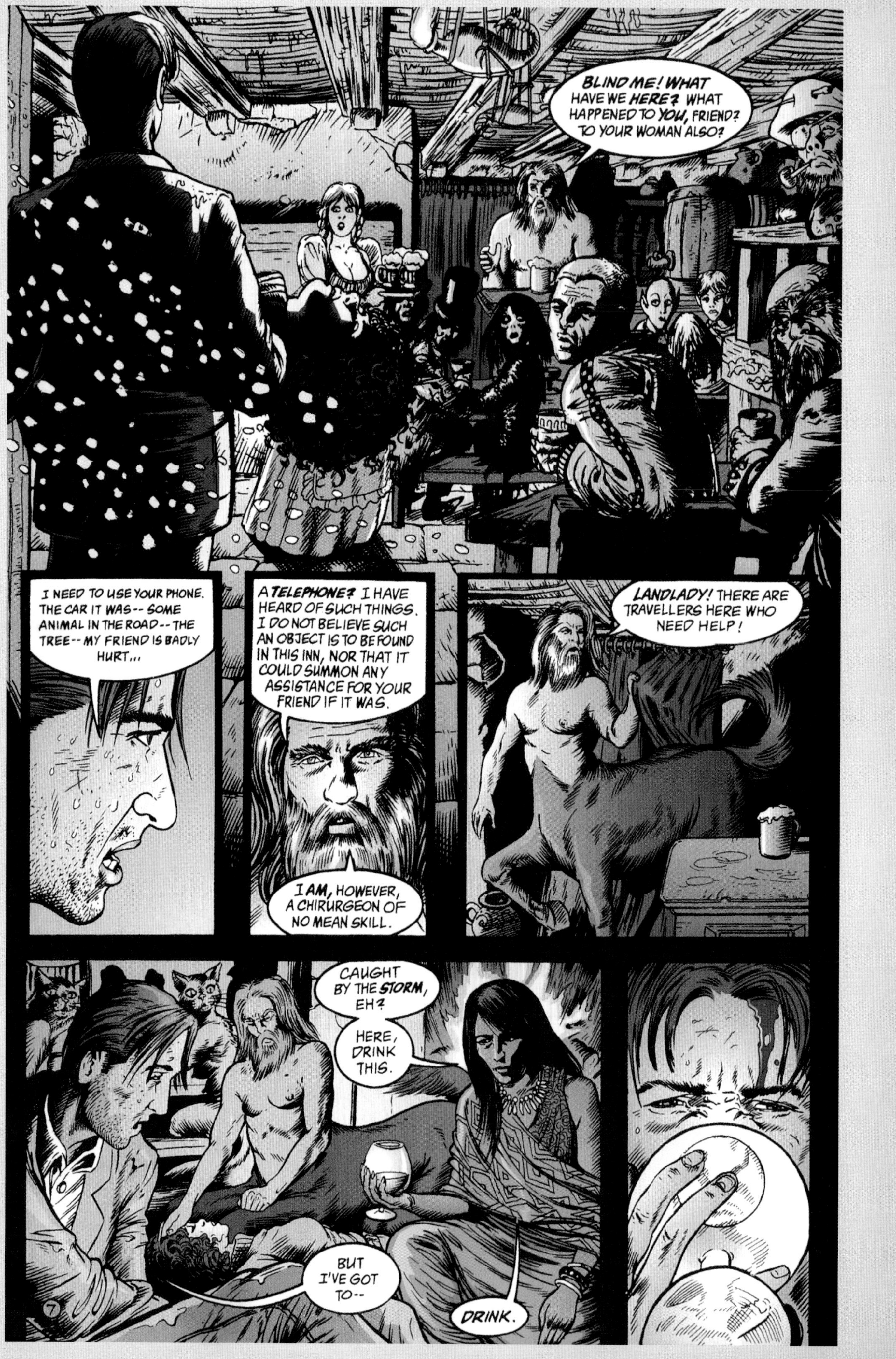

BLIND ME! WHAT HAVE WE HERE? WHAT HAPPENED TO YOU, FRIEND? TO YOUR WOMAN ALSO?
I NEED TO USE YOUR PHONE. THE CAR IT WAS-- SOME ANIMAL IN THE ROAD-- THE TREE-- MY FRIEND IS BADLY HURT...
A TELEPHONE? I HAVE HEARD OF SUCH THINGS. I DO NOT BELIEVE SUCH AN OBJECT IS TO BE FOUND IN THIS INN, NOR THAT IT COULD SUMMON ANY ASSISTANCE FOR YOUR FRIEND IF IT WAS.
I AM, HOWEVER, A CHIRURGEON OF NO MEAN SKILL.
LANDLADY! THERE ARE TRAVELLERS HERE WHO NEED HELP!
CAUGHT BY THE STORM, EH?
HERE, DRINK THIS.
BUT I'VE GOT TO--
DRINK.
7

PAGES 131–133 The tale of the dead Endless sister (count the standing figures of the family on the excerpt's third page and it is apparent that Despair is the sister in question) is first mentioned. Artwork by Shea Anton Pensa and Vince Locke. Daniel Vozzo, colorist.

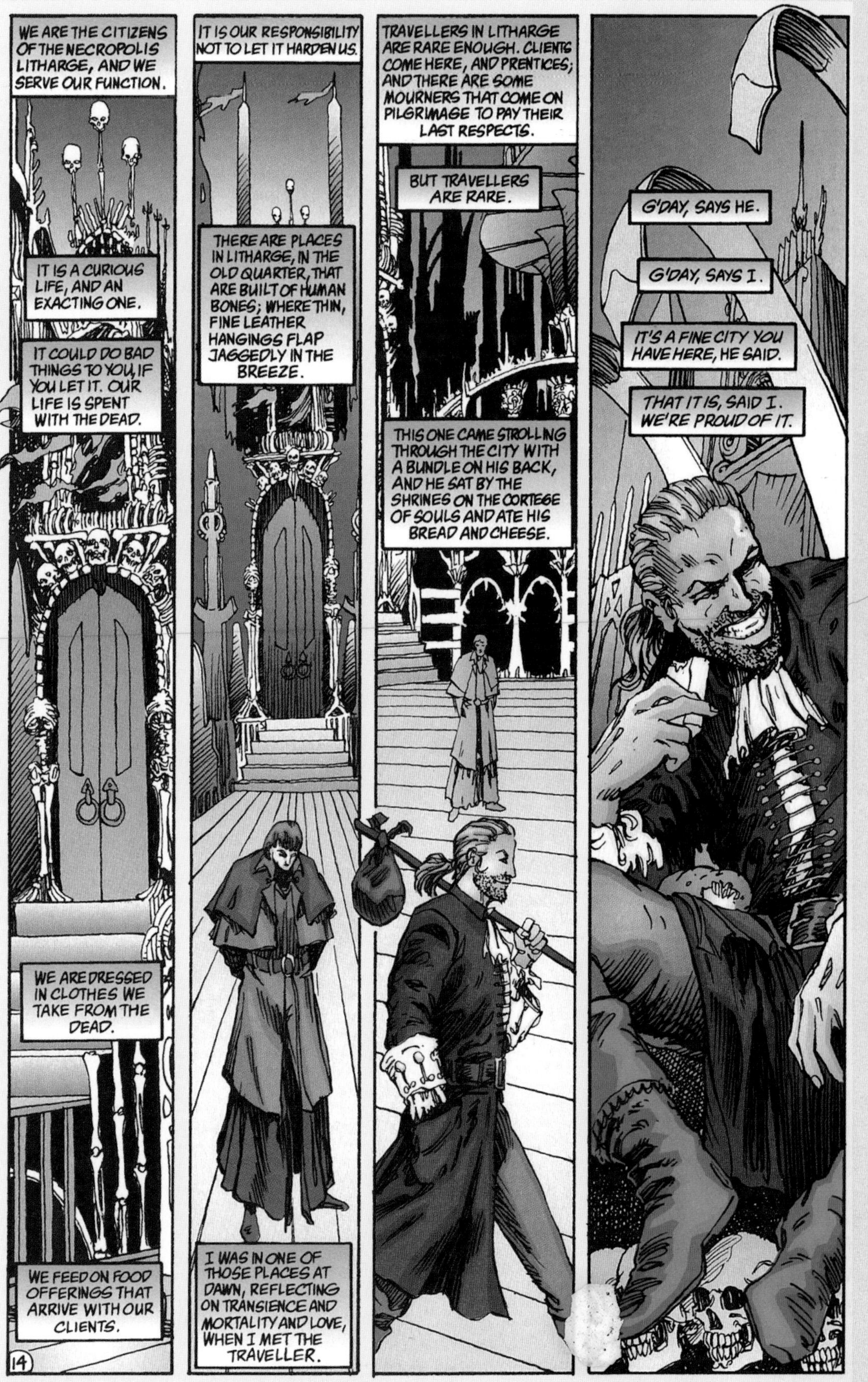
WE ARE THE CITIZENS OF THE NECROPOLIS LITHARGE, AND WE SERVE OUR FUNCTION.
IT IS A CURIOUS LIFE, AND AN EXACTING ONE.
IT COULD DO BAD THINGS TO YOU, IF YOU LET IT. OUR LIFE IS SPENT WITH THE DEAD.
WE ARE DRESSED IN CLOTHES WE TAKE FROM THE DEAD.
WE FEED ON FOOD OFFERINGS THAT ARRIVE WITH OUR CLIENTS.
14
IT IS OUR RESPONSIBILITY NOT TO LET IT HARDEN US.
THERE ARE PLACES IN LITHARGE, IN THE OLD QUARTER, THAT ARE BUILT OF HUMAN BONES; WHERE THIN, FINE LEATHER HANGINGS FLAP JAGGEDLY IN THE BREEZE.
I WAS IN ONE OF THOSE PLACES AT DAWN, REFLECTING ON TRANSIENCE AND MORTALITY AND LOVE, WHEN I MET THE TRAVELLER.
TRAVELLERS IN LITHARGE ARE RARE ENOUGH. CLIENTS COME HERE, AND PRENTICES; AND THERE ARE SOME MOURNERS THAT COME ON PILGRIMAGE TO PAY THEIR LAST RESPECTS.
BUT TRAVELLERS ARE RARE.
THIS ONE CAME STROLLING THROUGH THE CITY WITH A BUNDLE ON HIS BACK, AND HE SAT BY THE SHRINES ON THE CORTEGE OF SOULS AND ATE HIS BREAD AND CHEESE.
G'DAY, SAYS HE.
G'DAY, SAYS I.
IT'S A FINE CITY YOU HAVE HERE, HE SAID.
THAT IT IS, SAID I. WE'RE PROUD OF IT.

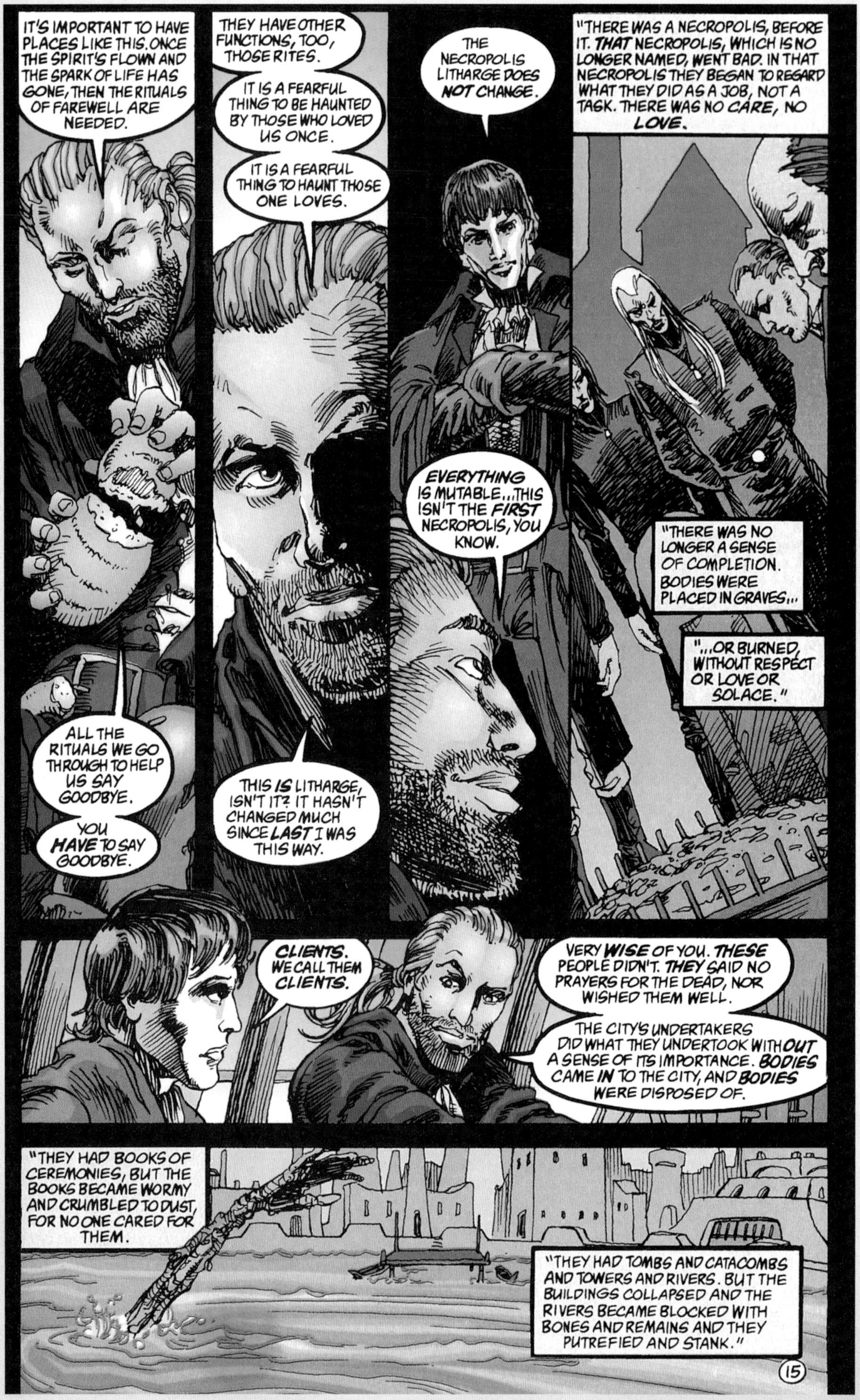
IT'S IMPORTANT TO HAVE PLACES LIKE THIS. ONCE THE SPIRIT'S FLOWN AND THE SPARK OF LIFE HAS GONE, THEN THE RITUALS OF FAREWELL ARE NEEDED.
THEY HAVE OTHER FUNCTIONS, TOO, THOSE RITES.
IT IS A FEARFUL THING TO BE HAUNTED BY THOSE WHO LOVED US ONCE.
IT IS A FEARFUL THING TO HAUNT THOSE ONE LOVES.
THE NECROPOLIS LITHARGE DOES NOT CHANGE.
"THERE WAS A NECROPOLIS, BEFORE IT. THAT NECROPOLIS, WHICH IS NO LONGER NAMED, WENT BAD. IN THAT NECROPOLIS THEY BEGAN TO REGARD WHAT THEY DID AS A JOB, NOT A TASK. THERE WAS NO CARE, NO LOVE.
EVERYTHING IS MUTABLE... THIS ISN'T THE FIRST NECROPOLIS, YOU KNOW.
"THERE WAS NO LONGER A SENSE OF COMPLETION. BODIES WERE PLACED IN GRAVES...
"...OR BURNED, WITHOUT RESPECT OR LOVE OR SOLACE."
ALL THE RITUALS WE GO THROUGH TO HELP US SAY GOODBYE.
YOU HAVE TO SAY GOODBYE.
THIS IS LITHARGE, ISN'T IT? IT HASN'T CHANGED MUCH SINCE LAST I WAS THIS WAY.
CLIENTS. WE CALL THEM CLIENTS.
VERY WISE OF YOU. THESE PEOPLE DIDN'T. THEY SAID NO PRAYERS FOR THE DEAD, NOR WISHED THEM WELL.
THE CITY'S UNDERTAKERS DID WHAT THEY UNDERTOOK WITHOUT A SENSE OF ITS IMPORTANCE. BODIES CAME IN TO THE CITY, AND BODIES WERE DISPOSED OF.
"THEY HAD BOOKS OF CEREMONIES, BUT THE BOOKS BECAME WORMY AND CRUMBLED TO DUST, FOR NO ONE CARED FOR THEM.
"THEY HAD TOMBS AND CATACOMBS AND TOWERS AND RIVERS. BUT THE BUILDINGS COLLAPSED AND THE RIVERS BECAME BLOCKED WITH BONES AND REMAINS AND THEY PUTREFIED AND STANK."
15

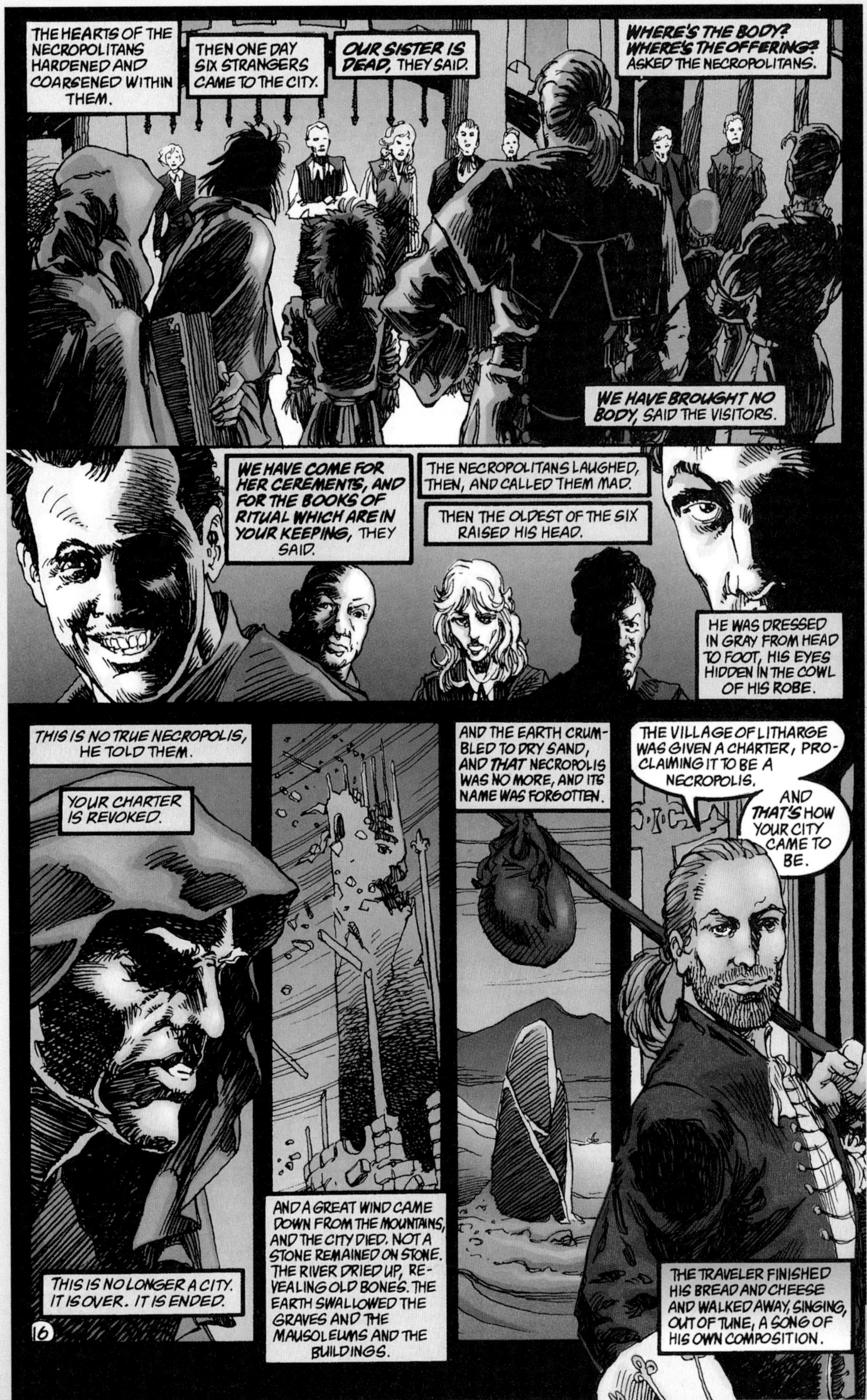
THE HEARTS OF THE NECROPOLITANS HARDENED AND COARSENED WITHIN THEM.
THEN ONE DAY SIX STRANGERS CAME TO THE CITY.
OUR SISTER IS DEAD, THEY SAID.
WHERE'S THE BODY? WHERE'S THE OFFERING? ASKED THE NECROPOLITANS.
WE HAVE BROUGHT NO BODY, SAID THE VISITORS.
WE HAVE COME FOR HER CEREMENTS, AND FOR THE BOOKS OF RITUAL WHICH ARE IN YOUR KEEPING, THEY SAID.
THE NECROPOLITANS LAUGHED, THEN, AND CALLED THEM MAD.
THEN THE OLDEST OF THE SIX RAISED HIS HEAD.
HE WAS DRESSED IN GRAY FROM HEAD TO FOOT, HIS EYES HIDDEN IN THE COWL OF HIS ROBE.
THIS IS NO TRUE NECROPOLIS, HE TOLD THEM.
YOUR CHARTER IS REVOKED.
THIS IS NO LONGER A CITY. IT IS OVER. IT IS ENDED.
16
AND A GREAT WIND CAME DOWN FROM THE MOUNTAINS, AND THE CITY DIED. NOT A STONE REMAINED ON STONE. THE RIVER DRIED UP, REVEALING OLD BONES. THE EARTH SWALLOWED THE GRAVES AND THE MAUSOLEUMS AND THE BUILDINGS.
AND THE EARTH CRUMBLED TO DRY SAND, AND THAT NECROPOLIS WAS NO MORE, AND ITS NAME WAS FORGOTTEN.
THE VILLAGE OF LITHARGE WAS GIVEN A CHARTER, PROCLAIMING IT TO BE A NECROPOLIS.
AND THAT'S HOW YOUR CITY CAME TO BE.
THE TRAVELER FINISHED HIS BREAD AND CHEESE AND WALKED AWAY, SINGING, OUT OF TUNE, A SONG OF HIS OWN COMPOSITION.

PAGES 134–135 The procession in the sky. From "Cerements." Artwork by Gary Amaro and Tony Harris. Daniel Vozzo, colorist.

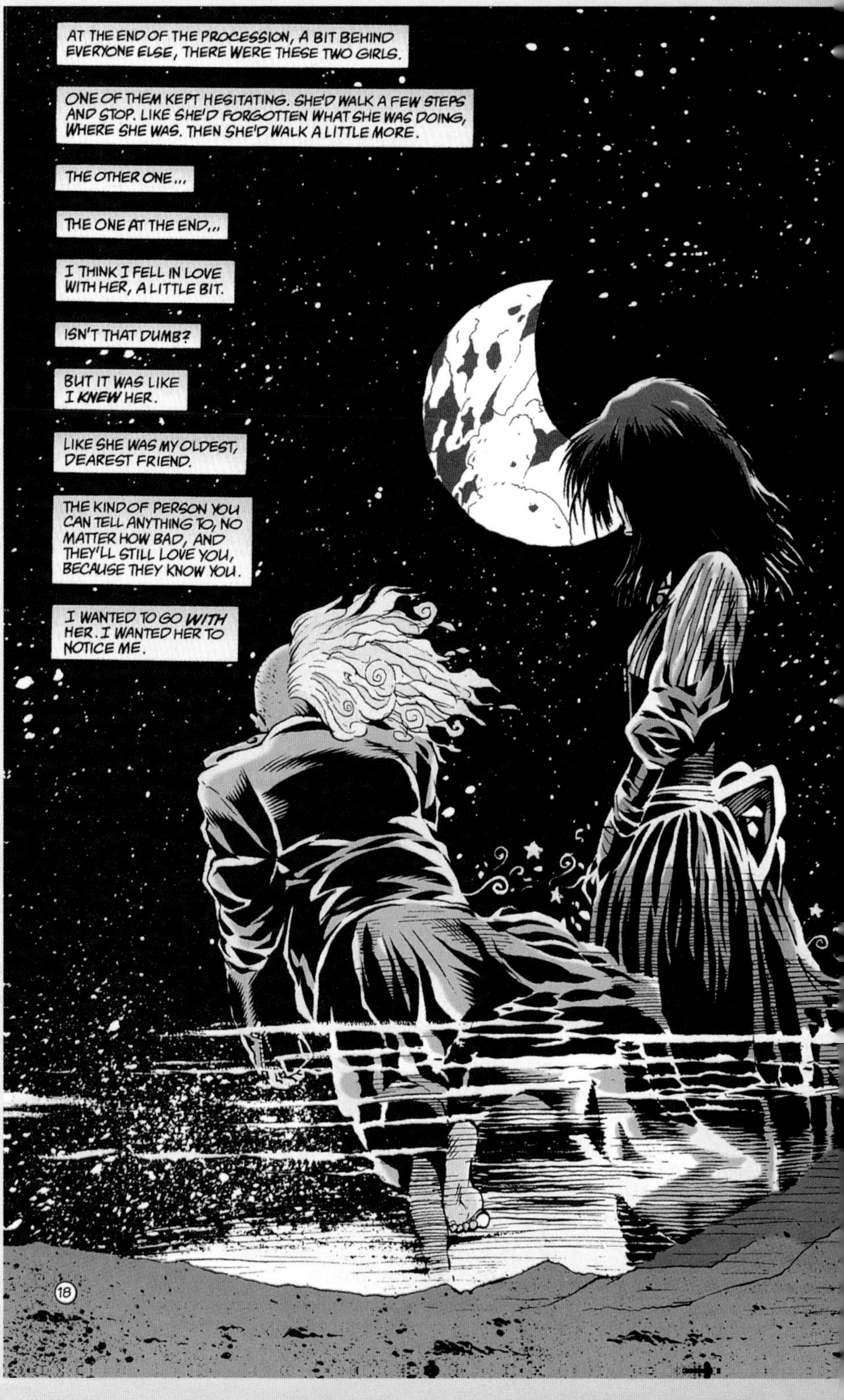
AT THE END OF THE PROCESSION, A BIT BEHIND EVERYONE ELSE, THERE WERE THESE TWO GIRLS.
ONE OF THEM KEPT HESITATING. SHE'D WALK A FEW STEPS AND STOP. LIKE SHE'D FORGOTTEN WHAT SHE WAS DOING, WHERE SHE WAS. THEN SHE'D WALK A LITTLE MORE.
THE OTHER ONE...
THE ONE AT THE END...
I THINK I FELL IN LOVE WITH HER, A LITTLE BIT.
ISN'T THAT DUMB?
BUT IT WAS LIKE I KNEW HER.
LIKE SHE WAS MY OLDEST, DEAREST FRIEND.
THE KIND OF PERSON YOU CAN TELL ANYTHING TO, NO MATTER HOW BAD, AND THEY'LL STILL LOVE YOU, BECAUSE THEY KNOW YOU.
I WANTED TO GO WITH HER. I WANTED HER TO NOTICE ME.
18

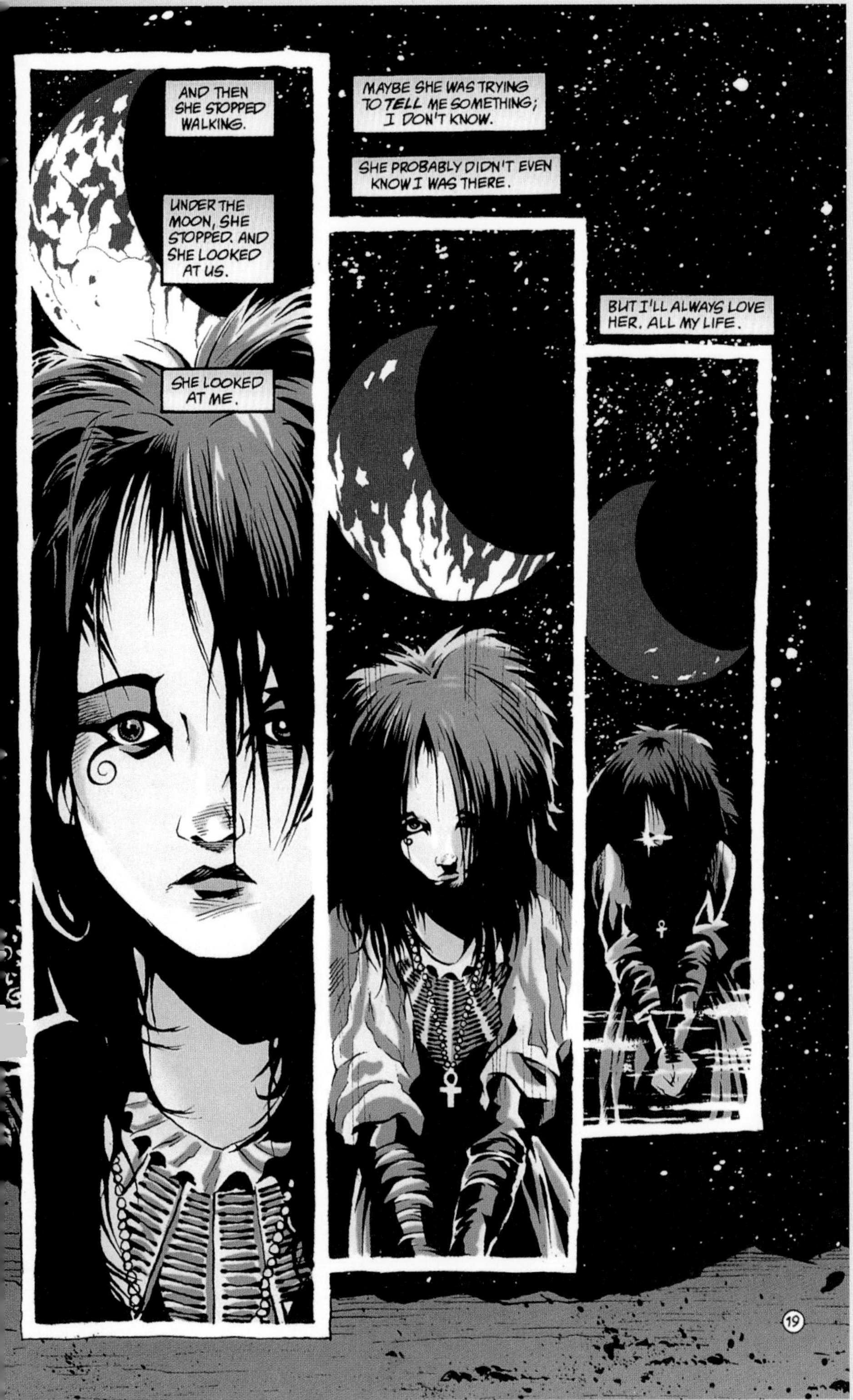
AND THEN SHE STOPPED WALKING.
UNDER THE MOON, SHE STOPPED. AND SHE LOOKED AT US.
SHE LOOKED AT ME.
MAYBE SHE WAS TRYING TO TELL ME SOMETHING; I DON'T KNOW.
SHE PROBABLY DIDN'T EVEN KNOW I WAS THERE.
BUT I'LL ALWAYS LOVE HER. ALL MY LIFE.
19

PAGES 136–137 Charlene questions why all the stories are about boys. In the next collection, *The Kindly Ones*, women will take center stage. Artwork by Bryan Talbot and Mark Buckingham. Daniel Vozzo, colorist.

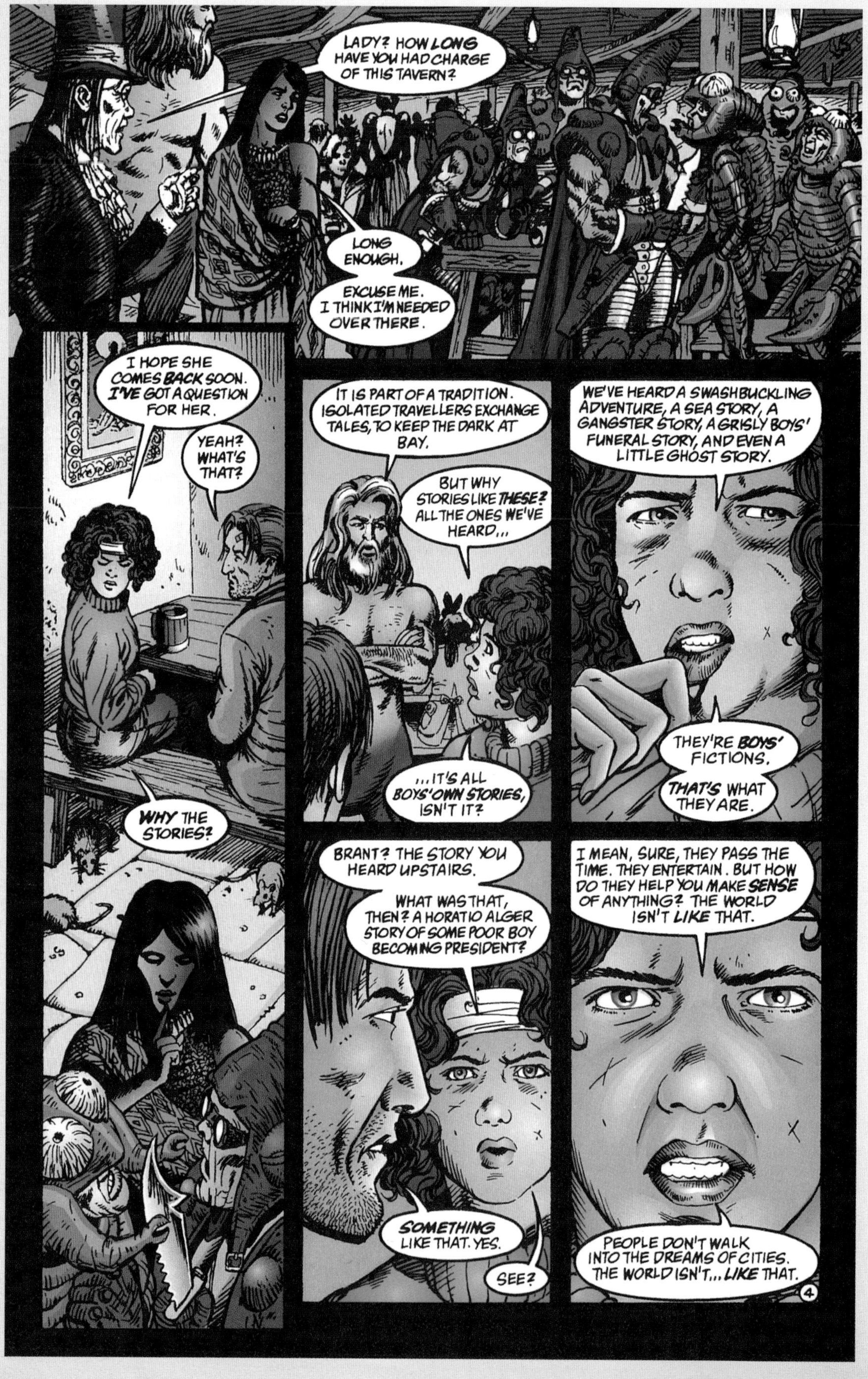
LADY? HOW LONG HAVE YOU HAD CHARGE OF THIS TAVERN?
LONG ENOUGH.
EXCUSE ME. I THINK I'M NEEDED OVER THERE.
I HOPE SHE COMES BACK SOON. I'VE GOT A QUESTION FOR HER.
YEAH? WHAT'S THAT?
WHY THE STORIES?
IT IS PART OF A TRADITION. ISOLATED TRAVELLERS EXCHANGE TALES, TO KEEP THE DARK AT BAY.
BUT WHY STORIES LIKE THESE? ALL THE ONES WE'VE HEARD...
...IT'S ALL BOYS' OWN STORIES, ISN'T IT?
WE'VE HEARD A SWASHBUCKLING ADVENTURE, A SEA STORY, A GANGSTER STORY, A GRISLY BOYS' FUNERAL STORY, AND EVEN A LITTLE GHOST STORY.
THEY'RE BOYS' FICTIONS.
THAT'S WHAT THEY ARE.
BRANT? THE STORY YOU HEARD UPSTAIRS.
WHAT WAS THAT, THEN? A HORATIO ALGER STORY OF SOME POOR BOY BECOMING PRESIDENT?
SOMETHING LIKE THAT. YES.
SEE?
I MEAN, SURE, THEY PASS THE TIME. THEY ENTERTAIN. BUT HOW DO THEY HELP YOU MAKE SENSE OF ANYTHING? THE WORLD ISN'T LIKE THAT.
PEOPLE DON'T WALK INTO THE DREAMS OF CITIES. THE WORLD ISN'T... LIKE THAT.
4

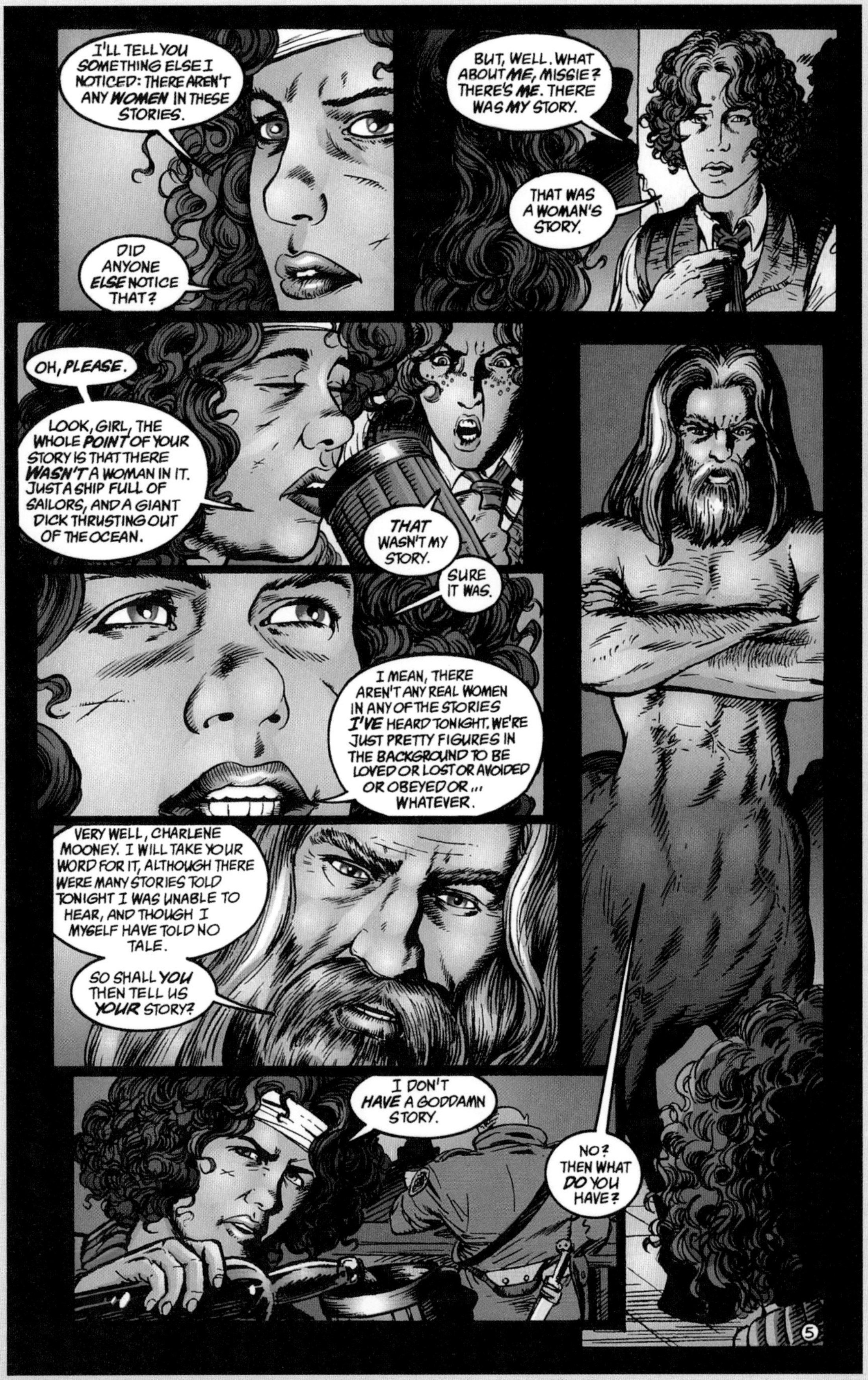
I'LL TELL YOU SOMETHING ELSE I NOTICED: THERE AREN'T ANY WOMEN IN THESE STORIES.
DID ANYONE ELSE NOTICE THAT?
BUT, WELL. WHAT ABOUT ME, MISSIE? THERE'S ME. THERE WAS MY STORY.
THAT WAS A WOMAN'S STORY.
OH, PLEASE.
LOOK, GIRL, THE WHOLE POINT OF YOUR STORY IS THAT THERE WASN'T A WOMAN IN IT. JUST A SHIP FULL OF SAILORS, AND A GIANT DICK THRUSTING OUT OF THE OCEAN.
THAT WASN'T MY STORY.
SURE IT WAS.
I MEAN, THERE AREN'T ANY REAL WOMEN IN ANY OF THE STORIES I'VE HEARD TONIGHT. WE'RE JUST PRETTY FIGURES IN THE BACKGROUND TO BE LOVED OR LOST OR AVOIDED OR OBEYED OR ... WHATEVER.
VERY WELL, CHARLENE MOONEY. I WILL TAKE YOUR WORD FOR IT, ALTHOUGH THERE WERE MANY STORIES TOLD TONIGHT I WAS UNABLE TO HEAR, AND THOUGH I MYSELF HAVE TOLD NO TALE.
SO SHALL YOU THEN TELL US YOUR STORY?
I DON'T HAVE A GODDAMN STORY.
NO? THEN WHAT DO YOU HAVE?
5

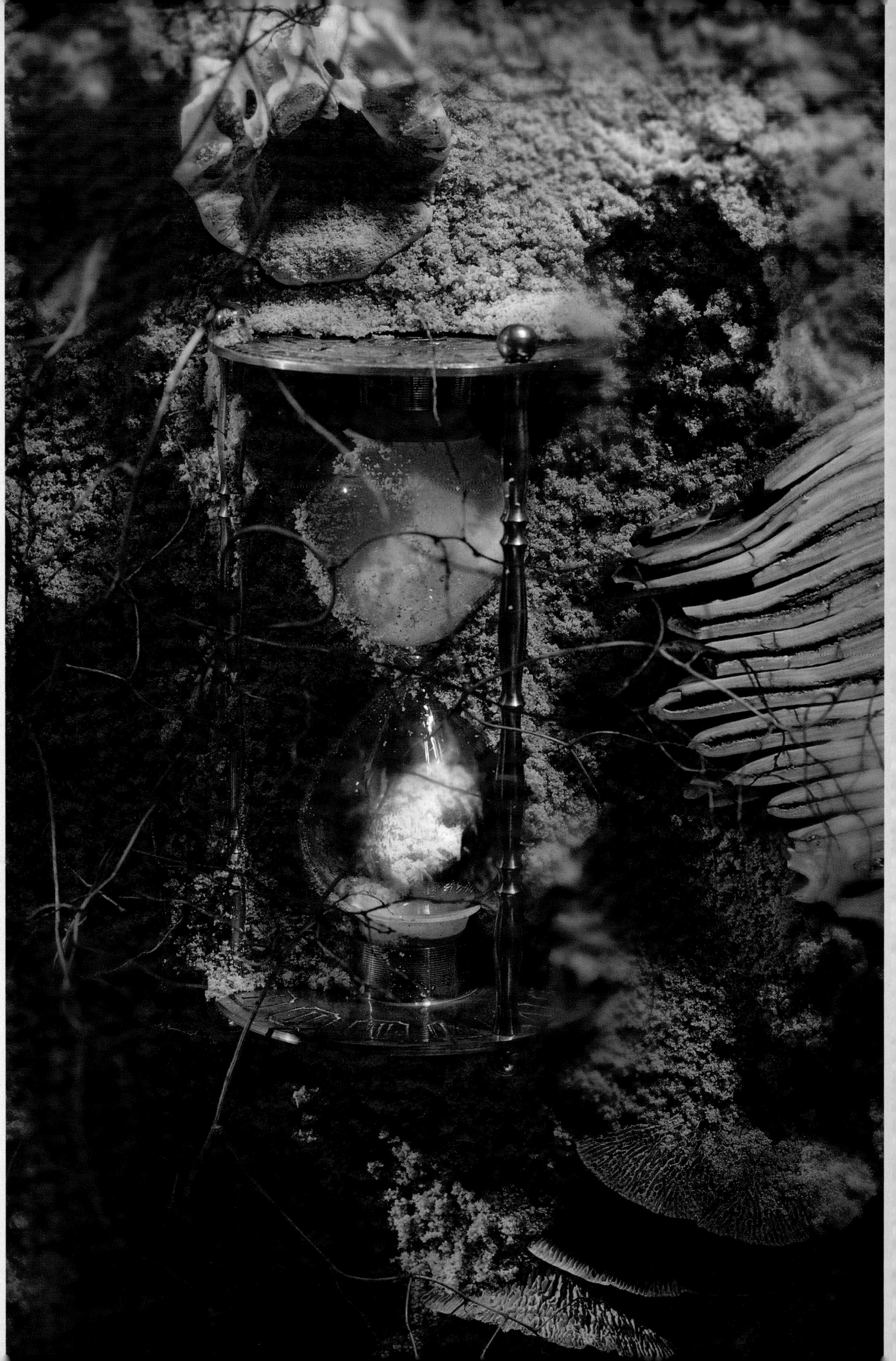

CHAPTER *10*

THE KINDLY ONES

IN WHICH LYTA HALL EXACTS HER REVENGE AND THE FATE OF THE DREAM KING IS REVEALED.

The Kindly Ones is the longest and most novelistic of the story arcs. It is the exact opposite of the brief "boy's only" adventure stories of *Worlds' End.* It takes thirteen chapters, plus a wounded mother (Lyta Hall), a maiden in love (Nuala), and a deceptively youthful crone (Thessaly, who despite her looks is long post-menopausal), to bring *The Sandman*'s saga to its tragic close.

This maiden-mother-crone triad, replayed throughout the series, reminds us by the frequency of its repetition that the Fates are aspects of the Furies, are aspects of the Gorgons, are aspects of our girlfriends, sisters, mothers, daughters – are aspects of ourselves.

As the eternal triad of feminine power keeps reconfiguring, we are being prepared for a different kind of reconfiguration, as the aspect of Dream of the Endless we have journeyed with all this long way – the brooding, taciturn, surprisingly gentle Morpheus – is about to take his older sister's hand for the very last time.

The Kindly Ones isn't everybody's cup of tea – there were, at the time of its first publication as a monthly comic, grumbles about the drawn-out plotline and artist Marc Hempel's bold, geometrical style. But while I've never gone so far as to tattoo any of Hempel's characters on my flesh (unlike the lady who walked up to him, interrupting us at one convention, to ask him to draw a picture on her arm that would later be permanently tattooed), I find the expressive cleverness of his pen a real temptation. In my opinion, the darkly exquisite blend of story and art in this collection is rivaled only by "Ramadan," and by the final collection, *The Wake.*

PAGE 138 Cover, *The Sandman* no. 64. Artwork by Dave McKean.

PAGES 140–141 Neil jots down *The Kindly Ones'* "Story So Far," in his thumbnail comic for *The Sandman* no. 64

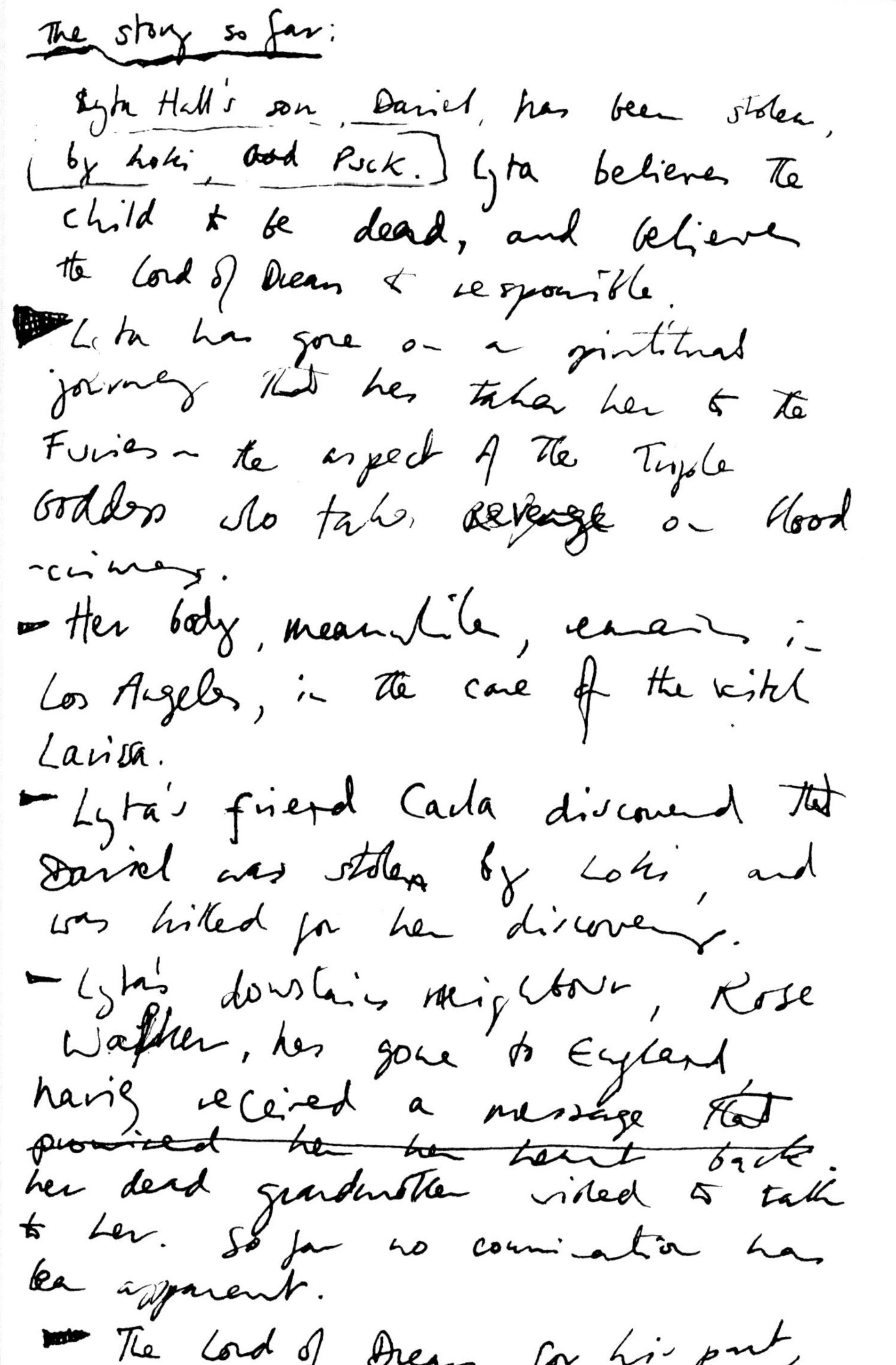
The story so far:

Lyta Hall's son, Daniel, has been stolen, by Loki, and Puck. Lyta believes the child to be dead, and believes the Lord of Dreams is responsible.

- Lyta has gone on a spiritual journey that has taken her to the Furies – the aspect of the Triple Goddess who takes revenge on blood-crimes.
- Her body, meanwhile, remains in Los Angeles, in the care of the witch Larissa.
- Lyta's friend Carla discovered that Daniel was stolen by Loki, and was killed for her discovery.
- Lyta's downstairs neighbour, Rose Walker, has gone to England having received a message that ~~promised her her heart back.~~ her dead grandmother wished to talk to her. So far no communication has been apparent.
- The Lord of Dreams, for his part, has despatched Matthew the Raven and

a newly decapitated Corinthian to
find Daniel and bring him
to the Dreaming.

▸ Daniel was last seen placed on
a fire by Loki and the Puck.

▸ ~~the oldest~~ the youngest of the Endless, Delirium,
visited Destiny, the oldest, seeking
her lost dog, and received
some ambiguous advice...

                    Now Read On.

BELOW The world becomes distorted for Lyta as she embarks on her quest to find her son. Artwork by Marc Hempel and D'Israeli. Daniel Vozzo, colorist.

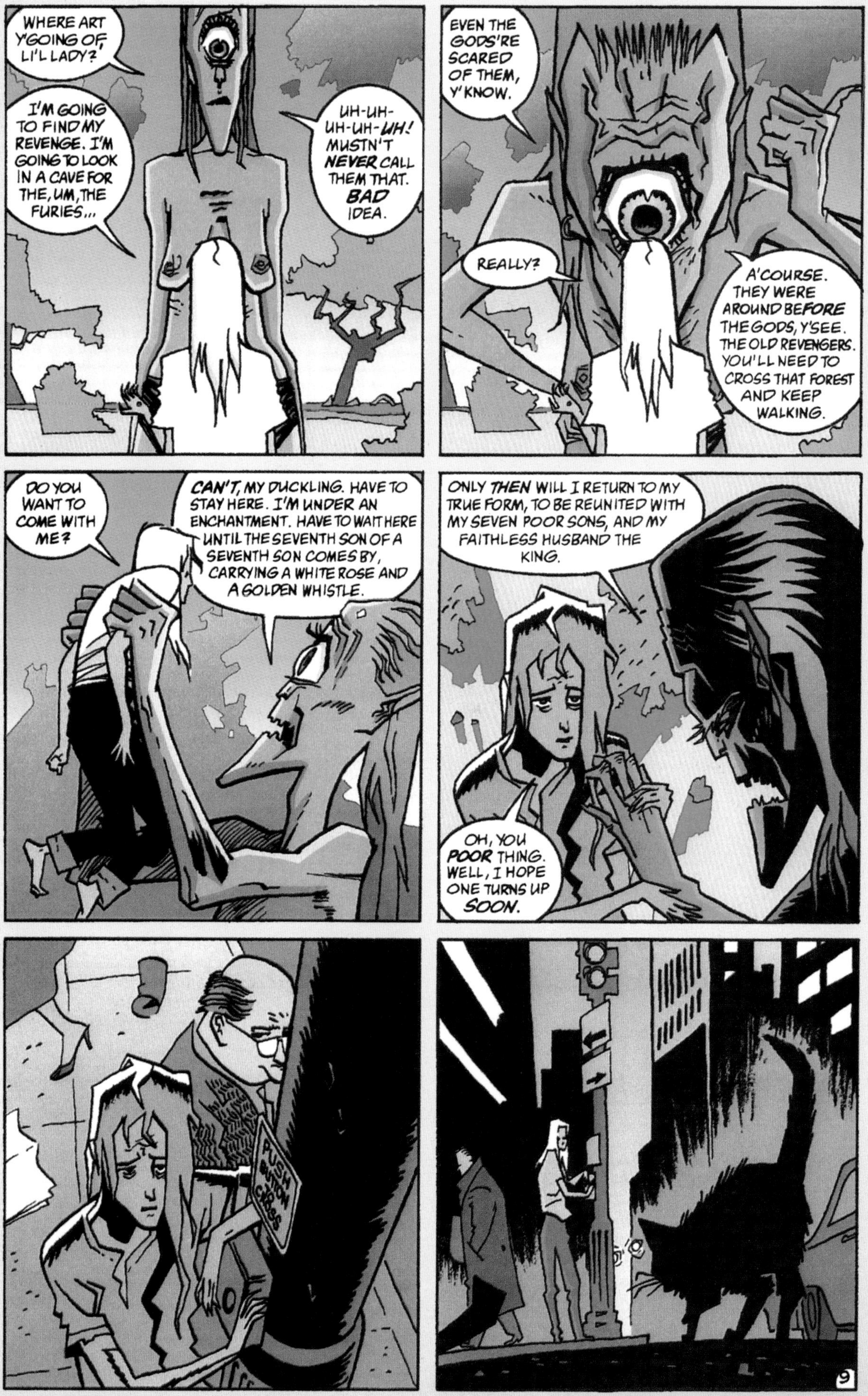
WHERE ART Y'GOING OF, LI'L LADY?
I'M GOING TO FIND MY REVENGE. I'M GOING TO LOOK IN A CAVE FOR THE, UM, THE FURIES...
UH-UH-UH-UH-UH! MUSTN'T NEVER CALL THEM THAT. BAD IDEA.
EVEN THE GODS'RE SCARED OF THEM, Y'KNOW.
REALLY?
A'COURSE. THEY WERE AROUND BEFORE THE GODS, Y'SEE. THE OLD REVENGERS. YOU'LL NEED TO CROSS THAT FOREST AND KEEP WALKING.
DO YOU WANT TO COME WITH ME?
CAN'T, MY DUCKLING. HAVE TO STAY HERE. I'M UNDER AN ENCHANTMENT. HAVE TO WAIT HERE UNTIL THE SEVENTH SON OF A SEVENTH SON COMES BY, CARRYING A WHITE ROSE AND A GOLDEN WHISTLE.
ONLY THEN WILL I RETURN TO MY TRUE FORM, TO BE REUNITED WITH MY SEVEN POOR SONS, AND MY FAITHLESS HUSBAND THE KING.
OH, YOU POOR THING. WELL, I HOPE ONE TURNS UP SOON.
PUSH BUTTON TO CROSS
9

BELOW The beginning of the end, featuring – who else but the Fates. Artwork by Marc Hempel. Daniel Vozzo, colorist.

"I READ THE BOOK *DUNE MESSIAH* BEFORE I EVER READ *DUNE.* WHICH MAY HAVE BEEN A GOOD THING, AS EVERYONE HATES *DUNE MESSIAH* AND LOVES *DUNE.* BUT I THOUGHT THAT *DUNE MESSIAH* WAS A FASCINATING BOOK AND I WAS DISAPPOINTED IN *DUNE.* I WAS INTERESTED IN THE CHARACTER OF DUNCAN IDAHO BECAUSE HE WAS RE-CREATED; HE WAS NOT THE FIRST ONE OF HIM. SIMILARLY, HAVING TWO INCARNATIONS OF THE CORINTHIAN SIGNALS AND SETS UP FOR WHAT WE'RE GOING TO DO WITH SANDMAN." —NEIL GAIMAN

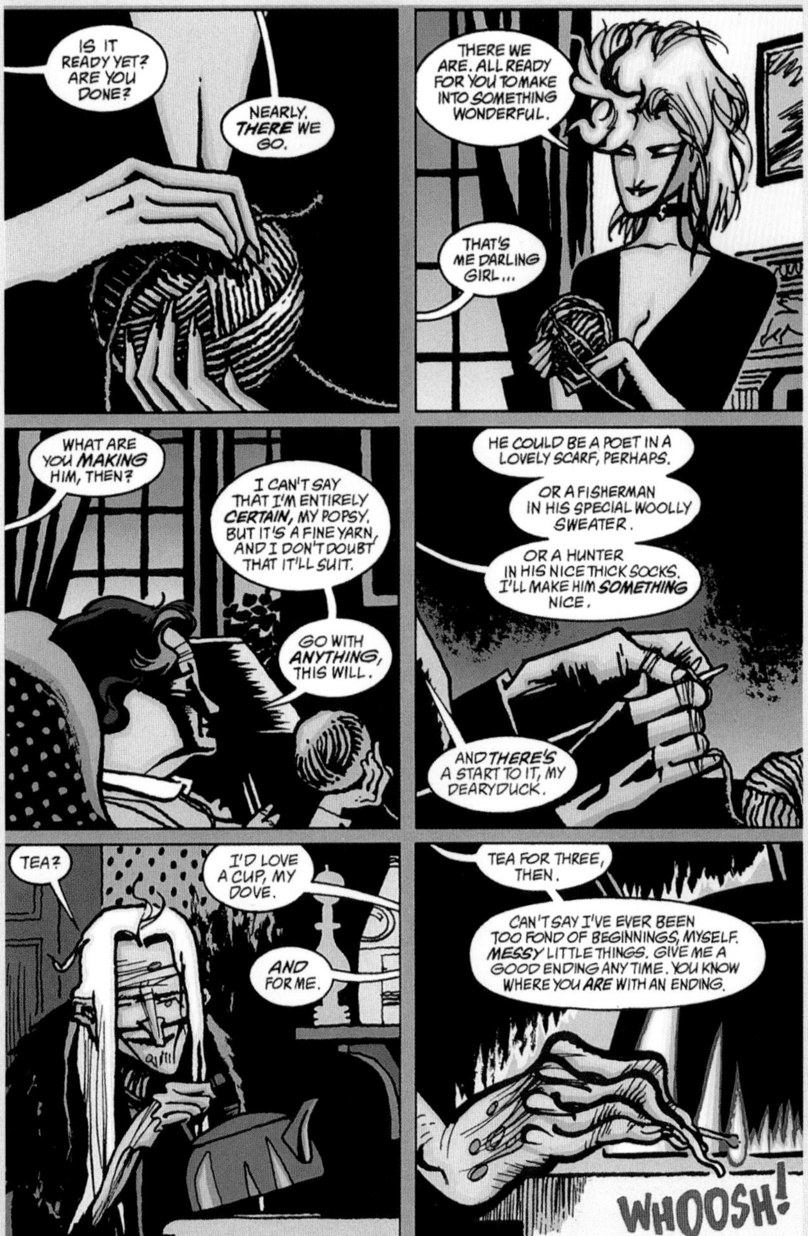
IS IT READY YET? ARE YOU DONE?
NEARLY. THERE WE GO.
THERE WE ARE. ALL READY FOR YOU TO MAKE INTO SOMETHING WONDERFUL.
THAT'S ME DARLING GIRL...
WHAT ARE YOU MAKING HIM, THEN?
I CAN'T SAY THAT I'M ENTIRELY CERTAIN, MY POPSY, BUT IT'S A FINE YARN, AND I DON'T DOUBT THAT IT'LL SUIT.
GO WITH ANYTHING, THIS WILL.
HE COULD BE A POET IN A LOVELY SCARF, PERHAPS.
OR A FISHERMAN IN HIS SPECIAL WOOLLY SWEATER.
OR A HUNTER IN HIS NICE THICK SOCKS. I'LL MAKE HIM SOMETHING NICE.
AND THERE'S A START TO IT, MY DEARYDUCK.
TEA?
I'D LOVE A CUP, MY DOVE.
AND FOR ME.
TEA FOR THREE, THEN.
CAN'T SAY I'VE EVER BEEN TOO FOND OF BEGINNINGS, MYSELF. MESSY LITTLE THINGS. GIVE ME A GOOD ENDING ANY TIME. YOU KNOW WHERE YOU ARE WITH AN ENDING.
WHOOSH!

little things.

      Give me a good ending any time. You know where you are with an ending.

PAGE 2 PANEL 1

SAME GRID, SAME PLACE, SAME SCENE. IT'S ALL VERY DOMESTIC, MARC. ALL VERY SWEET AND REASSURING. THREE LADIES IN A LITTLE COTTAGE, HAVING A DISCUSSION THAT COULD, QUITE POSSIBLY, BE ABOUT MAKING WOOLLY GARMENTS FOR PEOPLE. THE MOTHER, SITTING IN HER CHAIR. SHE'S GOT ABOUT AN INCH OF KNITTING ON HER NEEDLES NOW. BALL OF YARN IN HER LAP (AND THE END OF THAT YARN STILL GOING OFF-PANEL). A HUGE BLACK CAT WITH GREEN EYES IS TWINING BETWEEN HER LEGS.

Mother: Now then, you mustn't say things like that. You know you don't mean them.

      purl one, plain one, purl two together...

Mother: Why, that's what I like about making things for people. You can start off in Birmingham and finish in, well, Tangyanika or somewhere.

PAGE 2 PANEL 2

IN THE KITCHEN. THE OLD HAG (WELL, LET'S NOT MINCE WORDS, THAT'S WHAT SHE IS). SHE HAS AN ENORMOUS TEA POT, AND IS SPOONING TEA LEAVES INTO IT. THE KETTLE IS STEAMING.

Mother (off): That's not messy, my cherub. That's exciting.

Crone: Exciting my aunt banana!

      What's so exciting about it?

Mother (off): Well, every one we make's unique. Never seen before. Never seen again.

PAGE 2 PANEL 3

THE CRONE, BUT IN CLOSE-UP. SHE'S POURING BOILING WATER FROM THE KETTLE INTO THE TEA-POT. LOTS OF STEAM. WE'RE LOOKING AT THE WATER AND THE KETTLE AND THE POT, MAINLY.

CRONE: HMMPH. I DON'T KNOW WHY THAT'S EXCITING. IT'S NOT LIKE ANYONE NOTICES WHAT WE DO. NOT LIKE ANYONE CARES.

Crone: And they're always complaining: they don't like the fit of it; too loose -- too tight -- too different -- too much like everyone else's.

PAGE 2 PANEL 4

THE CRONE. SHE'S RAISED HER ARMS HIGH, IS WIGGLING HER FINGERS AROUND, PRETENDING TO BE SOMEONE COMPLAINING. HER RAGGEDY SKIRTS ARE FLAPPING. SHE'S TALKING, WHITE HAIR BLOWING AROUND HER HEAD.

Crone: It's never what they want, and if we give them what they think they want they like it less than ever.

Crone: "I never thought it would be like this." "Why can't it be like the one I had before?"

      I don't know why we bother.

PAGES 144–145 Neil's ability to describe visuals comes across clearly in this script page and final artwork. Artwork by Marc Hempel and D'Israeli. Daniel Vozzo, colorist.

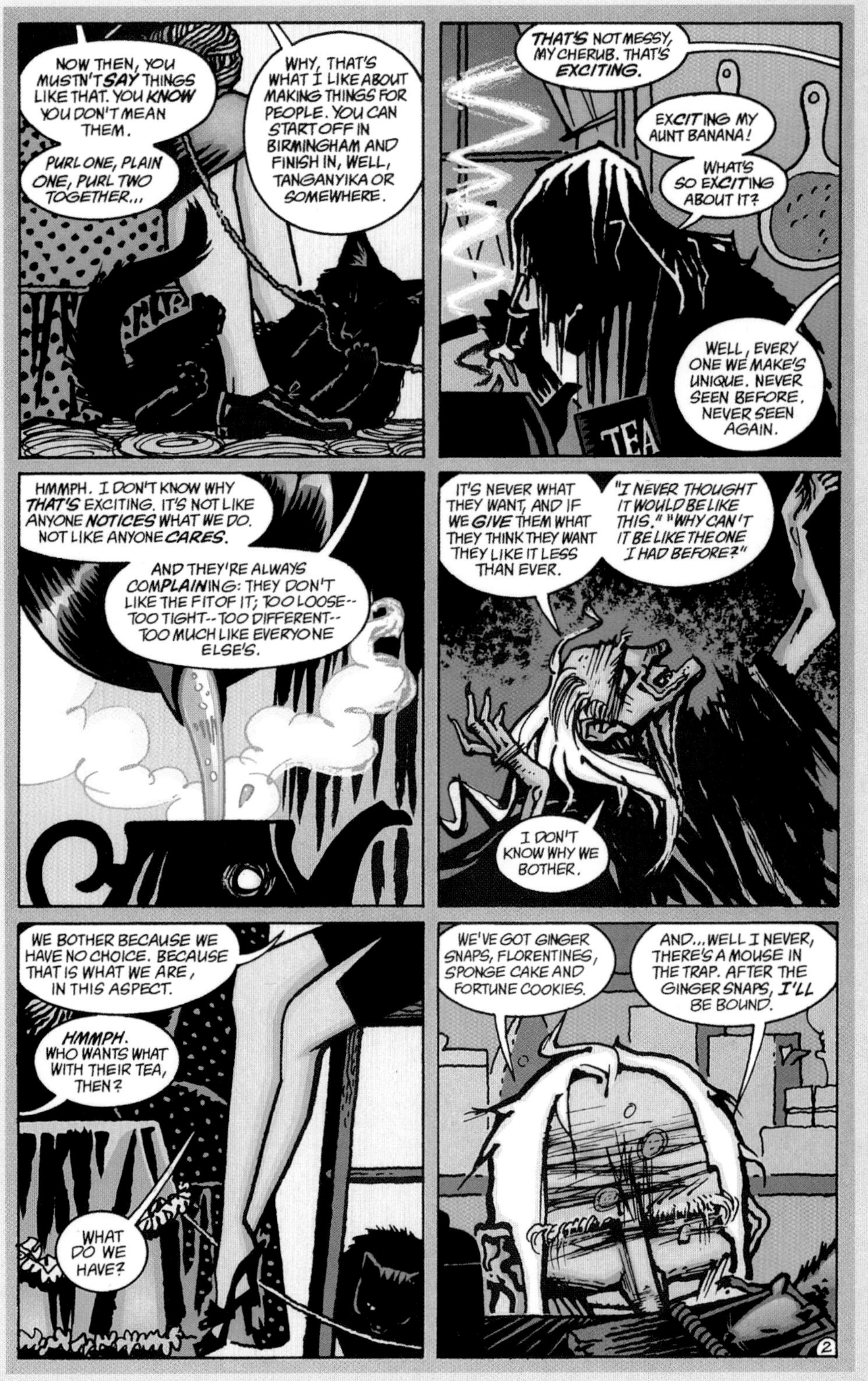
NOW THEN, YOU MUSTN'T SAY THINGS LIKE THAT. YOU KNOW YOU DON'T MEAN THEM.
PURL ONE, PLAIN ONE, PURL TWO TOGETHER...
WHY, THAT'S WHAT I LIKE ABOUT MAKING THINGS FOR PEOPLE. YOU CAN START OFF IN BIRMINGHAM AND FINISH IN, WELL, TANGANYIKA OR SOMEWHERE.
THAT'S NOT MESSY, MY CHERUB. THAT'S EXCITING.
EXCITING MY AUNT BANANA!
WHAT'S SO EXCITING ABOUT IT?
WELL, EVERY ONE WE MAKE'S UNIQUE. NEVER SEEN BEFORE. NEVER SEEN AGAIN.
TEA
HMMPH. I DON'T KNOW WHY THAT'S EXCITING. IT'S NOT LIKE ANYONE NOTICES WHAT WE DO. NOT LIKE ANYONE CARES.
AND THEY'RE ALWAYS COMPLAINING: THEY DON'T LIKE THE FIT OF IT; TOO LOOSE-- TOO TIGHT-- TOO DIFFERENT-- TOO MUCH LIKE EVERYONE ELSE'S.
IT'S NEVER WHAT THEY WANT, AND IF WE GIVE THEM WHAT THEY THINK THEY WANT THEY LIKE IT LESS THAN EVER.
"I NEVER THOUGHT IT WOULD BE LIKE THIS." "WHY CAN'T IT BE LIKE THE ONE I HAD BEFORE?"
I DON'T KNOW WHY WE BOTHER.
WE BOTHER BECAUSE WE HAVE NO CHOICE. BECAUSE THAT IS WHAT WE ARE, IN THIS ASPECT.
HMMPH. WHO WANTS WHAT WITH THEIR TEA, THEN?
WHAT DO WE HAVE?
WE'VE GOT GINGER SNAPS, FLORENTINES, SPONGE CAKE AND FORTUNE COOKIES.
AND... WELL I NEVER, THERE'S A MOUSE IN THE TRAP. AFTER THE GINGER SNAPS, I'LL BE BOUND.
2

The plot in *The Kindly Ones* is as simple as misunderstanding: Lyta's son, Daniel, has been stolen (though not, as she believes, by the Sandman). She goes mad with the single-minded need for revenge, entering her own personal reality storm, in which prostitutes are swashbucklers, an alley cat is Puss in Boots, and the traffic light is a Cyclops.

PAGES 146–147 Lyta meets with the witches. Artwork by Marc Hempel and D'Israeli. Daniel Vozzo, colorist.

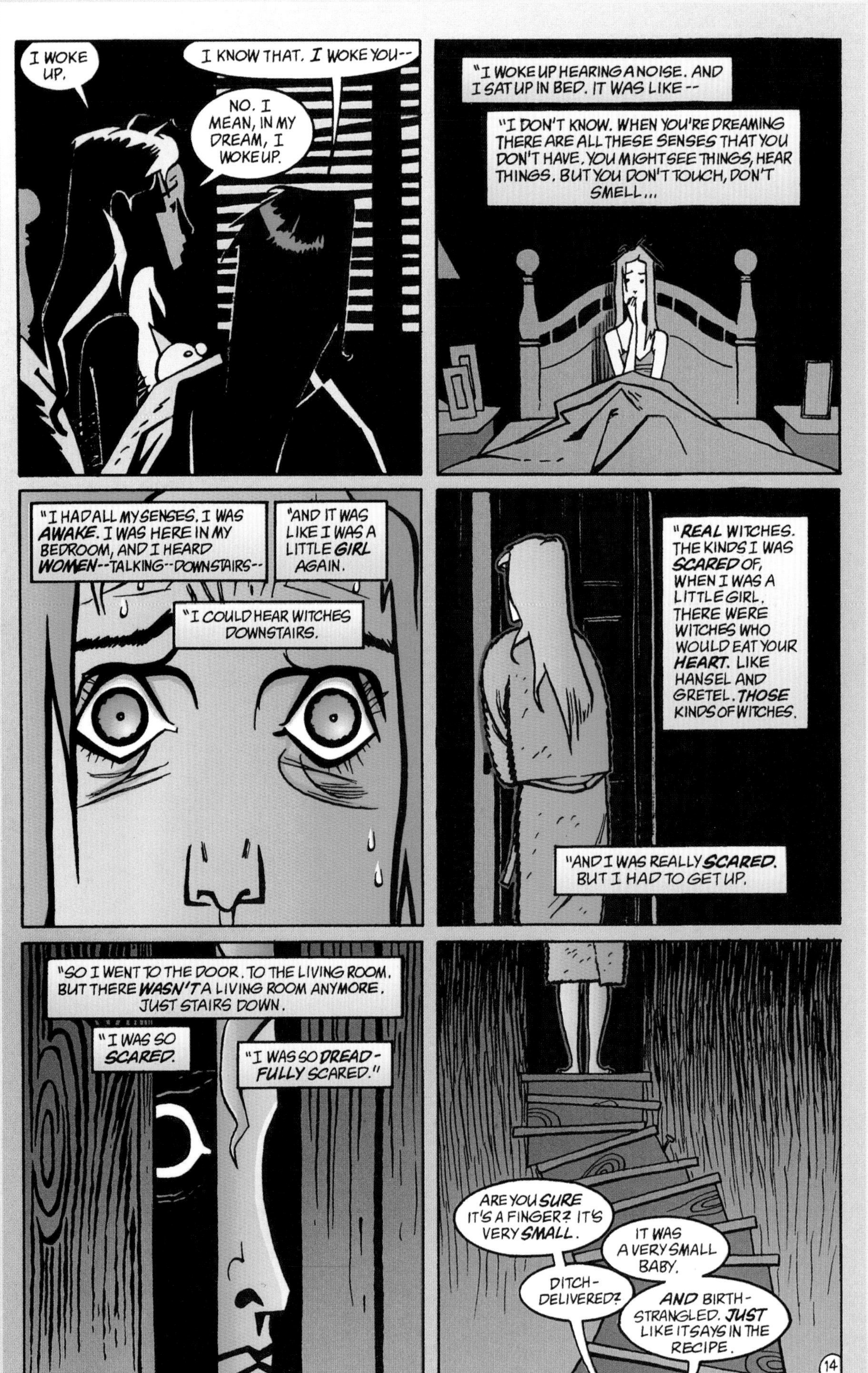
I WOKE UP.
I KNOW THAT. I WOKE YOU--
NO. I MEAN, IN MY DREAM, I WOKE UP.
"I WOKE UP HEARING A NOISE. AND I SAT UP IN BED. IT WAS LIKE --
"I DON'T KNOW. WHEN YOU'RE DREAMING THERE ARE ALL THESE SENSES THAT YOU DON'T HAVE. YOU MIGHT SEE THINGS, HEAR THINGS. BUT YOU DON'T TOUCH, DON'T SMELL...
"I HAD ALL MY SENSES. I WAS AWAKE. I WAS HERE IN MY BEDROOM, AND I HEARD WOMEN--TALKING--DOWNSTAIRS--
"AND IT WAS LIKE I WAS A LITTLE GIRL AGAIN.
"I COULD HEAR WITCHES DOWNSTAIRS.
"REAL WITCHES. THE KINDS I WAS SCARED OF, WHEN I WAS A LITTLE GIRL. THERE WERE WITCHES WHO WOULD EAT YOUR HEART. LIKE HANSEL AND GRETEL. THOSE KINDS OF WITCHES.
"AND I WAS REALLY SCARED. BUT I HAD TO GET UP.
"SO I WENT TO THE DOOR. TO THE LIVING ROOM. BUT THERE WASN'T A LIVING ROOM ANYMORE. JUST STAIRS DOWN.
"I WAS SO SCARED.
"I WAS SO DREAD-FULLY SCARED."
ARE YOU SURE IT'S A FINGER? IT'S VERY SMALL.
IT WAS A VERY SMALL BABY.
DITCH-DELIVERED?
AND BIRTH-STRANGLED. JUST LIKE IT SAYS IN THE RECIPE.
14

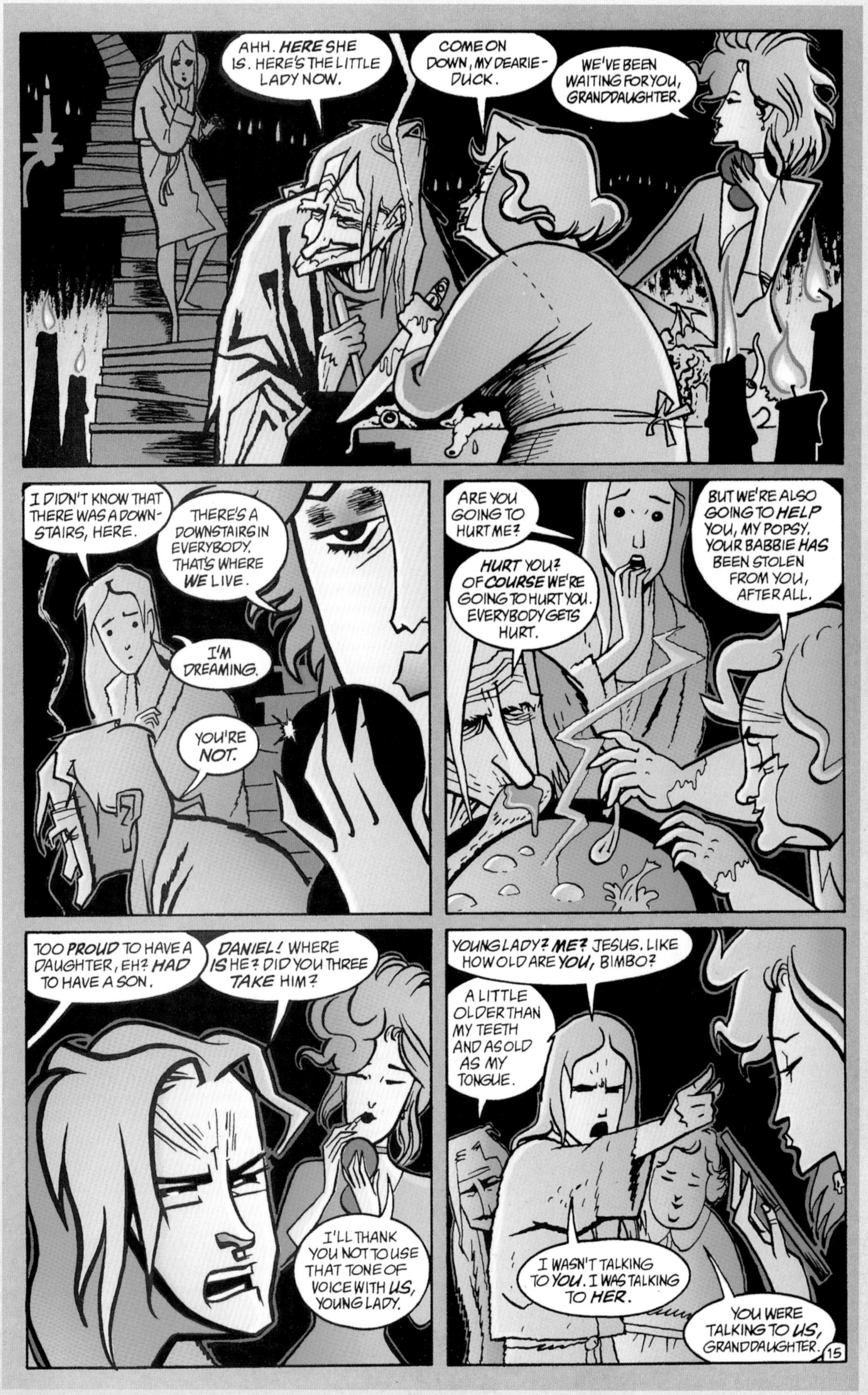
AHH. HERE SHE IS. HERE'S THE LITTLE LADY NOW.
COME ON DOWN, MY DEARIE-DUCK.
WE'VE BEEN WAITING FOR YOU, GRANDDAUGHTER.
I DIDN'T KNOW THAT THERE WAS A DOWNSTAIRS, HERE.
THERE'S A DOWNSTAIRS IN EVERYBODY. THAT'S WHERE WE LIVE.
I'M DREAMING.
YOU'RE NOT.
ARE YOU GOING TO HURT ME?
HURT YOU? OF COURSE WE'RE GOING TO HURT YOU. EVERYBODY GETS HURT.
BUT WE'RE ALSO GOING TO HELP YOU, MY POPSY. YOUR BABBIE HAS BEEN STOLEN FROM YOU, AFTER ALL.
TOO PROUD TO HAVE A DAUGHTER, EH? HAD TO HAVE A SON.
DANIEL! WHERE IS HE? DID YOU THREE TAKE HIM?
I'LL THANK YOU NOT TO USE THAT TONE OF VOICE WITH US, YOUNG LADY.
YOUNG LADY? ME? JESUS. LIKE HOW OLD ARE YOU, BIMBO?
A LITTLE OLDER THAN MY TEETH AND AS OLD AS MY TONGUE.
I WASN'T TALKING TO YOU. I WAS TALKING TO HER.
YOU WERE TALKING TO US, GRANDDAUGHTER.
15

BELOW Marc Hempel's simple, bold lines make this advertisement all the more striking.

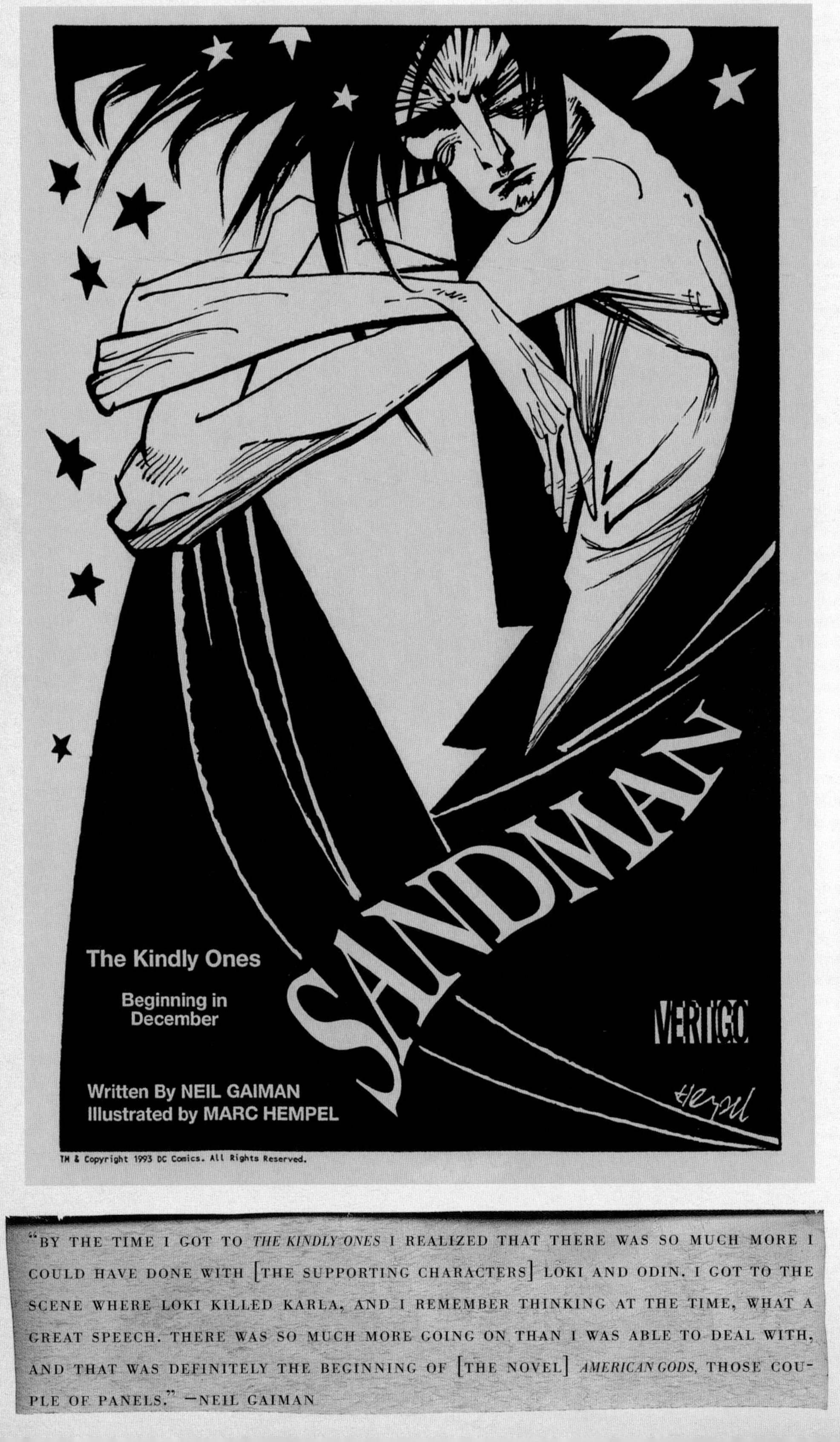
SANDMAN
The Kindly Ones
Beginning in December
VERTIGO
Written By NEIL GAIMAN
Illustrated by MARC HEMPEL
Hempel
TM & Copyright 1993 DC Comics. All Rights Reserved.

"BY THE TIME I GOT TO *THE KINDLY ONES* I REALIZED THAT THERE WAS SO MUCH MORE I COULD HAVE DONE WITH [THE SUPPORTING CHARACTERS] LOKI AND ODIN. I GOT TO THE SCENE WHERE LOKI KILLED KARLA, AND I REMEMBER THINKING AT THE TIME, WHAT A GREAT SPEECH. THERE WAS SO MUCH MORE GOING ON THAN I WAS ABLE TO DEAL WITH, AND THAT WAS DEFINITELY THE BEGINNING OF [THE NOVEL] *AMERICAN GODS*, THOSE COUPLE OF PANELS." —NEIL GAIMAN

BELOW In *The Kindly Ones*, chapter 7, Lyta reveals what she has in store for Dream. Artwork by Marc Hempel. Daniel Vozzo, colorist.

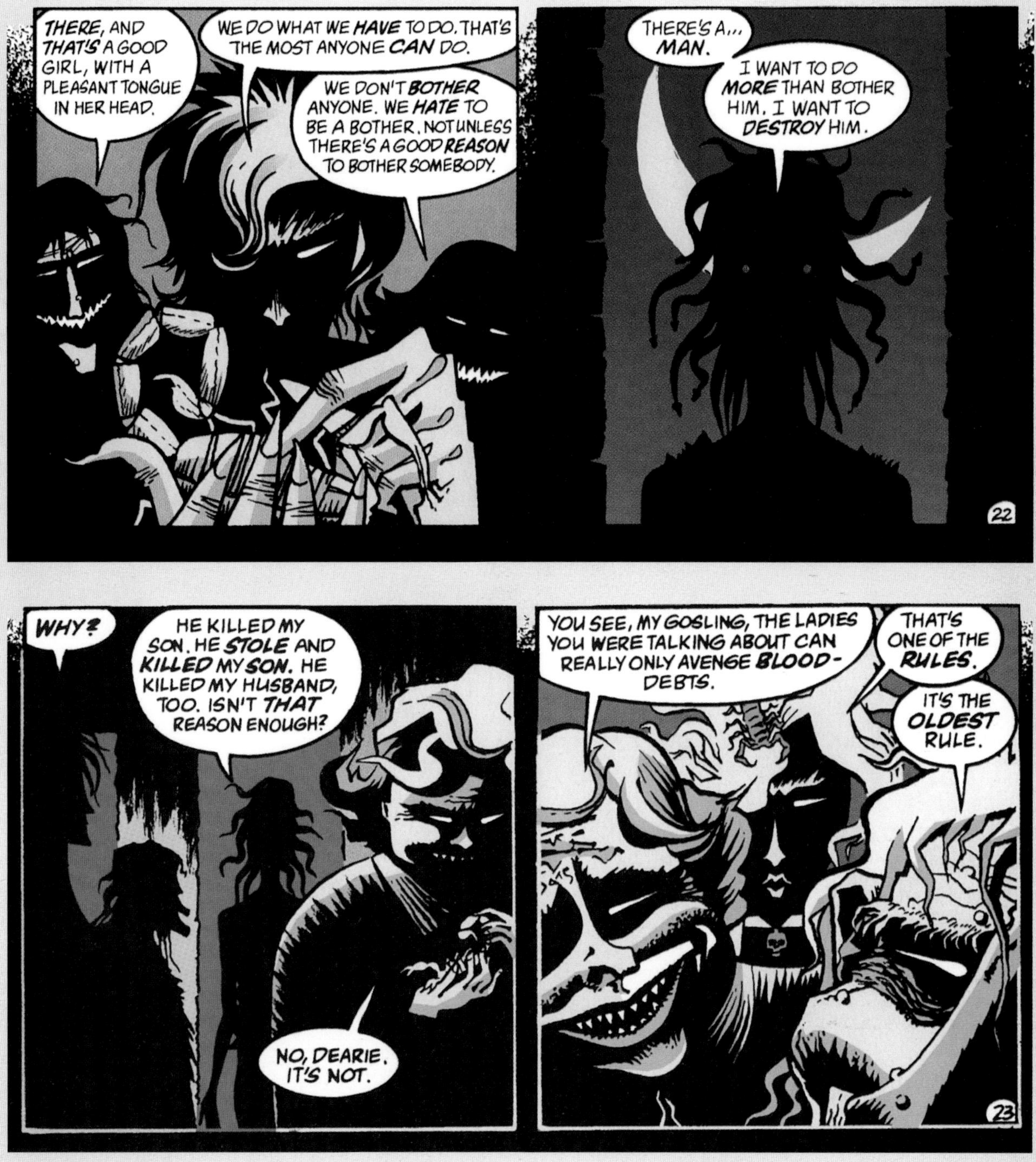
THERE, AND THAT'S A GOOD GIRL, WITH A PLEASANT TONGUE IN HER HEAD.
WE DO WHAT WE HAVE TO DO. THAT'S THE MOST ANYONE CAN DO.
WE DON'T BOTHER ANYONE. WE HATE TO BE A BOTHER. NOT UNLESS THERE'S A GOOD REASON TO BOTHER SOMEBODY.
THERE'S A... MAN.
I WANT TO DO MORE THAN BOTHER HIM. I WANT TO DESTROY HIM.
22
WHY?
HE KILLED MY SON. HE STOLE AND KILLED MY SON. HE KILLED MY HUSBAND, TOO. ISN'T THAT REASON ENOUGH?
NO, DEARIE. IT'S NOT.
YOU SEE, MY GOSLING, THE LADIES YOU WERE TALKING ABOUT CAN REALLY ONLY AVENGE BLOOD-DEBTS.
THAT'S ONE OF THE RULES.
IT'S THE OLDEST RULE.
23

On her quest for vengeance, Lyta makes her way past many female helpers until she comes, at last, to the witchiest of all: the Erinyes, sisters so dread that those who know them take care to call them the Kindly Ones. By the time Lyta arrives at their threshold, her own hair has twined into snakes, and she is less and more than herself. She has surrendered some part of her personality, or possibly her soul: She has gained access to some elemental, archetypal, wildly empowering female rage. Or perhaps a better word for it would be . . . fury.

BELOW Danish artist Teddy Kristiansen, his work shown here, also contributed to *The Kindly Ones'* brilliantly executed art. Daniel Vozzo, colorist.

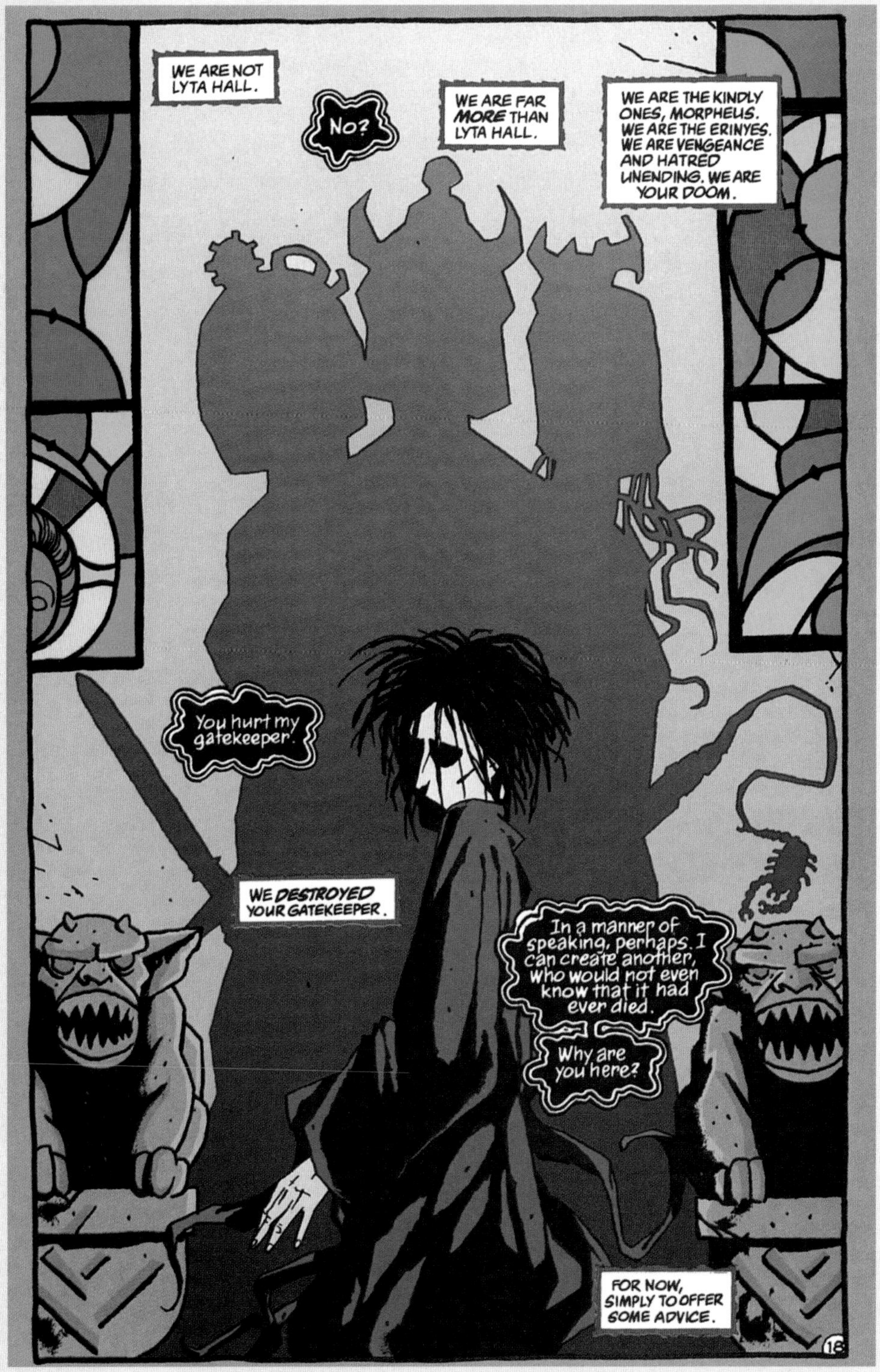
WE ARE NOT LYTA HALL.
No?
WE ARE FAR MORE THAN LYTA HALL.
WE ARE THE KINDLY ONES, MORPHEUS. WE ARE THE ERINYES. WE ARE VENGEANCE AND HATRED UNENDING. WE ARE YOUR DOOM.
You hurt my gatekeeper.
WE DESTROYED YOUR GATEKEEPER.
In a manner of speaking, perhaps. I can create another, who would not even know that it had ever died.
Why are you here?
FOR NOW, SIMPLY TO OFFER SOME ADVICE.
18

Creatively, *The Kindly Ones* operates at a pitch of such intensity that it feels like a high-wire act: At each turning point, you feel that surely now the story will put a foot wrong. A false note will be sounded. But *The Kindly Ones* never falters.

In the end, it is love that betrays Morpheus. His downfall is brought on by the love Lyta bears for her son, the love he rediscovers for his own son, and the love of that long-ago, dangerous gift: the fairy Nuala, who thinks she is saving her lord when she summons him to her side, hoping against hope that she can bind him to her with his promise to grant her one boon. The boon she seeks, of course, is the Sandman's love.

BELOW *The Kindly Ones*, chapter 10. Nuala summons Dream. Artwork by Marc Hempel and Richard Case. Daniel Vozzo, colorist.

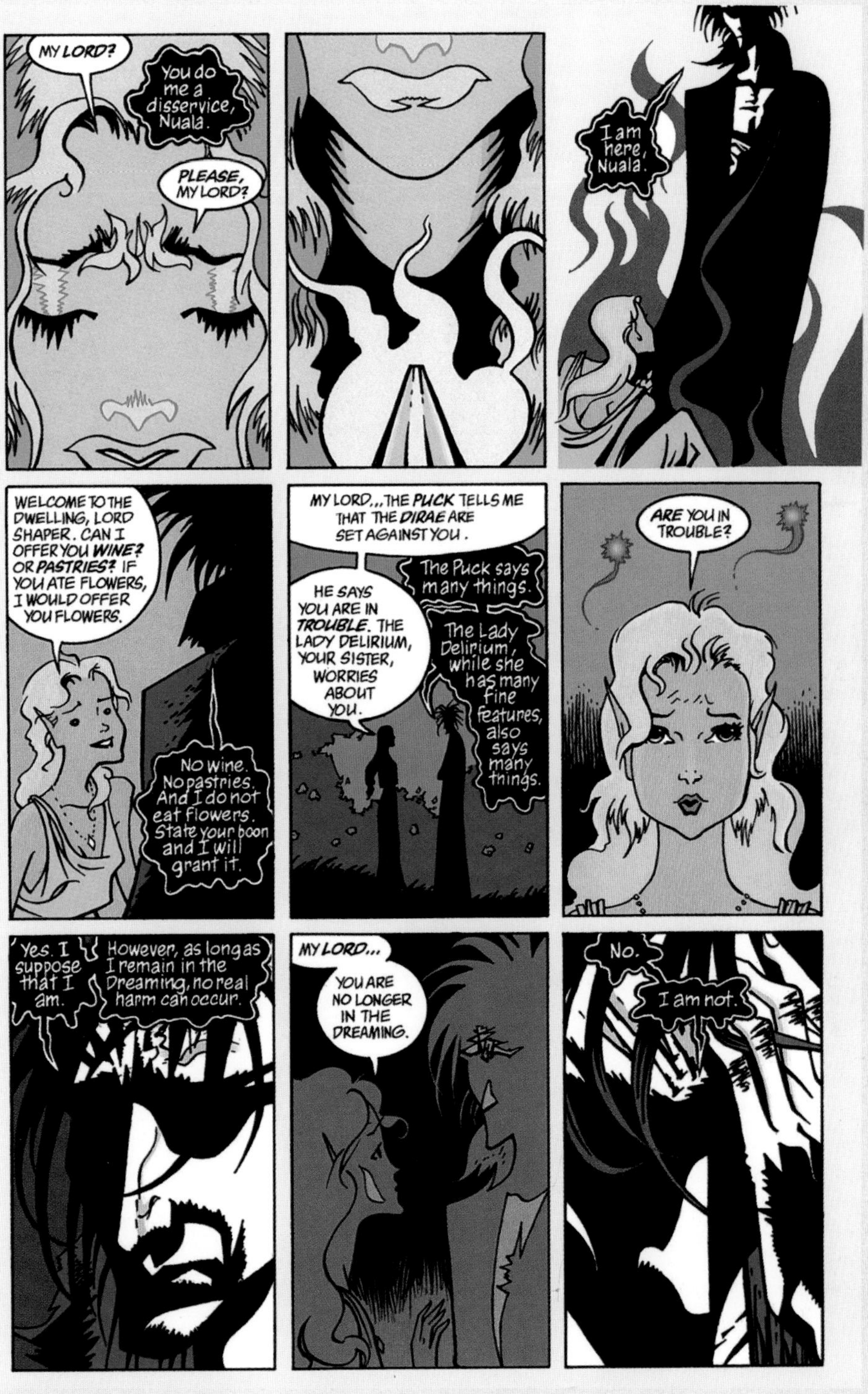
MY LORD?
You do me a disservice, Nuala.
PLEASE, MY LORD?
I am here, Nuala.
WELCOME TO THE DWELLING, LORD SHAPER. CAN I OFFER YOU WINE? OR PASTRIES? IF YOU ATE FLOWERS, I WOULD OFFER YOU FLOWERS.
No wine. No pastries. And I do not eat flowers. State your boon and I will grant it.
MY LORD,,, THE PUCK TELLS ME THAT THE DIRAE ARE SET AGAINST YOU.
The Puck says many things.
HE SAYS YOU ARE IN TROUBLE. THE LADY DELIRIUM, YOUR SISTER, WORRIES ABOUT YOU.
The Lady Delirium, while she has many fine features, also says many things.
ARE YOU IN TROUBLE?
Yes. I suppose that I am.
However, as long as I remain in the Dreaming, no real harm can occur.
MY LORD...
YOU ARE NO LONGER IN THE DREAMING.
No.
I am not.

Throughout the Sandman saga, Morpheus has gained in empathy and tolerance for the gray areas of relationships, but he has also retained a certain rigidity of purpose that is the prerogative of kings. Another word for it is nobility, with all the duties and expectation that word implies. Dream is not his brother Destruction; for him, abdication is not an option..

"The Sandman's flaw," says Neil, "is that he cannot get out of the way. He is a creature of rules and responsibilities. They are the things that empower him and the things that bind him." And so his story ends in tragedy – but really, he wouldn't have wanted it any other way.

BELOW The first page of the final chapter of *The Kindly Ones*. Artwork by Marc Hempel. Daniel Vozzo, colorist.

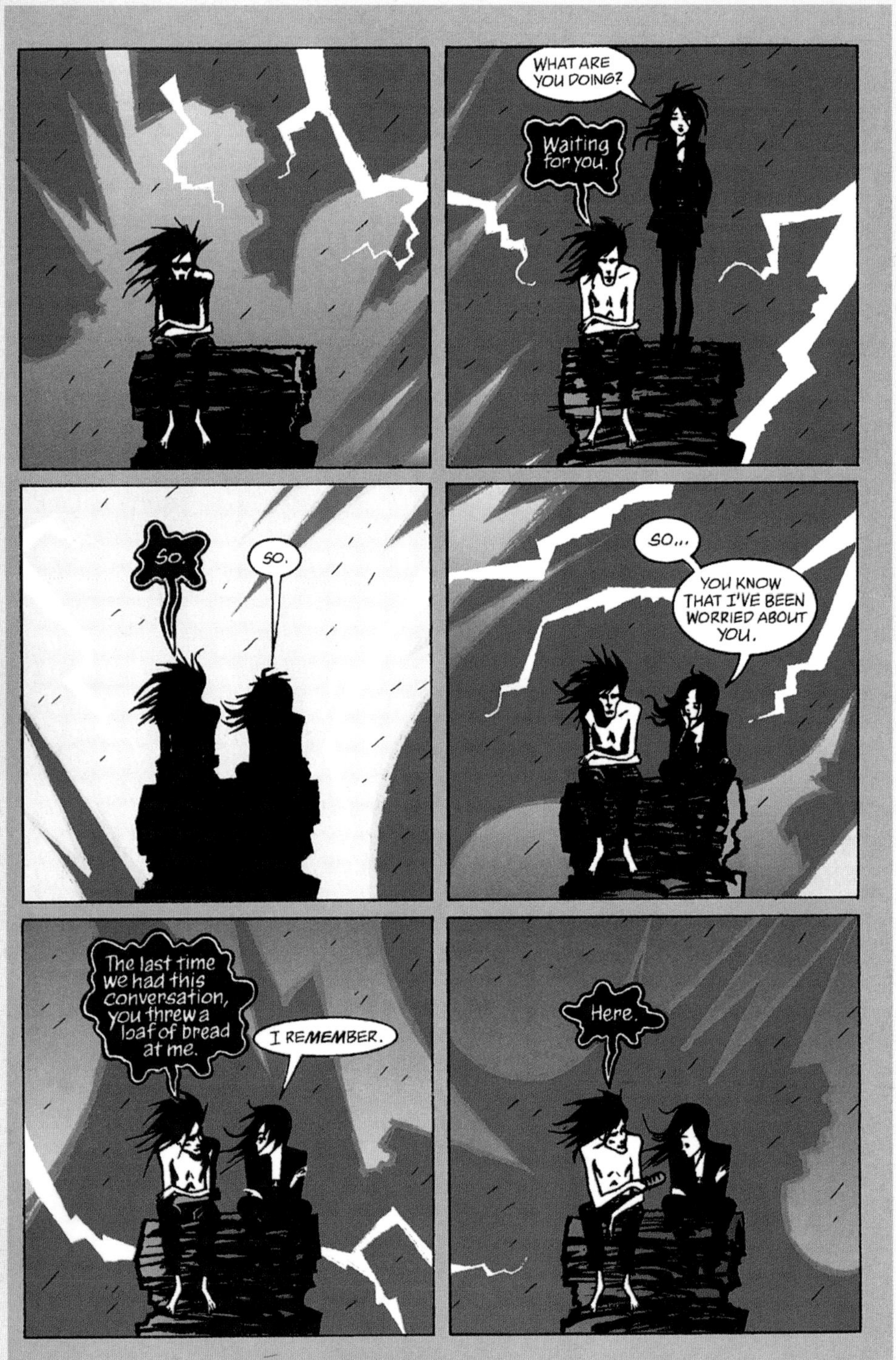
WHAT ARE YOU DOING?
Waiting for you.
So.
SO.
SO...
YOU KNOW THAT I'VE BEEN WORRIED ABOUT YOU.
The last time we had this conversation, you threw a loaf of bread at me.
I REMEMBER.
Here.

Undone by Nuala, the Sandman seems to draw some of his old hauteur back, demanding to know if she thinks his love a gift he can grant. But when Nuala reveals her love for him, Morpheus seems visibly shaken. He offers her what he can, a dream of his love; she tells him that she already possesses this.

In the end, his kingdom ravaged by the Kindly Ones, the Sandman sits alone and waits for the one he has always loved most – his sister, Death.

BELOW Matthew the Raven. Artwork by Michael Zulli.

ALISA KWITNEY: MATTHEW [THE RAVEN] WAS SUPPOSED TO DIE AT THE END OF *THE KINDLY ONES*.

NEIL GAIMAN: YEAH, THAT WAS YOUR FAULT. I JUST REMEMBER TELLING YOU I WAS GOING TO KILL HIM AT THE END OF KINDLY ONES AND YOU SAID, 'PLEASE DON'T. I'VE JUST NAMED MY SON MATTHEW.' THAT WAS THE ONLY TIME A CHARACTER GOT REPRIEVED. AND I ALSO KNEW I WAS GOING TO HAVE A LOT OF READERS SAYING, 'WE DON'T WANT THIS NEW GUY — WE WANT OUR OLD MOODY MORPEHUS.' I WANTED SOMEONE WHO COULD SAY THAT, AND MATTHEW HAD ALWAYS BEEN THE VOICE OF THE READER, WHOSE FUNCTION IT WAS TO SOMETIMES SAY, 'WHAT THE HELL IS GOING ON HERE?'

PAGES 154–155 Daniel transforms into the new Dream in *The Kindly Ones*, chapter 13. Artwork by Marc Hempel. Daniel Vozzo, colorist.

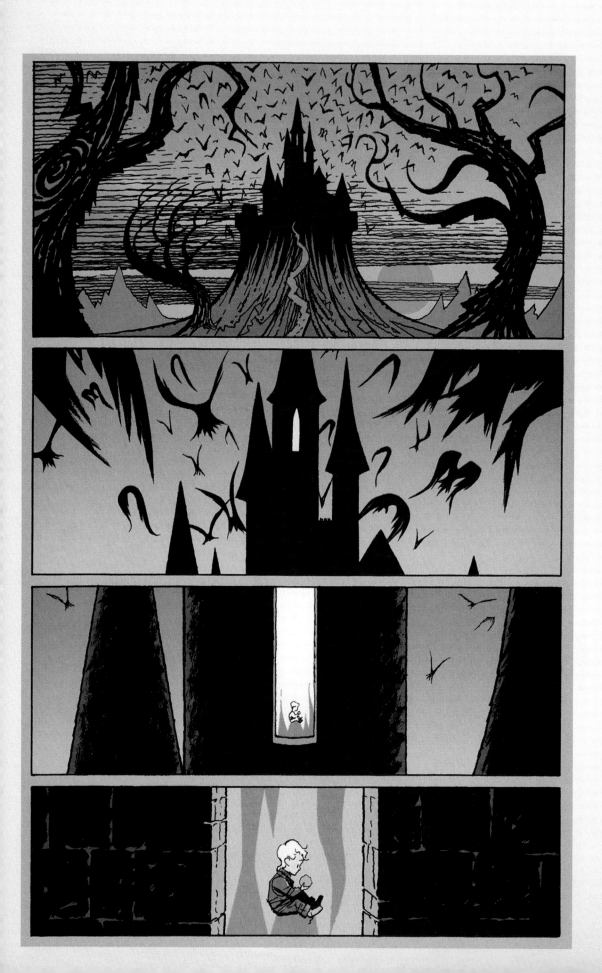

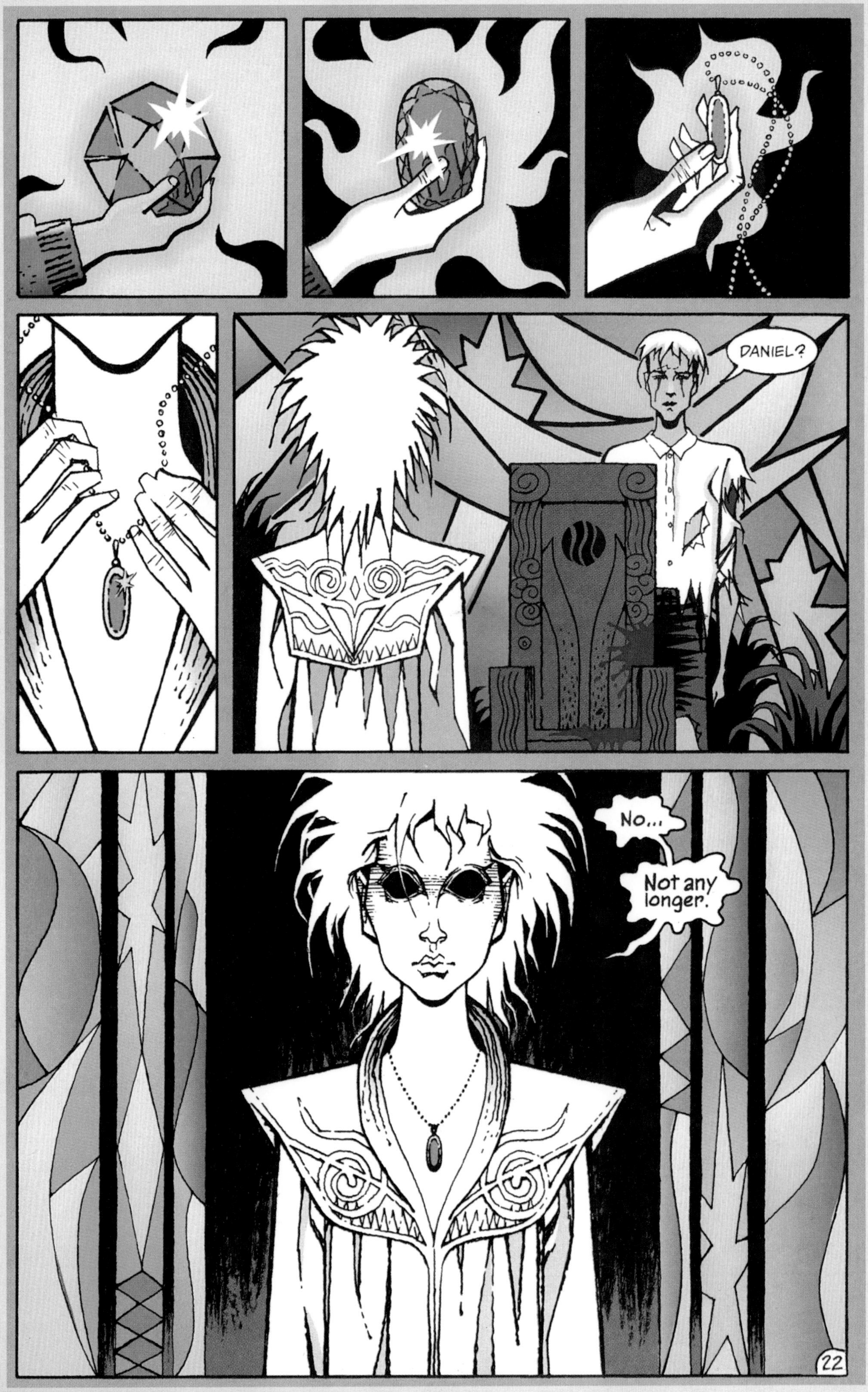
DANIEL?
No...
Not any longer.
22

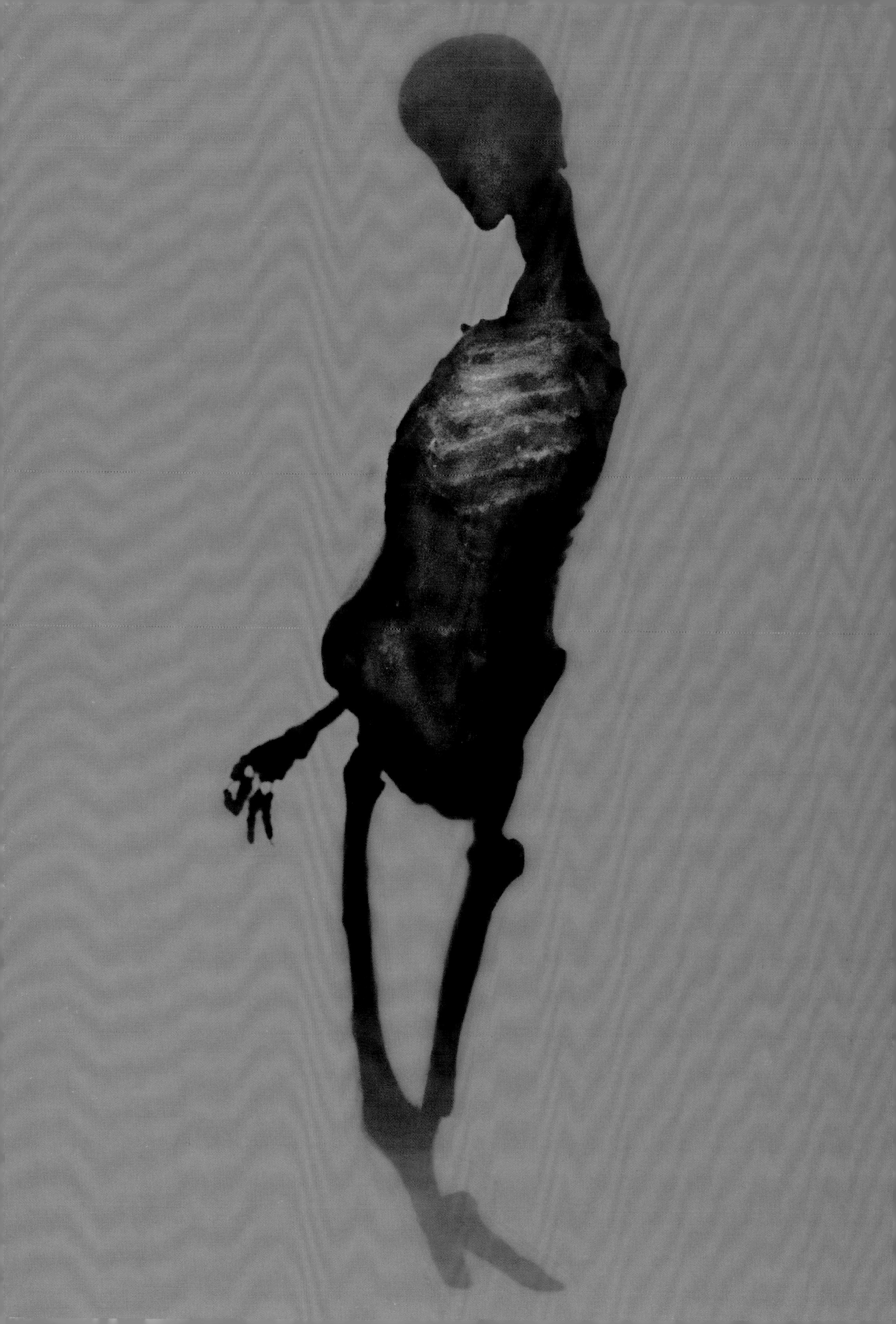

CHAPTER *11*

THE WAKE

IN WHICH WE BID FAREWELL TO AN OLD FRIEND, AND BECOME ACQUAINTED WITH THE NEW KING OF DREAMS.

Where *The Kindly Ones* is dark, *The Wake* is light; where *The Kindly Ones* is iconographic, *The Wake* is naturalistic; and where *The Kindly Ones* is fraught with tension, *The Wake* is somber, stately, an elegy in pencils for an unforgettable character and series.

Daniel, conceived in the realm of dreams – in a way conceived *of* dreams – is the obvious heir to Morpheus's throne. And though he has been transfigured from a baby into something that looks very much like Morpheus, it becomes clear that the new Dream is not Morpheus when he sees Lyta Hall. "Daniel?" she asks. "No," he replies. "What was mortal of Daniel was burned away: What was immortal was . . . transfigured." Again, disbelieving, Lyta reaches out her hands, a grieving mother who has lost her infant and now stands face to face with a young man who wears his face. "Daniel?" "No," says the new Dream. "I am sorry. Not Daniel." And then, instead of taking vengeance, he embraces her and puts his mark on her to protect her from any who would do her harm. This is the Dream of a new faith, as it were; this is a Dream who believes in forgiveness.

So what exactly is the new Dream's relationship to Daniel? According to Neil, that of an Oak tree to an Acorn. The baby Daniel was the seed; the new Dream is that promise come to fruition.

PAGE 156 Cover, *The Sandman* no. 73. Artwork by Dave McKean.

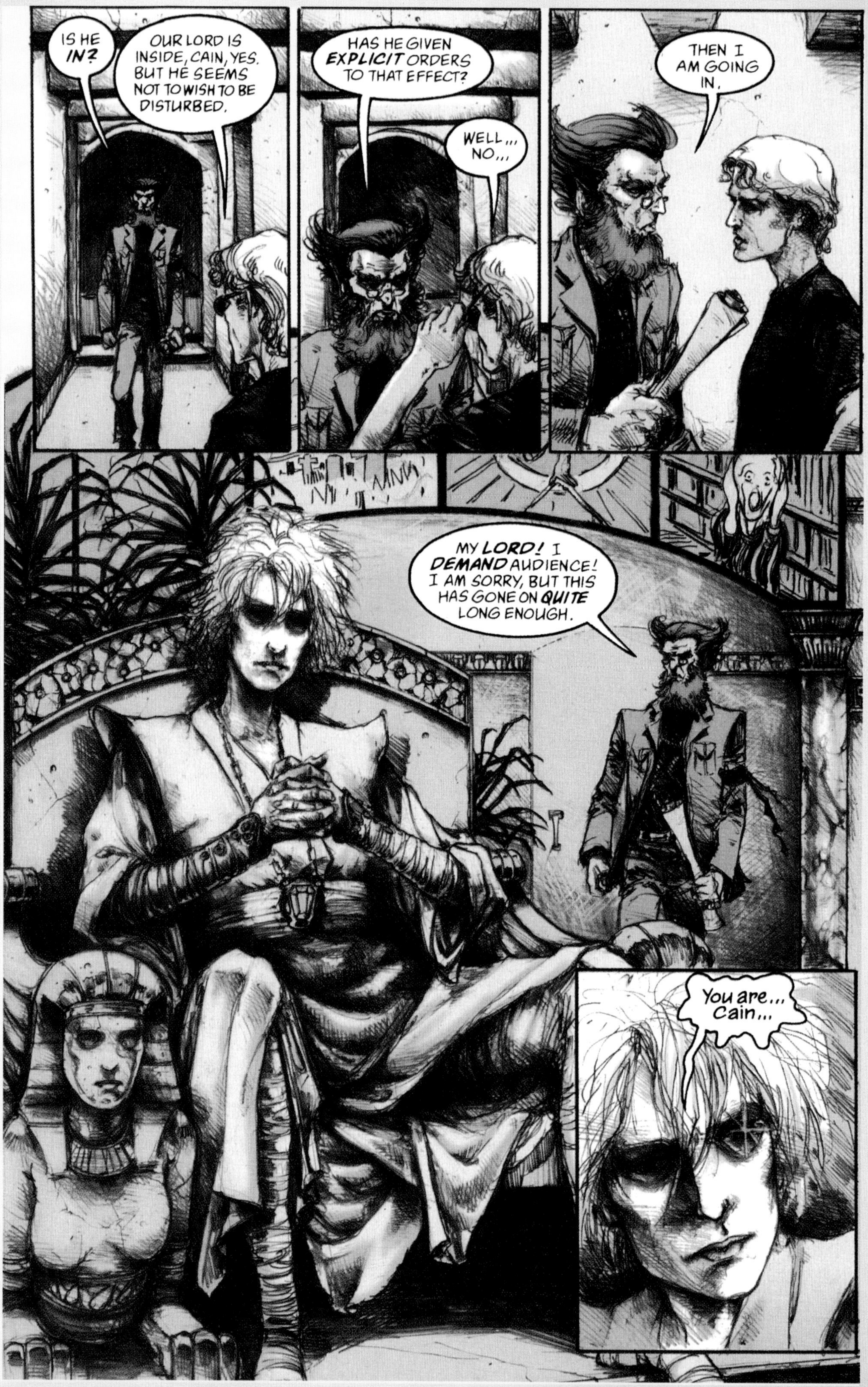
IS HE IN?
OUR LORD IS INSIDE, CAIN, YES. BUT HE SEEMS NOT TO WISH TO BE DISTURBED.
HAS HE GIVEN EXPLICIT ORDERS TO THAT EFFECT?
WELL... NO...
THEN I AM GOING IN.
MY LORD! I DEMAND AUDIENCE! I AM SORRY, BUT THIS HAS GONE ON QUITE LONG ENOUGH.
You are... Cain...

PAGE 158 Michael Zulli is a superb penciler whose delicate pencils are not best served by the need for his art to be reinterpreted in ink. His talent shines here as his remarkable line work, long admired in the editorial offices, finally sees the light of day. Artwork by Michael Zulli. Daniel Vozzo, colorist. PAGES 159–161 Dream's funeral procession: Note Death's red dress; the Chinese boy, surely Nada's new incarnation; and Orpheus as figurehead for the funeral barge. Artwork by Michael Zulli. Daniel Vozzo, colorist.

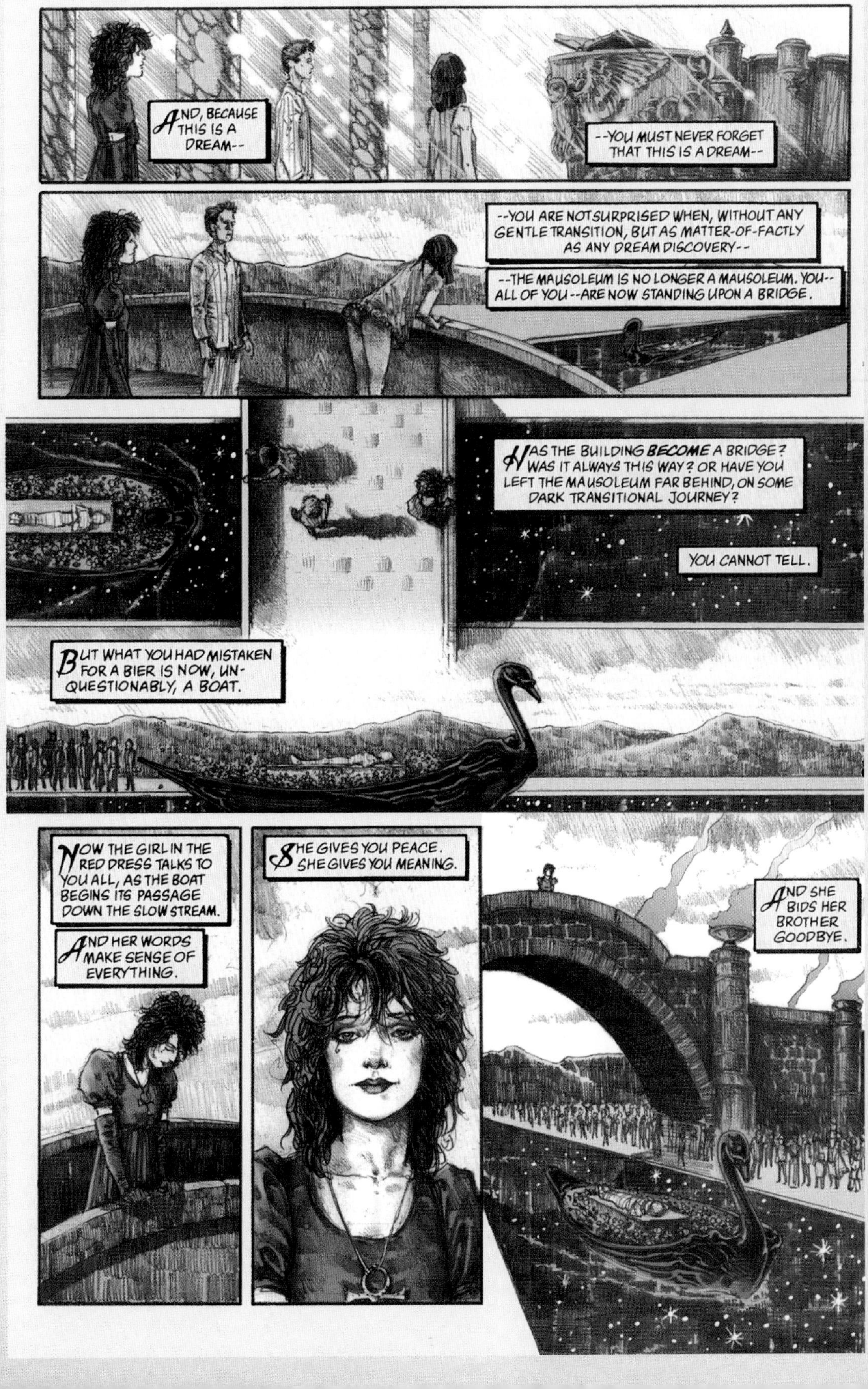
AND, BECAUSE THIS IS A DREAM--
--YOU MUST NEVER FORGET THAT THIS IS A DREAM--
--YOU ARE NOT SURPRISED WHEN, WITHOUT ANY GENTLE TRANSITION, BUT AS MATTER-OF-FACTLY AS ANY DREAM DISCOVERY--
--THE MAUSOLEUM IS NO LONGER A MAUSOLEUM. YOU--ALL OF YOU--ARE NOW STANDING UPON A BRIDGE.
HAS THE BUILDING BECOME A BRIDGE? WAS IT ALWAYS THIS WAY? OR HAVE YOU LEFT THE MAUSOLEUM FAR BEHIND, ON SOME DARK TRANSITIONAL JOURNEY?
YOU CANNOT TELL.
BUT WHAT YOU HAD MISTAKEN FOR A BIER IS NOW, UNQUESTIONABLY, A BOAT.
NOW THE GIRL IN THE RED DRESS TALKS TO YOU ALL, AS THE BOAT BEGINS ITS PASSAGE DOWN THE SLOW STREAM.
AND HER WORDS MAKE SENSE OF EVERYTHING.
SHE GIVES YOU PEACE. SHE GIVES YOU MEANING.
AND SHE BIDS HER BROTHER GOODBYE.

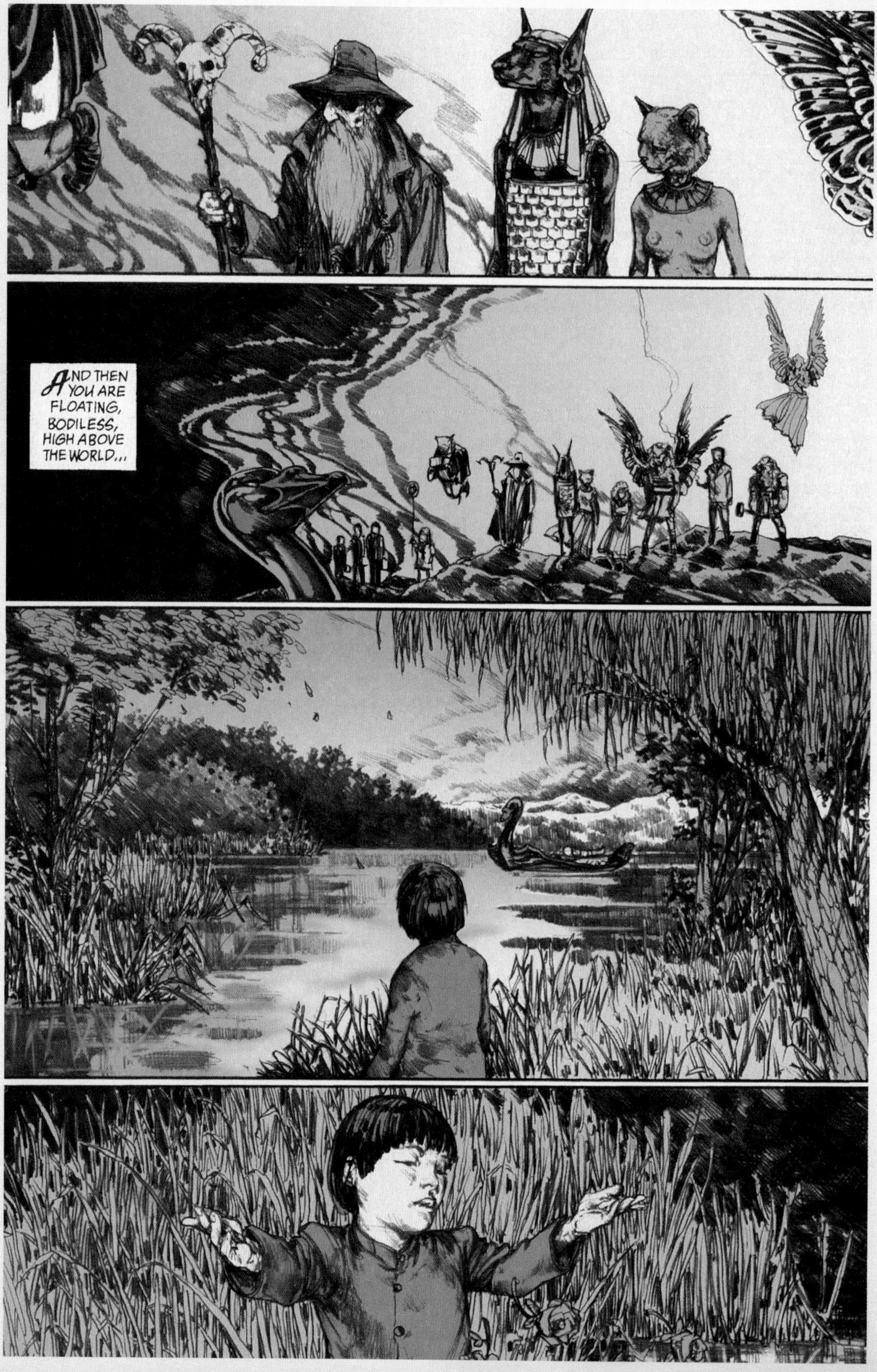
AND THEN YOU ARE FLOATING, BODILESS, HIGH ABOVE THE WORLD...

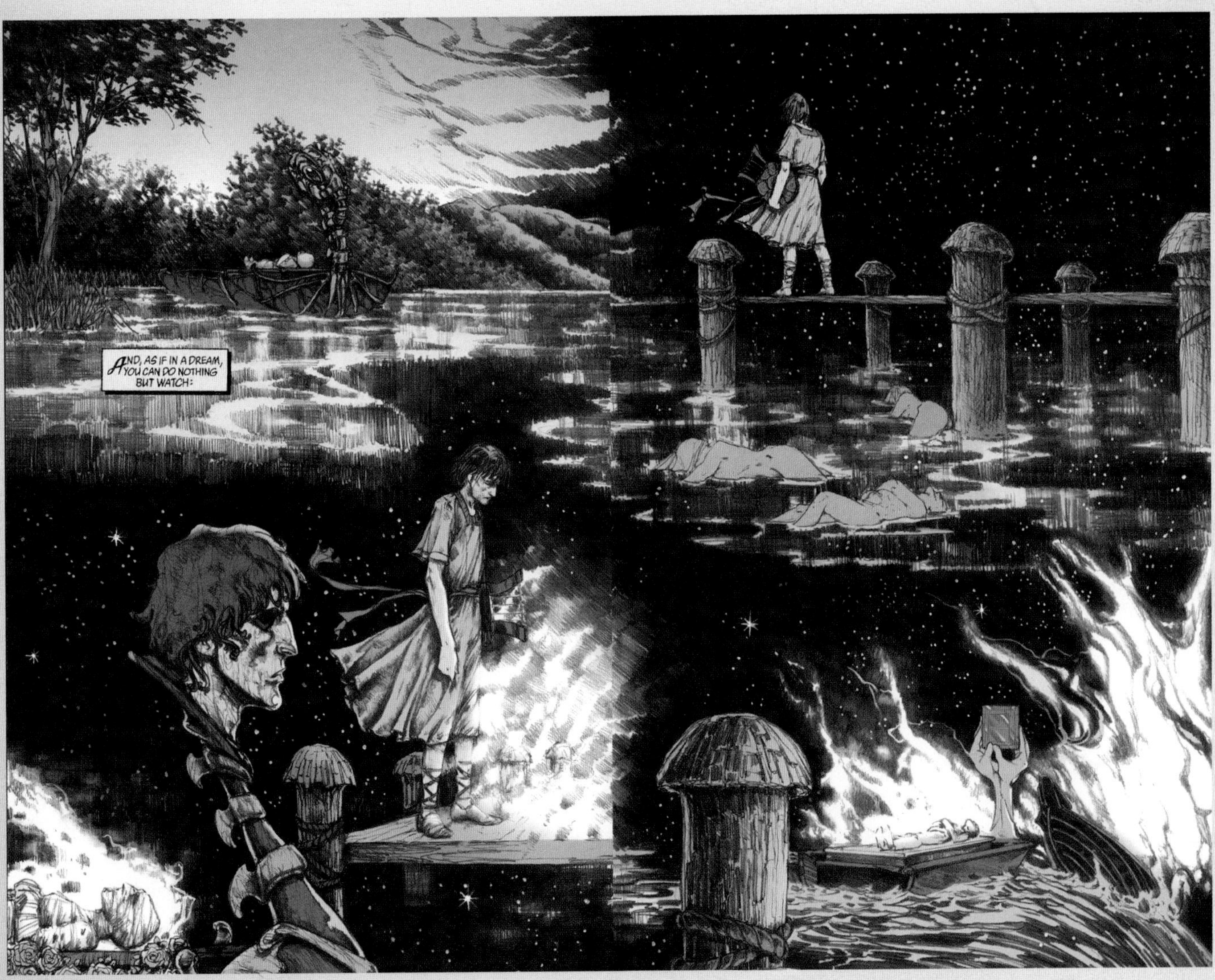
AND, AS IF IN A DREAM, YOU CAN DO NOTHING BUT WATCH:

BELOW A young Dream, not so much pale as luminous, sits and waits as worlds of dreamers mourn his predecessor in the second chapter of *The Wake*. Artwork by Michael Zulli.

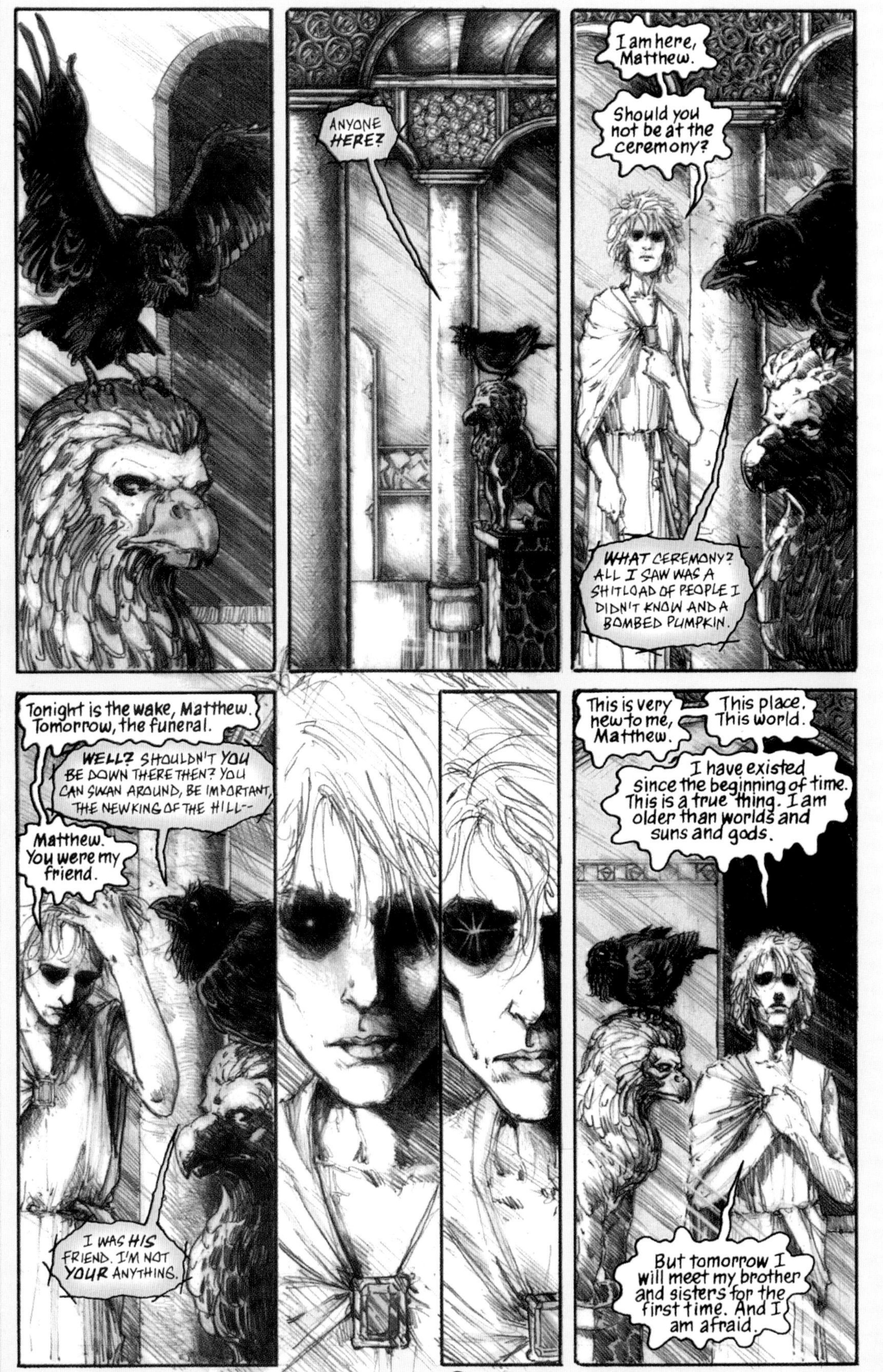
ANYONE HERE?
I am here, Matthew.
Should you not be at the ceremony?
WHAT CEREMONY? ALL I SAW WAS A SHITLOAD OF PEOPLE I DIDN'T KNOW AND A BOMBED PUMPKIN.
Tonight is the wake, Matthew. Tomorrow, the funeral.
WELL? SHOULDN'T YOU BE DOWN THERE THEN? YOU CAN SWAN AROUND, BE IMPORTANT, THE NEW KING OF THE HILL--
Matthew. You were my friend.
I WAS HIS FRIEND. I'M NOT YOUR ANYTHING.
This is very new to me, Matthew.
This place. This world.
I have existed since the beginning of time. This is a true thing. I am older than worlds and suns and gods.
But tomorrow I will meet my brother and sisters for the first time. And I am afraid.
49

PAGES 163–164 Death and Hob discuss – death. From *The Wake's* "Sunday Mourning." Artwork by Michael Zulli. Daniel Vozzo, colorist.

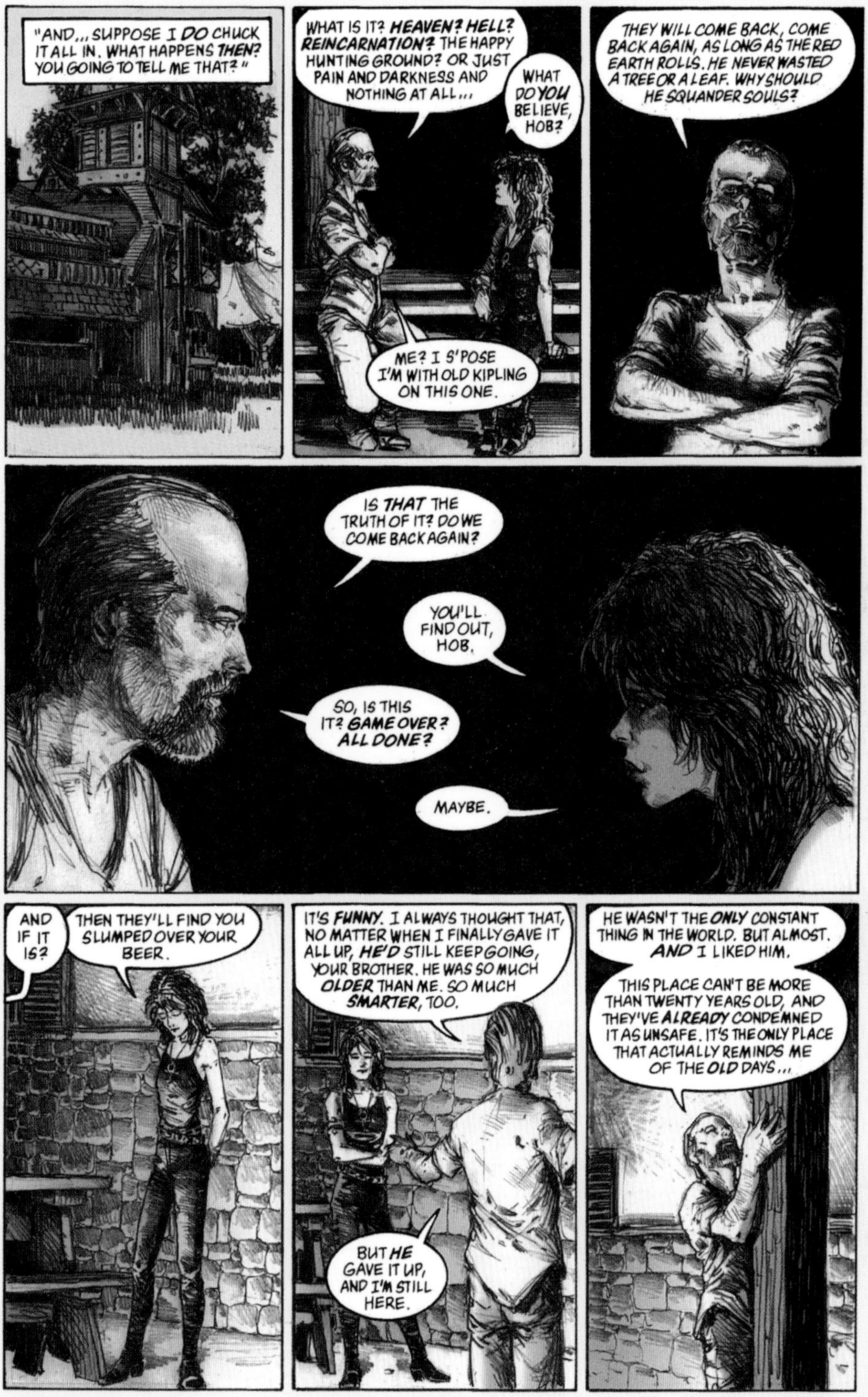
"AND,,, SUPPOSE I DO CHUCK IT ALL IN. WHAT HAPPENS THEN? YOU GOING TO TELL ME THAT?"
WHAT IS IT? HEAVEN? HELL? REINCARNATION? THE HAPPY HUNTING GROUND? OR JUST PAIN AND DARKNESS AND NOTHING AT ALL...
WHAT DO YOU BELIEVE, HOB?
ME? I S'POSE I'M WITH OLD KIPLING ON THIS ONE.
THEY WILL COME BACK, COME BACK AGAIN, AS LONG AS THE RED EARTH ROLLS. HE NEVER WASTED A TREE OR A LEAF. WHY SHOULD HE SQUANDER SOULS?
IS THAT THE TRUTH OF IT? DO WE COME BACK AGAIN?
YOU'LL FIND OUT, HOB.
SO, IS THIS IT? GAME OVER? ALL DONE?
MAYBE.
AND IF IT IS?
THEN THEY'LL FIND YOU SLUMPED OVER YOUR BEER.
IT'S FUNNY. I ALWAYS THOUGHT THAT, NO MATTER WHEN I FINALLY GAVE IT ALL UP, HE'D STILL KEEP GOING, YOUR BROTHER. HE WAS SO MUCH OLDER THAN ME. SO MUCH SMARTER, TOO.
BUT HE GAVE IT UP, AND I'M STILL HERE.
HE WASN'T THE ONLY CONSTANT THING IN THE WORLD. BUT ALMOST. AND I LIKED HIM.
THIS PLACE CAN'T BE MORE THAN TWENTY YEARS OLD, AND THEY'VE ALREADY CONDEMNED IT AS UNSAFE. IT'S THE ONLY PLACE THAT ACTUALLY REMINDS ME OF THE OLD DAYS...

With the old Dream dead, you would think there would be little material left to include in this collection. On the contrary, some of *The Sandman*'s finest moments occur after Morpheus's departure. There is the bittersweet tale of Hob Gadling's misadventures at a Renaissance festival; there is Jon J Muth's Chinese tale, "Exiles" ("But I have had dreams about dreams about dreams"); and there is the final chapter, "The Tempest."

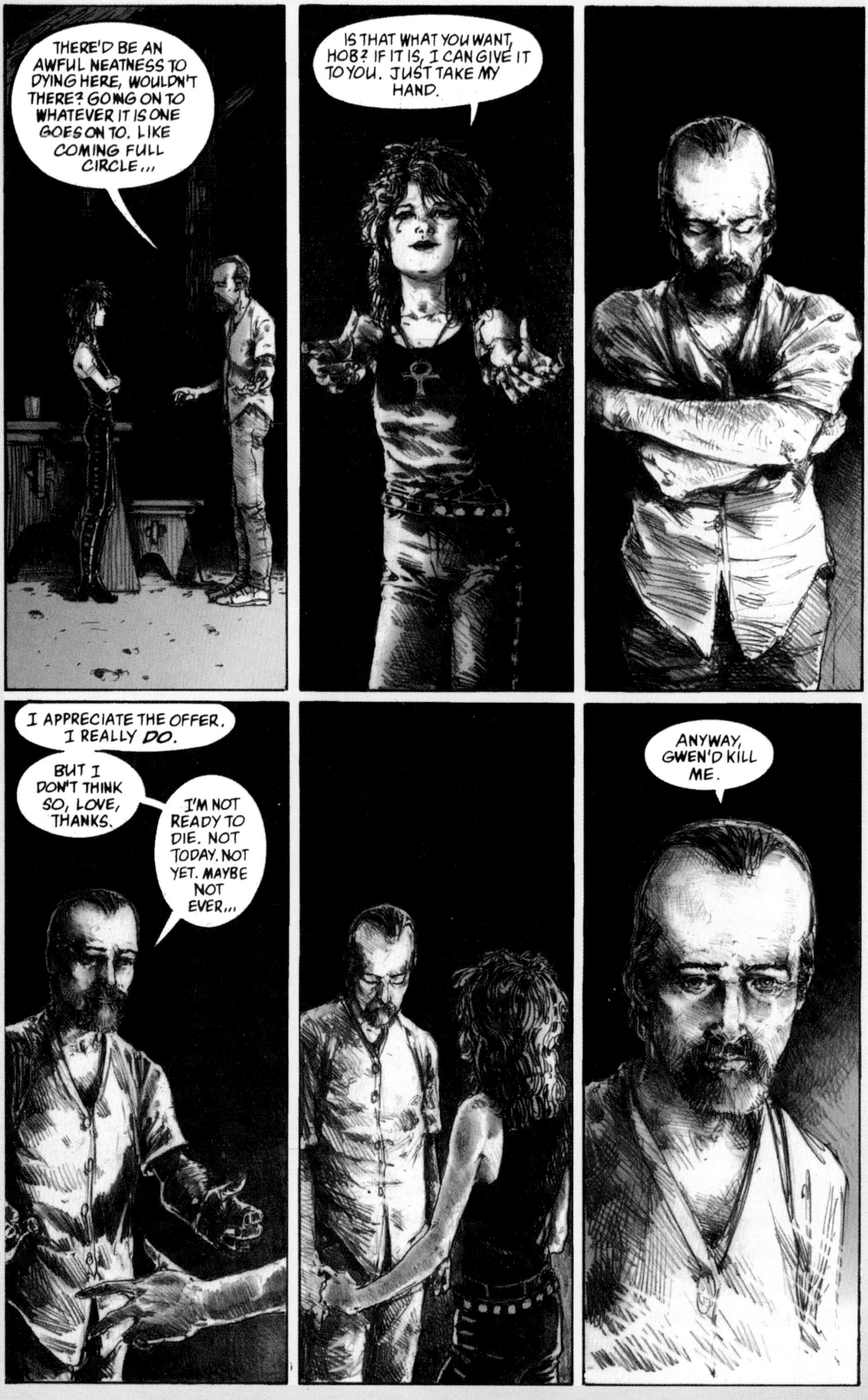
THERE'D BE AN AWFUL NEATNESS TO DYING HERE, WOULDN'T THERE? GOING ON TO WHATEVER IT IS ONE GOES ON TO. LIKE COMING FULL CIRCLE...
IS THAT WHAT YOU WANT, HOB? IF IT IS, I CAN GIVE IT TO YOU. JUST TAKE MY HAND.
I APPRECIATE THE OFFER. I REALLY DO.
BUT I DON'T THINK SO, LOVE, THANKS.
I'M NOT READY TO DIE. NOT TODAY. NOT YET. MAYBE NOT EVER...
ANYWAY, GWEN'D KILL ME.

BELOW "Exiles," shown here, pre- and post-dates Morpheus's demise, as does "The Tempest." Artwork by Jon J Muth.

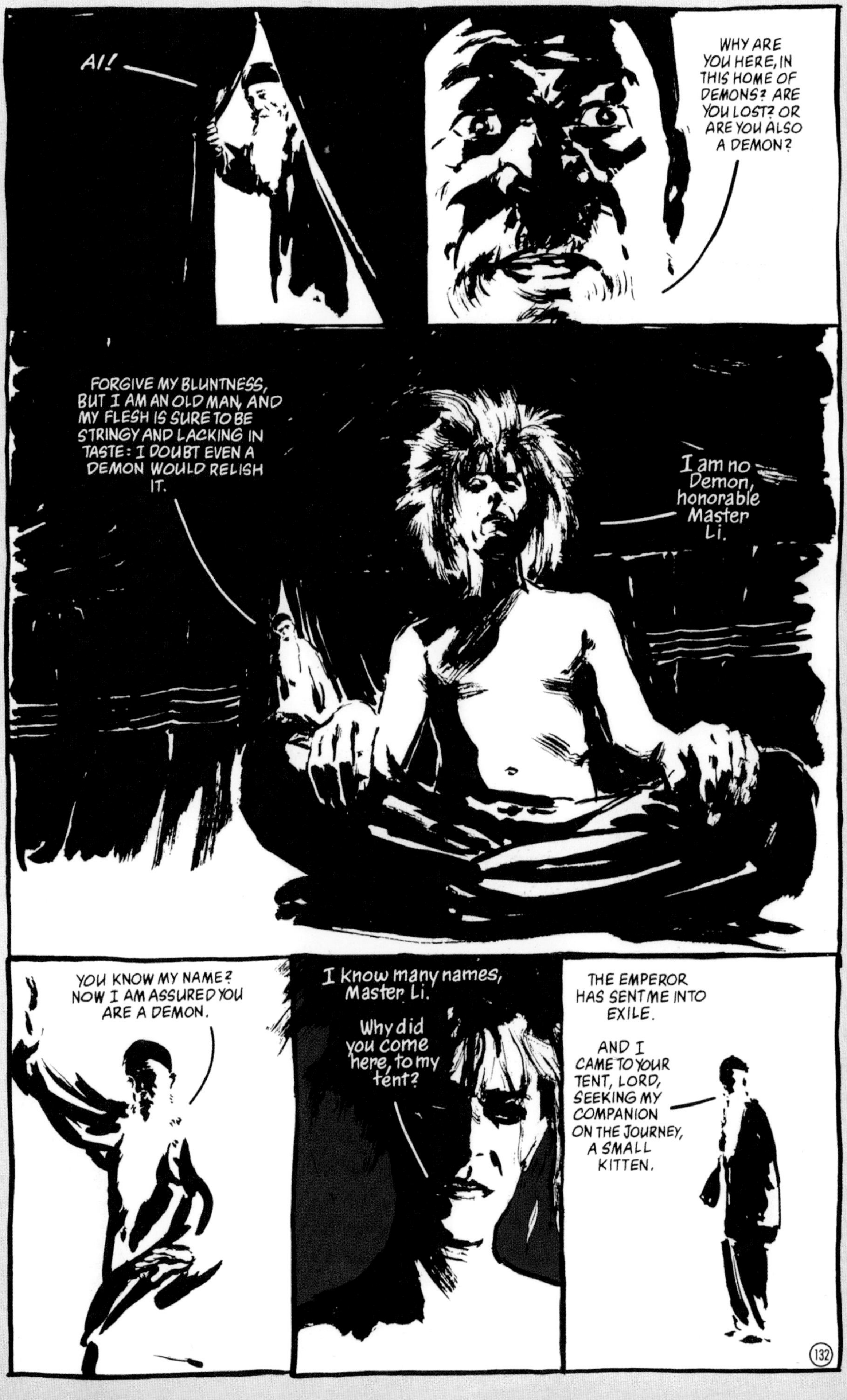
AI!
WHY ARE YOU HERE, IN THIS HOME OF DEMONS? ARE YOU LOST? OR ARE YOU ALSO A DEMON?
FORGIVE MY BLUNTNESS, BUT I AM AN OLD MAN, AND MY FLESH IS SURE TO BE STRINGY AND LACKING IN TASTE: I DOUBT EVEN A DEMON WOULD RELISH IT.
I am no Demon, honorable Master Li.
YOU KNOW MY NAME? NOW I AM ASSURED YOU ARE A DEMON.
I know many names, Master Li.
Why did you come here, to my tent?
THE EMPEROR HAS SENT ME INTO EXILE.
AND I CAME TO YOUR TENT, LORD, SEEKING MY COMPANION ON THE JOURNEY, A SMALL KITTEN.
132

PAGES 166–167 Will Shakespeare in conversation with Dream. From "The Tempest," the final monthly issue of *The Sandman*. Artwork by Charles Vess and John Ridgway. Daniel Vozzo, colorist.

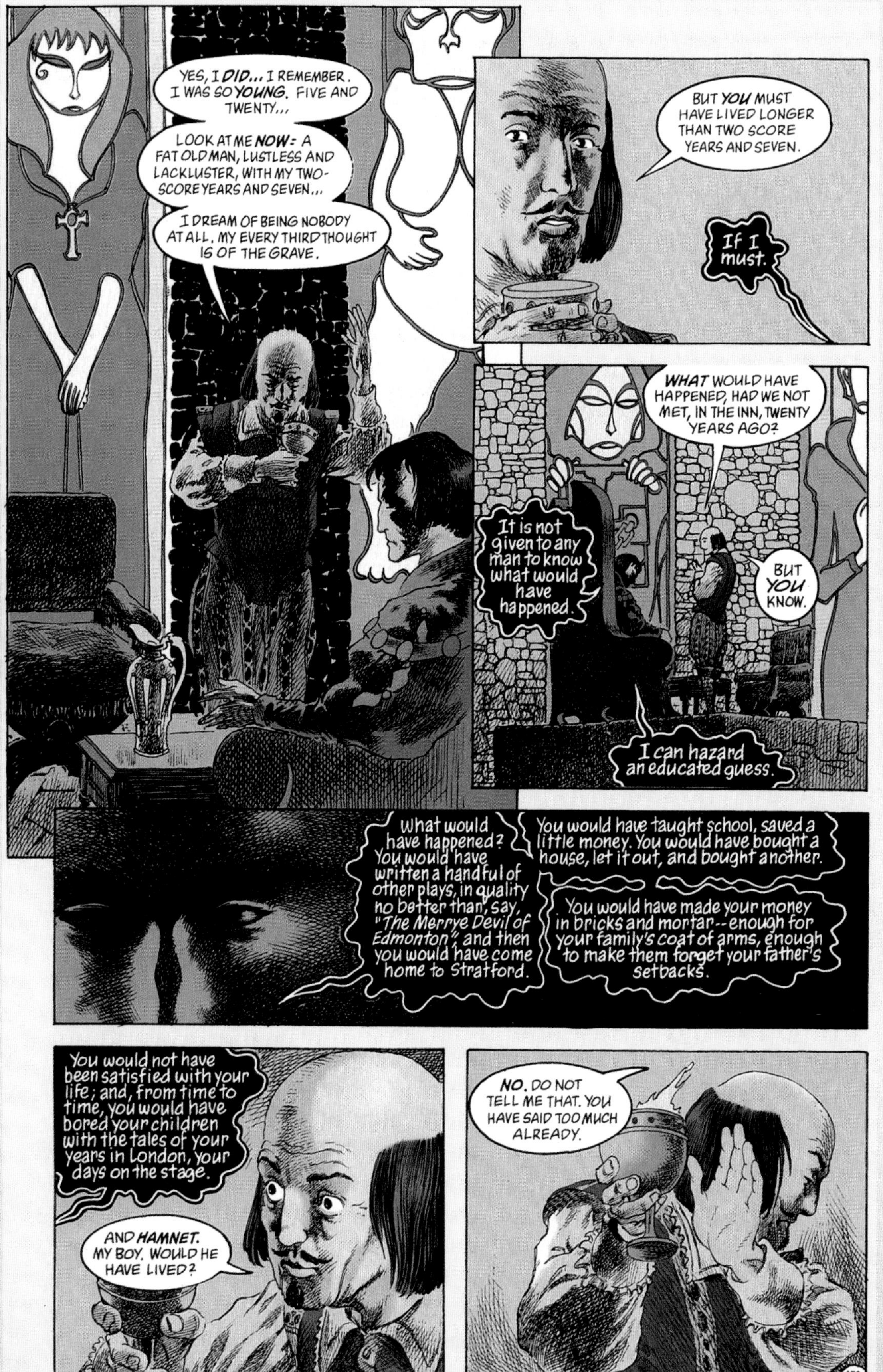
YES, I DID... I REMEMBER. I WAS SO YOUNG. FIVE AND TWENTY...
LOOK AT ME NOW: A FAT OLD MAN, LUSTLESS AND LACKLUSTER, WITH MY TWO-SCORE YEARS AND SEVEN...
I DREAM OF BEING NOBODY AT ALL. MY EVERY THIRD THOUGHT IS OF THE GRAVE.
BUT YOU MUST HAVE LIVED LONGER THAN TWO SCORE YEARS AND SEVEN.
If I must.
WHAT WOULD HAVE HAPPENED, HAD WE NOT MET, IN THE INN, TWENTY YEARS AGO?
It is not given to any man to know what would have happened.
BUT YOU KNOW.
I can hazard an educated guess.
What would have happened? You would have written a handful of other plays, in quality no better than, say, "The Merrye Devil of Edmonton", and then you would have come home to Stratford.
You would have taught school, saved a little money. You would have bought a house, let it out, and bought another.
You would have made your money in bricks and mortar--enough for your family's coat of arms, enough to make them forget your father's setbacks.
You would not have been satisfied with your life; and, from time to time, you would have bored your children with the tales of your years in London, your days on the stage.
AND HAMNET. MY BOY. WOULD HE HAVE LIVED?
NO. DO NOT TELL ME THAT. YOU HAVE SAID TOO MUCH ALREADY.
179

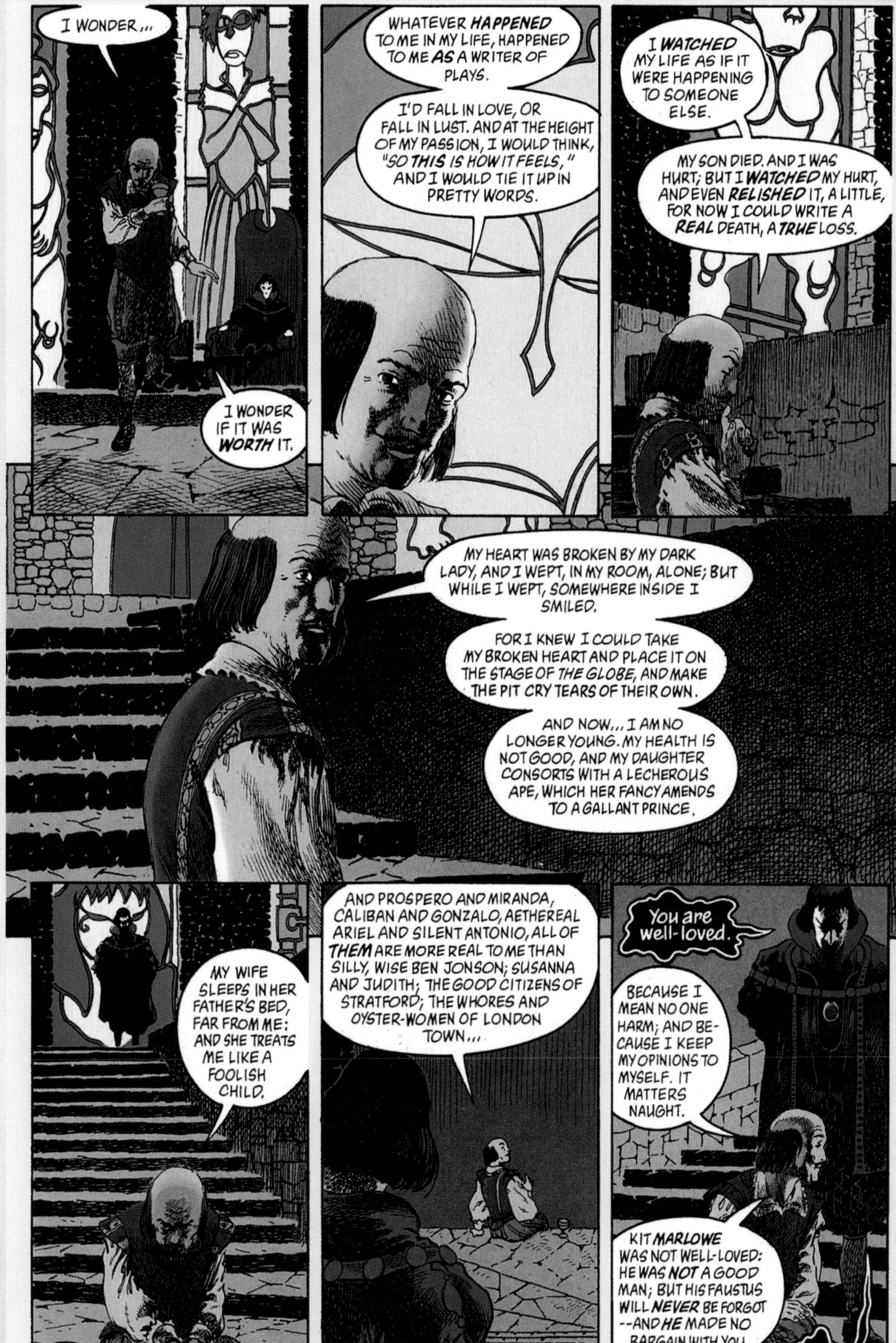

I WONDER...
I WONDER IF IT WAS WORTH IT.
WHATEVER HAPPENED TO ME IN MY LIFE, HAPPENED TO ME AS A WRITER OF PLAYS.
I'D FALL IN LOVE, OR FALL IN LUST. AND AT THE HEIGHT OF MY PASSION, I WOULD THINK, "SO THIS IS HOW IT FEELS," AND I WOULD TIE IT UP IN PRETTY WORDS.
I WATCHED MY LIFE AS IF IT WERE HAPPENING TO SOMEONE ELSE.
MY SON DIED. AND I WAS HURT; BUT I WATCHED MY HURT, AND EVEN RELISHED IT, A LITTLE, FOR NOW I COULD WRITE A REAL DEATH, A TRUE LOSS.
MY HEART WAS BROKEN BY MY DARK LADY, AND I WEPT, IN MY ROOM, ALONE; BUT WHILE I WEPT, SOMEWHERE INSIDE I SMILED.
FOR I KNEW I COULD TAKE MY BROKEN HEART AND PLACE IT ON THE STAGE OF THE GLOBE, AND MAKE THE PIT CRY TEARS OF THEIR OWN.
AND NOW... I AM NO LONGER YOUNG. MY HEALTH IS NOT GOOD, AND MY DAUGHTER CONSORTS WITH A LECHEROUS APE, WHICH HER FANCY AMENDS TO A GALLANT PRINCE.
MY WIFE SLEEPS IN HER FATHER'S BED, FAR FROM ME: AND SHE TREATS ME LIKE A FOOLISH CHILD.
AND PROSPERO AND MIRANDA, CALIBAN AND GONZALO, AETHEREAL ARIEL AND SILENT ANTONIO, ALL OF THEM ARE MORE REAL TO ME THAN SILLY, WISE BEN JONSON; SUSANNA AND JUDITH; THE GOOD CITIZENS OF STRATFORD; THE WHORES AND OYSTER-WOMEN OF LONDON TOWN...
You are well-loved.
BECAUSE I MEAN NO ONE HARM; AND BECAUSE I KEEP MY OPINIONS TO MYSELF. IT MATTERS NAUGHT.
KIT MARLOWE WAS NOT WELL-LOVED: HE WAS NOT A GOOD MAN; BUT HIS FAUSTUS WILL NEVER BE FORGOT --AND HE MADE NO BARGAIN WITH YOU.
You think not?
180

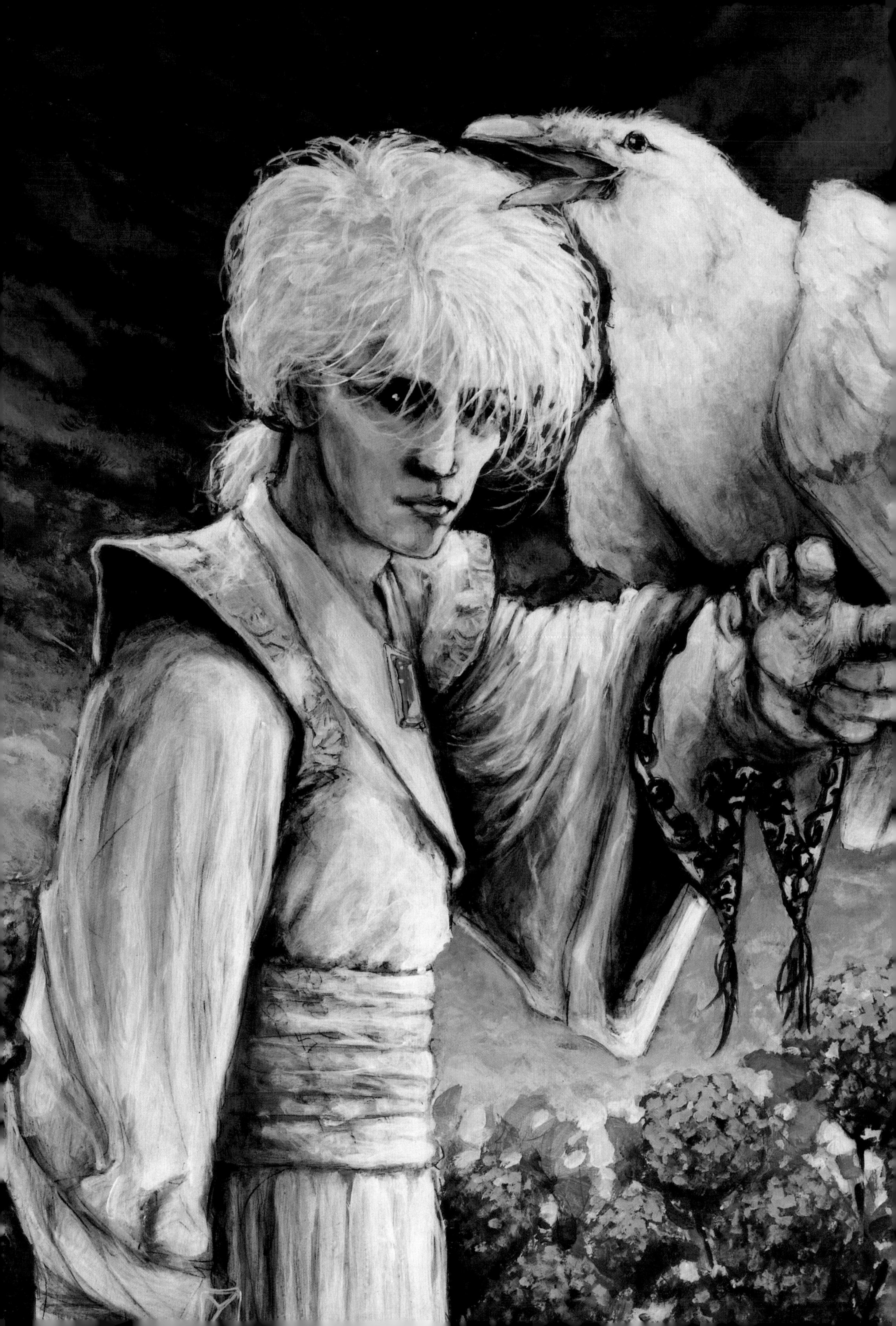

PAGE 168 Daniel and his raven Tethys. An original piece by Michael Zulli. BELOW Dream. Artwork by Charles Vess.

HOB GADLING, LIKE MAD HETTIE, IS A MORTAL WHO HAS LIVED A VERY, VERY LONG TIME. ASKED HOW HE KNOWS SO MUCH ABOUT THESE FOLK, NEIL MAINTAINS THAT HE IS NOT A MEMBER OF THIS SELECT GROUP (REPORTS OF NEIL SIGHTINGS BY THE SURVIVORS OF THE *TITANIC* DISASTER NOTWITHSTANDING): "THE NARRATOR OF ALL THE *SANDMAN* CAPTIONS WHO GOT TO TALK ABOUT THE FACT THAT THERE ARE ONLY A CERTAIN NUMBER OF PEOPLE WHO KNOW WHAT MAMMOTHS SMELL LIKE — THAT GUY IS NOT ME. WHO HE IS I DO NOT KNOW."

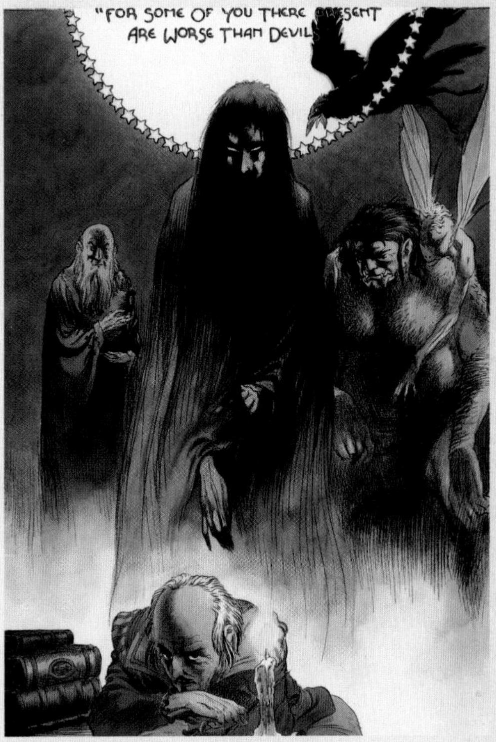
"FOR SOME OF YOU THERE
ARE WORSE THAN DEVIL

In "The Tempest," Neil takes a moment to speak more autobiographically than we have ever seen him do before. It really isn't possible to read Will Shakespeare's lament about the bargain he has made with words and not read something personal into it.

"I *watched* my life as if it were happening to someone else," says Shakespeare, as he wonders if the bargain he made long ago with the Sandman was worth it. And we know, even without Morpheus's implicit reminder, that all writers make bargains, even the ones who don't go around raping the muse.

"Why did you not want a tragedy?" Shakespeare continues. "Something lofty, something dark, a tale of a noble hero with a tragic flaw?" The answer is, Morpheus wanted a tale of graceful ends, of escape. Who wanted the tragedy, then? Presumably, it was us, because that's what we got.

"I am prince of stories," Morpheus tells Shakespeare, "but I have no story of my own." It's a moment of surpassing irony, and Neil Gaiman spent nine years earning every drop of it.

The final line of *The Sandman* series reads, "Neil Gaiman. October 1987–January, 1996." And we readers know that during those years — a good chunk of a working writer's life — Neil Gaiman breathed his gift of life into *The Sandman*.

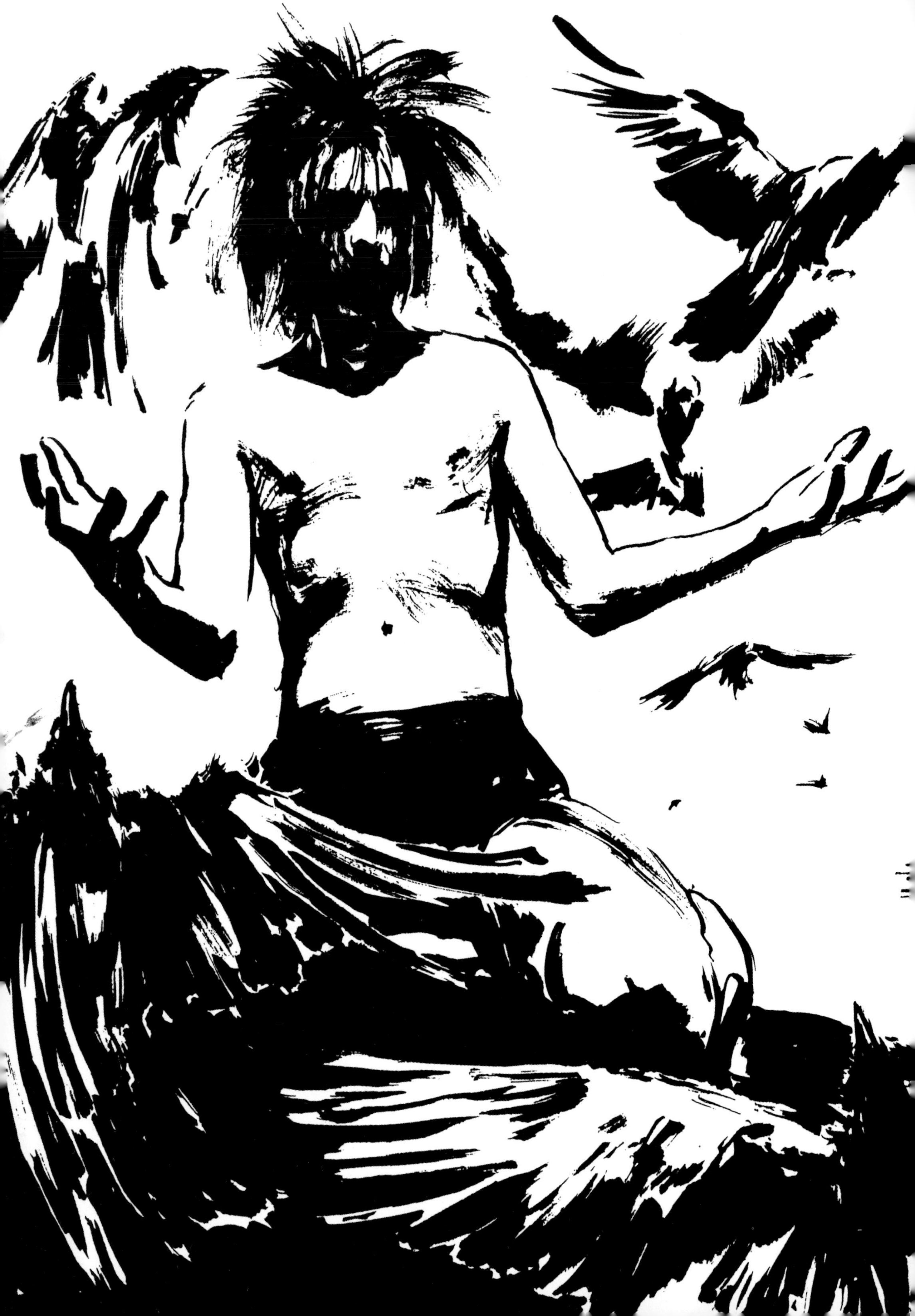

CHAPTER 12

APOCRYPHA

The Sandman's legacy is vast and still growing: There have been two *Death* miniseries written by Neil Gaiman. And other creative teams have utilized the characters – in a *Dreaming* monthly spin-off, a *Lucifer* monthly spin-off, as well as shorter tales of the Corinthian and other *Sandman* characters. (Most of these are now available as collected trade paperbacks.)

And not all of Morpheus's stories have been told, as Neil demonstrated when he collaborated with the internationally acclaimed artist Yoshitaka Amano on *The Dream Hunters*. Published in 1999, this gloriously painted Japanese fable of the Sandman proves that the character has not lost his appeal – neither to audiences nor to his creator, Neil Gaiman.

And Neil has more stories in the works. Coinciding with the tenth anniversary of DC Comics' VERTIGO imprint, *Endless Nights*, a hardcover graphic novel, was released. The book is a collection of stories, each focusing on one member of the Endless. Keeping with the tradition of the series, the artwork for each story has been executed by a separate talent. The roster of high-profile and European artists includes Moebius illustrating a Destiny story, Bill Sienkiewicz illustrating Delirium, Milo Manara illustrating Desire, Miguelanxo Prado illustrating a Sandman story, Barron Storey illustrating Despair, P. Craig Russell illustrating the Death story, and Gaetano Liberatore illustrating Destruction, the cover is by the one and only Dave McKean.

Nearly fifteen years after his release from captivity, Morpheus continues to captivate us, and we have yet to take the full measure of the new king, who says he is not Daniel, but seems to come closer to being mortal than any of his family has before.

PAGE 170 Dream. Artwork by John J Muth.

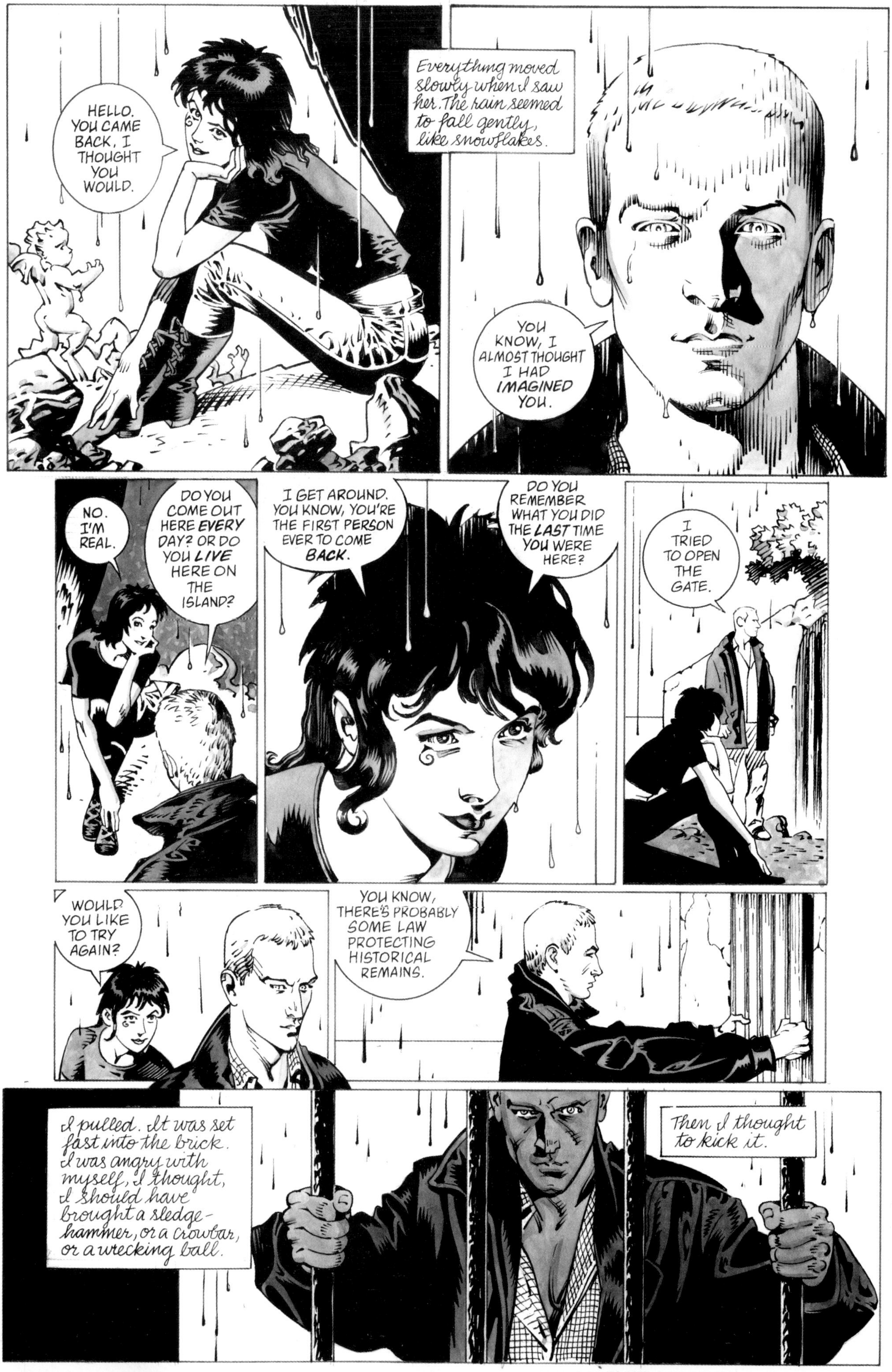
HELLO. YOU CAME BACK, I THOUGHT YOU WOULD.
Everything moved slowly when I saw her. The rain seemed to fall gently, like snowflakes.
YOU KNOW, I ALMOST THOUGHT I HAD IMAGINED YOU.
NO. I'M REAL.
DO YOU COME OUT HERE EVERY DAY? OR DO YOU LIVE HERE ON THE ISLAND?
I GET AROUND. YOU KNOW, YOU'RE THE FIRST PERSON EVER TO COME BACK.
DO YOU REMEMBER WHAT YOU DID THE LAST TIME YOU WERE HERE?
I TRIED TO OPEN THE GATE.
WOULD YOU LIKE TO TRY AGAIN?
YOU KNOW, THERE'S PROBABLY SOME LAW PROTECTING HISTORICAL REMAINS.
I pulled. It was set fast into the brick. I was angry with myself, I thought, I should have brought a sledge-hammer, or a crowbar, or a wrecking ball.
Then I thought to kick it.

page 172 A page by P. Craig Russell's page for Endless Nights. below Miguelanxo Prado's sketches of Death and Desire for Endless Nights.

BELOW The Sandman Library has been translated into twelve different languages in fourteen countries. Shown here is a German edition of *Death*. BELOW RIGHT A sampling of the many *Sandman* merchandise products from DC Direct. PAGE 175 The Japanese edition of *The Sandman: The Dream Hunters*. Artwork by Yoshitaka Amano.

SANDMAN SPECIAL
DEATH - THE TIME OF YOUR LIFE VERTIGO
DEATH - THE TIME OF YOUR LIFE VERTIGO
DEATH
THE TIME OF YOUR LIFE
DIE ZEIT DEINES LEBENS
NEIL GAIMAN
CHRIS BACHALO+MARK BUCKINGHAM+MARK PENNINGTON+DAVE MCKEAN
FeestUSA

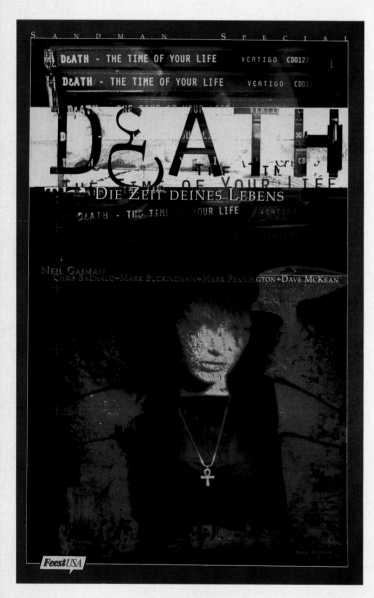

I wonder as I lay this manuscript to rest about all the as-yet-untold stories. Did Charlene ever discover her own tale? What happens next to Lyta Hall, touched by madness, transfigured by the Furies, and marked by Dream? And what of the twelve dreamstones, created long ago – the greatest of which was Morpheus's ruby, and the least of which was an emerald, an eagle stone, which has now become the new Dream's focus of power?

In Lucien's library in the Dreaming are all the titles of all the books never written. Let us hope they disappear one by one and take shape here, in the waking world. There aren't enough stories of the sort that keep this tired reader up late at night, holding off one sort of dream – with another.

the SANDMAN
サンドマン
Neil Gaiman / Yoshitaka Amano
夢の狩人
ニール・ゲイマン◎作
夢枕 獏◎訳
天野喜孝◎画
The Dream Hunters
VERTIGO
DC COMICS

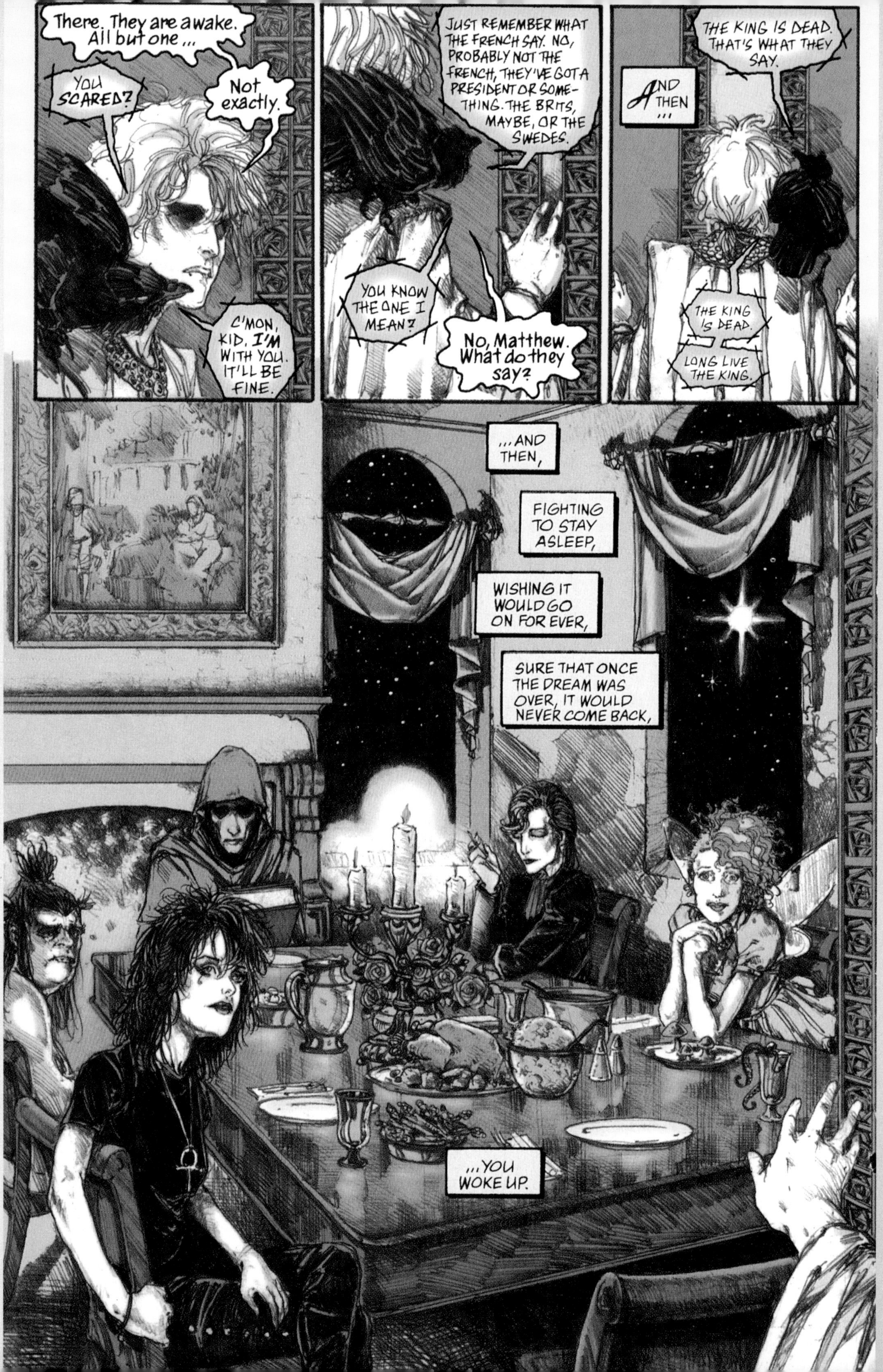
There. They are awake. All but one...
YOU SCARED?
Not exactly.
C'MON, KID. I'M WITH YOU. IT'LL BE FINE.
JUST REMEMBER WHAT THE FRENCH SAY. NO, PROBABLY NOT THE FRENCH, THEY'VE GOT A PRESIDENT OR SOMETHING. THE BRITS, MAYBE, OR THE SWEDES.
YOU KNOW THE ONE I MEAN?
No, Matthew. What do they say?
THE KING IS DEAD. THAT'S WHAT THEY SAY.
AND THEN...
THE KING IS DEAD.
LONG LIVE THE KING.
...AND THEN,
FIGHTING TO STAY ASLEEP,
WISHING IT WOULD GO ON FOR EVER,
SURE THAT ONCE THE DREAM WAS OVER, IT WOULD NEVER COME BACK,
...YOU WOKE UP.

PAGE 176 The new Dream meets the family. Artwork by Michael Zulli. Daniel Vozzo, colorist. BELOW As with all myths and legends, when you get to the end, there's only one thing to do – start at the beginning again. In-house promotional poster. Artwork by Michael Zulli.

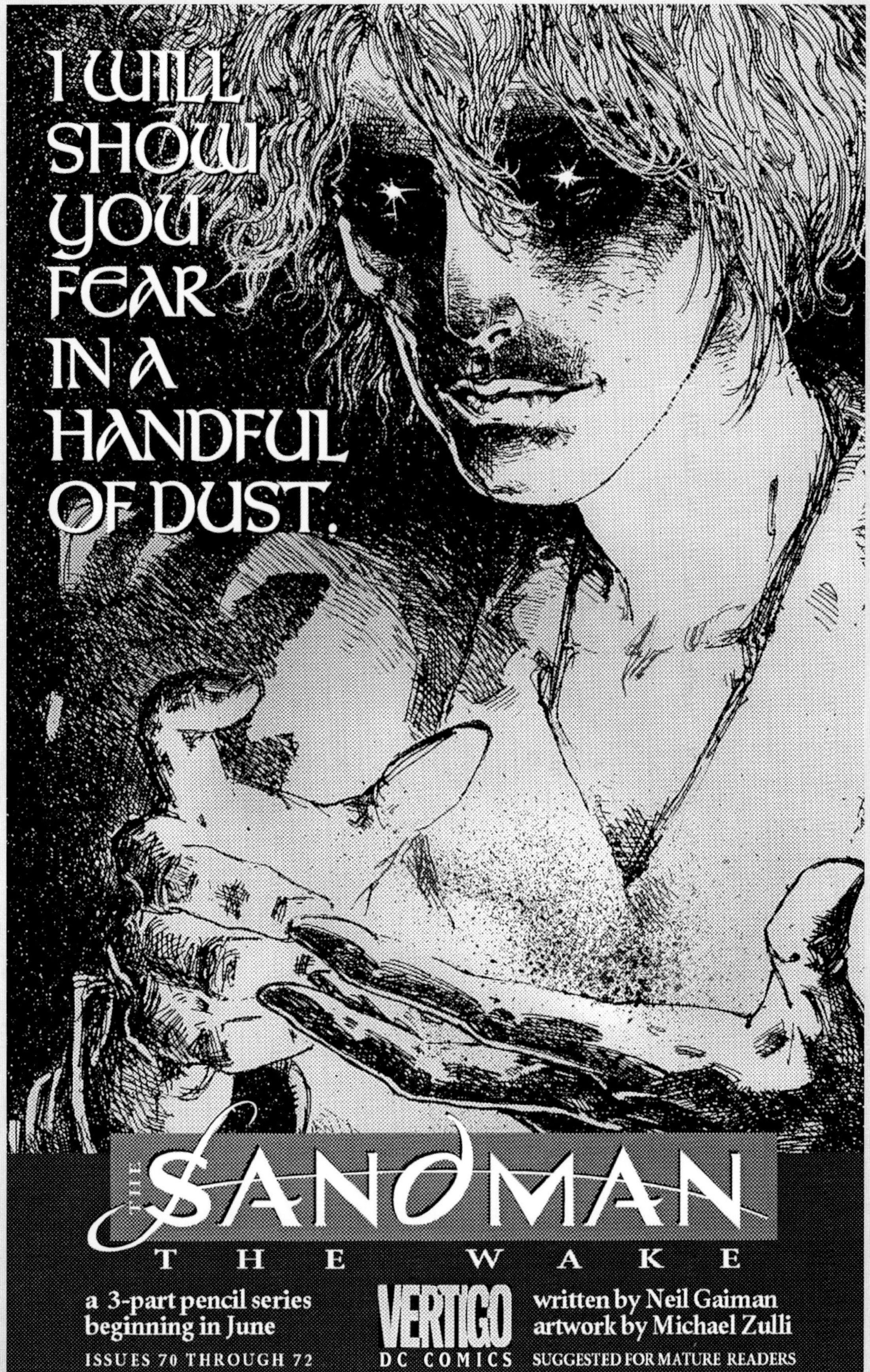
I WILL SHOW YOU FEAR IN A HANDFUL OF DUST.
THE SANDMAN
THE WAKE
a 3-part pencil series beginning in June
ISSUES 70 THROUGH 72
VERTIGO
DC COMICS
written by Neil Gaiman
artwork by Michael Zulli
SUGGESTED FOR MATURE READERS

ACKNOWLEDGMENTS.

I would like to thank Karen Berger for getting me into VERTIGO in the first place, Steve Korté for his endless patience (no pun intended), Rich Thomas for astute and gentle close editing, Hy Bender for creating the truly definitive work of Sandman scholarship, and Neil Gaiman for guidance, advice, and generally operating as one of my frontal lobes on this project.

— Alisa Kwitney